Beer

PAIRING

© 2015 Quarto Publishing Group USA Inc.
Text © 2015 Julia Herz and Gwen Conley
Photography © 2015 Jackie Dodd, unless otherwise noted

First published in 2015 by Voyageur Press, an imprint of Quarto Publishing Group USA Inc.,
400 First Avenue North, Suite 400, Minneapolis, MN 55401 USA.
Telephone: (612) 344-8100 Fax: (612) 344-8692

quartoknows.com
Visit our blogs at quartoknows.com

Voyageur Press titles are also available at discounts in bulk quantity for industrial or sales-promotional use. For details contact the Special Sales Manager at Quarto Publishing Group USA Inc., 400 First Avenue North, Suite 400, Minneapolis, MN 55401 USA.

10 9 8 7 6 5 4 3 2

ISBN: 978-0-7603-4843-7

Library of Congress Cataloging-in-Publication Data

Herz, Julia, 1968-
  Beer pairing : the essential guide from the pairing pros / Julia Herz, Gwen Conley.
    pages cm
  ISBN 978-0-7603-4843-7 (hardback)
 1. Beer. 2. Food and beer pairing. I. Conley, Gwen, 1966- II. Title.
 TP577.H475 2015
 641.2'3--dc23
                    2015020146

Acquiring Editor: Thom O'Hearn
Project Manager: Caitlin Fultz
Art Director: Cindy Samargia Laun
Book Design and Layout: Amelia LeBarron

Printed in China

Cicerone® is a registered certification mark and service mark of the Craft Beer Institute in the United States and a registered trademark and service mark in the European Union and Canada.

Beer

PAIRING

The Essential Guide
from the Pairing Pros

JULIA HERZ &
GWEN CONLEY

Voyageur
Press

CONTENTS

FOREWORD

To the barbarians living beyond the borders of ancient Greece, beer personified humankind's ability to force a wild and dangerous world to submit to our will. Represented by an image of a man on horseback stabbing a dragon, we know him as Saint George, but he is far older than that. If you peel back the layers of Christianity, this warrior is the barley god Sabazius, his act a metaphor for willfully bending raw nature into something sublime, even transcendental. We share the belief of these ancient people that beer is a fundamental comfort of civilization.

For millennia, beer was a replenishing quaff and nourishing staple—truly a liquid form of the bread it accompanied. Life was a struggle for most, and beer brought some comfort and amusement. Beer and food shared the table for sure, but only as simple, habitual pleasures, springing from the land and people who lived on it. An excerpt of an old harvest poem paints this picture:

> Ye shall see first the large and chief,
> Foundation of your feast, fat beef:
> With upper stories, mutton, veal,
> And bacon (which makes full the meal),
> With sev'ral dishes standing by,
> As here a custard, there a pie,
> . . . .
> If smirking wine be wanting here,
> There's that which drowns all care, stout beer . . .

Robert Herrick, 1591–1674

The Enlightenment brought renewed interest in classical authors such as Cicero, who wrote in passionate detail about gastronomy. Eventually technology and a humanist attitude fueled a highly refined culinary art via legendary chefs such as Carême and Escoffier. In France, this movement clutched wine close to its bosom, finding little use for beer.

Just across the border, however, Belgian beer had long been a beloved partner for the luscious food there. It took a more sophisticated turn as the rapid expansion of beer styles that occurred between the World Wars gave chefs and diners plenty to work with. As the beers adapted themselves to the food, *cuisine de la bière* became one of Belgium's distinguishing features and still inspires us today.

Things in North America were very different until quite recently. Like so much of the American food landscape, beer was industrialized into a homogeneous commodity. With a "don't think too much, just drink it" attitude from its purveyors, American beer cuisine for most of the twentieth century focused on washing down hot dogs and hamburgers. At its most wildly ambitious, beer found its way into things like fish batter or a pleasant cheese soup.

The late Michael Jackson was our bridge to European beer culture and its traditions, but he also encouraged us to find our own, new way. He visited frequently, seldom without engaging some unsuspecting chef in a beer pairing dinner. The end results were a bit uneven at times, but the very act was a revelation. Michael's passion and willingness to take risks for the sake of something better profoundly shaped the way people viewed beer and its role at the table.

As craft beer grew, it changed the way people thought about beer. The new brews sparkled with flavor, aroma, and personality. As the beer grew bolder, so did its drinkers, and people started to challenge the old assumptions: "What if beer is as good as wine?" And then, "I wonder what will happen if I put this barley wine with Stilton cheese?" At some point we dared to think, "Maybe beer is even better than wine at this."

It turned out that beer was very good indeed.

By the late 1990s, beer and food was a standard part of the canon. Beer dinners were everywhere. There was a lot of enthusiastic experimentation, and people started committing things to print. But since we were all just making it up as we went along, there was little agreement in how to put a particular beer and food pairing together.

Now that this movement is no longer in its infancy, we're seeing a bit more consensus. Collectively we have a lot of experience, so the common practice is better than ever. Our theories about why certain things work—or don't—are increasingly verified by science. It's taken a long time to get here, but we're ready for that next step. That brings us to this book.

A work like this is a bit of a balancing act. It has to translate the highly technical language of science into the experience-based world we all inhabit. It has to talk in generalities, even though every one of us experiences the world quite differently. It has to provide a standard vocabulary and a system with well-thought-out rules but not stifle creativity or limit flexibility. And it can't be content to simply tell you the way things are; it has to help you go out there, get your hands on the goods, and find out for yourself. This book does all that and more.

I suggest you not only read *Beer Pairing* but use it like a guide book, a lab manual, a diary, and a script. Beat it up, wear it out, and fill its margins with notes, because whatever the words say, they are of far more value to you when put into action.

One final thought on why this book is important: I often find that presenting beer and food to people breaks them loose of their daily habits and constructively challenges their assumptions. There are few things more exciting in life than helping people get to that weak moment where they are receptive to new ideas and can find thrills in things they may have unfairly rejected in the past. If there's one thing any movement needs to succeed, it's the power to change people's hearts and minds. That's the magic of beer and food.

So grab a beer, open your mind, and dig in. There is plenty to feast upon.

—Randy Mosher

INTRODUCTION

At its most basic, pairing is putting two things together. It can be a gathering of people paired with just the right music, turning the night into a party. It can be a hike paired with the perfect sunny day. It can be a warm chocolate chip cookie paired with a glass of milk. It can be warm, salty, crispy fish and chips paired with a fresh English-style extra special bitter. Look at us . . . we're on to beer and food pairing already!

Yes, in this book we're going to focus on beer and food pairings—and, moreover, on getting beers and foods to work together—because pairing is a practice that can enrich your day-to-day life in many ways. A perfect pairing makes two things greater than the sum of their parts. Its impact opens up the highest levels of satisfaction . . . dare we say bliss? And the beauty of pairing beer and food in particular is that it can be quite easy. Just by paying attention to likes and dislikes, by thinking about how individual elements work together, you can create new and more meaningful experiences.

Throughout *Beer Pairing* we want to open up your senses. This starts by living the slow-food way instead of the fast-food way, by savoring meals instead of speeding through them. We encourage you to pay attention to what already exists in your day-to-day life but is often missed.

As you slow down, you'll find the words *sensory evaluation* really aren't so intimidating. Sure, at first you may be surprised by the individual elements in ketchup (what exactly *are* you tasting besides tomatoes?). Yet when you slow down, you can look at the components and see vinegar, sugar, salt, maybe even clove, and start to see how ketchup plays with other foods and beverages. You'll discover that the acid and the umami-laden tomato are what make ketchup such a perfect companion for more than just fries and burgers. Plus you'll start to uncover the "why."

As you move through the chapters, you'll work your way through tasting beer as well as food, and you'll find yourself building your own sensory vocabulary. You'll move beyond *malty* to *notes of cashews, burnt toast, toffee*, and *honey* instead. Of course, there's so much more in store as well. We have exciting palate trips to challenge your senses. (Ever try an IPA with mangoes and sour pickles in the same sitting?) We'll cover some of the most popular beer styles and foolproof ways to pair with them. And of course, we'll explore cheese, chocolate, and other beer-friendly foods. Want to throw a full-on beer dinner, or want to get behind the stove and see how beer works in the kitchen? We'll cover that, too.

Yet these chapters aren't meant to be the last word on pairing—just the opposite. We want this book to be the start or expansion of your journey. After all, each one of us is unique. No two people perceive flavors in the exact same way. Realizing all of our sensory differences is what makes it obvious that eating and drinking—and thus, pairing—can never work with a one-size-fits-all approach. So we are going to teach you how to figure out what works and what doesn't work for *you*.

Disrupt your routines, avoid judgment, and stop thinking of specific foods and beers as something you simply like or dislike. "Be weird. Be random. Be who you are. Because you never know who would love the person you hide." That anonymous quote embodies exactly how we want you to pair beer and food.

Sometimes you will find pairings that are common but lovely. Sometimes you will find pairings that are terrible, but those are wonderful learning experiences that challenge you to find what will work. Eventually you'll find pairings that are groundbreaking knock-your-socks-off experiences that inspire you to keep tasting.

That tingle of excitement you'll feel is only the tip of your sensory curiosity. You are about to begin a lifelong learning journey, and we are here to help pave the way. Throughout our own lives we have been blessed by luck and by amazing mentors who sparked our interest in the what, why, and how of beer and food, and some of them share their wisdom with you in the book. Ours is a shared passion that we want to spread and continue to share in a monumental way. Join us! It's like being in a cult, except instead of drinking the Kool-Aid, we're going to analyze it and then decide what cheese to pair with it.

Cheers,
Gwen Conley and Julia Herz

TALKING ABOUT BEER AND PAIRING

We'd like to welcome you to the first chapter, to the first step on your beer and food pairing journey, with a beer. Seriously! In this chapter we are going to discuss what you smell and taste when you take a sip of beer. Why not make the experience interactive?

In the first section, we're going to discuss the major components of beer. We'll talk grain fresh from the malt house. We'll try to smell hops as if they were picked right off the vine. We'll look at yeast's effects under a microscope. Yes, we're that concerned with what these beautiful ingredients do when they come together with water and make beer!

Still, when we taste we're going to look at aroma and flavor informally. We'll use words you've heard before, though maybe not in the context of tasting. But that's the beauty of beer—you won't find any stuffiness. If a beer has notes of burnt toast and bubble gum, we will let you know to look for those descriptors. If the aroma blows you back with tropical fruits and a hint of catty, we'll let you know to look for that, too. Still, there will be words that are new to you in the other chapters of this book. Furthermore, we realize that some people will come to this book as beer or tasting experts while others are just starting their journey, so we thought it would be best to make sure we're on the same page by starting here, with terminology, in Chapter 1.

So come along with us . . . and don't forget to grab a beer and sip as you read along!

DESCRIBING BEER

Let's start with the reason why we're all here (that's beer!) and the ingredients that make up this marvelous drink. It's an understatement to say beer is an incredibly complex beverage. According to a recent study in the *Journal of Food Engineering*, beer is thought to contain more than 560 aromatic compounds. In practice, this means you may find yourself lost or overwhelmed after taking a sip of a beer, especially one that's strong or unfamiliar. Yet it's possible to cut through the noise and deconstruct just about any beer.

The secret to breaking down beer is the same secret for breaking down anything you're tasting: consider the ingredients individually. Lucky for us, the vast majority of beers start with just four main ingredients: malted barley, hops, yeast, and water. True, there is remarkable variation within those ingredients, not to mention in brewing practices and the fermentation process. Also true: some brewing cultures have stuck more rigidly to those ingredients while others have pushed the limits with sugars, wild yeasts, microorganisms, and other ingredients. But just as a chocolate chip cookie can be broken down into sugar, flour, eggs, butter, and chocolate, so too can beer be broken down into its components.

Note: The use of the term *craft beer* is largely up to each individual beer lover. However, as defined by the Brewers Association, a US craft brewer is "small," producing less than six million barrels of beer a year, and independently owned. That means the majority of breweries in the United States are considered craft. For us, the bottom line is it's always a good thing to support your local brewery. They're often an important part of the community—and of course, they're the place where you can get the freshest possible beer.

MALTS (BARLEY AND OTHER GRAINS)

Malt's Role: Malted barley and a few other grains provide the sugar source to produce wort, which is essentially sugar water, for the yeast to ferment. Although that is a simplified version of all that is involved, a complex sugary solution for the yeast is the goal. The grain types used can vary greatly: some may remain unmalted, and the malting process itself can turn the same grain into vastly different malts. No matter the country or the brewer, most beers do have a significant percentage of

Malted grains (most often barley) are the main fermentable used to make beer.

what's commonly referred to as a base malt. Base malts provide the majority of the enzymes necessary to convert starches into usable fermentable sugars, and they also help brewers with consistency from batch to batch (and among their many beer recipes). In addition to the base malt, the brewer also uses specialty malts and grains to achieve certain colors or flavor characteristics—like seasonings in a recipe.

Flavor and Aroma Notes: While there are subtle differences between different grain types, how long grains are kilned or roasted by the maltster tends to have the biggest effect on aroma and flavor. It's like bread in the toaster: you're more likely to notice if it's light or dark toast before you notice whether it's white or whole wheat.

Lighter malts will have notes such as toasted bread crust, biscuit, biscotti, and golden raisin, whereas dark-roasted malts will come across with roasted walnut or pecan, burnt toast,

— *Garrett Oliver* —

Garrett Oliver is not only the brewmaster of Brooklyn Brewery, he is one of the world's foremost experts when it comes to pairing. He is the editor of *The Oxford Companion to Beer* and the author of *The Brewmaster's Table*.

In your eyes, what is beer's standing in the food world and among food world thought leaders?

We've made a lot of progress, but unfortunately beer's standing in the restaurant world remains generally poor. Even as craft beer booms in the United States and throughout the world, the restaurant scene is still getting left behind. I think the restaurants don't realize that they're leaving a lot of money on the table. Craft beer is the only area of American food and drink where you can commonly walk into a restaurant and find that the patrons know more about the restaurant's beers than the restaurant does. I see it all the time.

And that, for the restaurant, is a disaster. Can you imagine this happening with wine? The patrons knowing the wine list better than the sommelier? No, of course that's tough to imagine. And it should be. I think there are two culprits—fear and lack of good educational opportunities. The fear is twofold: fear of not knowing what you're doing and fear of losing your wine sale,

often the tent pole of a restaurant's financials. The second fear, loss of the wine sale, is 100 percent false. I've been doing this for twenty-seven years, and no one's wine sales have ever dropped because they instituted a good craft beer list. What you get is a better restaurant, a higher check average, and a happier customer.

What do you want people to know about beer's pairing potential?

Essentially that beer is the absolute king of pairing potential, hands down, period, no argument. The reason is simple: brewing is cooking, and beer can have many ingredients. As a result, beer is essentially culinary. I can make a beer taste like chocolate, either by using roasted malts or even by actually adding chocolate. Wine is wonderful, but it has no such potential. Wine has one ingredient: grapes. And the grape is a nice ingredient, capable of making some brilliant drinks. But there is no way for wine to compete with a beverage that can use any fruit, any spice, can be highly bitter or acidic, and can carry flavors of roast and of caramel. If we wish, and this is particularly possible in the brewpub setting, we can create beers specifically meant to pair with particular dishes.

Why is pairing beer and food such a passion of yours?

Because it will improve your life, plain and simple. Making your meals a little more enjoyable every day is a small change, but it's a big deal. Great beer is a very affordable luxury. Many of the best beers in the world are less expensive than a fancy coffee. That's an amazing thing to have at your fingertips and to be able to enjoy every day. We make a drink that makes our customers a little bit happier and a little bit healthier every day.

What are the top tips for people interested in pairing food and beer?

1. Have fun. It's not an either/or situation between beer and wine. Almost every good brewer I know is also very knowledgeable about wine and food. It's about enjoying yourself, so be adventurous. It's beer, so thankfully you won't bankrupt yourself if you end up buying something that you don't care for. Get fifteen different beers, have some friends over, and make some cool discoveries.

2. Balance is the key to all things. If you want to have a nice pairing, the beer can't be massive and the food very delicate, or the other way around. One thing will just wipe out the other. Try to match the intensities of the beer and food, and you'll already be halfway there. Then see if you can "set the hook," in other words, find a part of the beer's flavor that you think will link up with a flavor in the food. For example, the roasted chocolatey flavors in a porter can work very nicely with the chiles and chocolate in a Mexican mole sauce. Remember, it's culinary, and pairing basically uses the same creativity that you use when cooking. So think like a chef, and you'll find some good pairings of your own.

3. Know your cheese. Not only is great cheese one of the most awesome foods there is, but it's wonderful with beer, a far better partner than wine.

4. A thing I've found: pretty much every sausage goes with every beer. So if you want to have a groundbreaking beer dinner . . . don't do sausages. It's cheating. But if you're just making yourself dinner, it's almost impossible to go wrong.

French roast coffee, dark chocolate, charcoal, and even pipe tobacco notes. Caramel malts, the malts that fall in between the lightest and darkest levels of malt, often deliver flavors of butterscotch, caramel, burnt sugar, molasses, cashew, toffee, sweet bread, and honey. There are also a variety of specialty malts with their own unique characteristics. For example, smoked malts can be used to add a hickory or peat character.

Malt and Pairing: As you can see from the flavor and aroma notes, malts have a broad spectrum of overlap with different foods. Toasty, biscuity malts find parallels with breads; caramel, toffee, and chocolate overlap with sweet sauces such as barbecue, as well as a wide variety of nuts and desserts; dark-roasted and smoky malts can connect with coffee, chocolate, or even grilled meat.

HOPS

Hops' Role: Hops provide bitterness, flavor, and aroma to beer, so they can be complicated to wrap your head around at first. A bitter beer is often referred to as "hoppy," for example. However, beer can be very low in bitterness but have a tropical or citrus aroma as the main characteristic. Since that comes from hops, you wouldn't be wrong to call that beer "hoppy," too.

When it comes to bitterness, brewers will generally let you know what International Bitterness Units (IBUs) their beers have. The scale ranges from a theoretical 0 to a theoretical 100. Once you get close to 100 IBUs, most palates can't perceive any further increases in bitterness. On the brewing side, hops are often evaluated by their alpha and beta acids, though the former contributes more directly to bitterness and is the factor brewers consider when crafting beers with targeted IBUs. In short, brewers have to use more of a hop with a low alpha acid to have

Hops are used by brewers similar to the way a chef uses herbs and spices.

the same bittering impact of a smaller amount of a hop with high alpha acids. You don't really need to know this for tasting, but you'll see "alpha" in beer names now and then, and it's generally a good sign the beer will be a hoppy one.

For bitterness, brewers typically add hops to their boil toward the beginning. The longer hops boil, the more alpha acids are extracted, creating the bitterness in the wort. However, for flavor and aroma, brewers add hops toward the end of the boil, after the boil is over, or even after fermentation (in a process known as dry hopping). The reason for this is that the essential oils in hops that give beer its aroma and flavor characteristics—at least 250 of which have been identified—are quite volatile. This means they evaporate and leave the beer quickly at higher temperatures. (Examples of these essential oils are humulene, myrcene, caryophyllene, and farnesene, or as we've memorized them, Hum My Car Faraway.)

As if all this weren't complex enough, esters are often formed when carboxylic acid reacts with alcohol. They are a byproduct of yeast fermentation. These esters can give the beer fruitlike aromas and flavors; some are very pleasant, like banana or tropical fruit, and some are not so pleasant, like nail polish.

Flavor and Aroma Notes: Hops contribute so much to beer, and it can be tough to separate the bitterness from the aroma. Yet the more you taste well-crafted hoppy beers, the more you'll be able to pick out specific flavor and aroma notes. You'll find many are fruity (apple, pear, mango, pineapple) or citrusy (orange, lemon, lime, grapefruit). Others are green with leafy, grassy, hay-like, resinous, floral, piney, woody, and even spruce-like qualities. There are also beers that feature unusual hops that don't follow any of these classic examples. You may taste black currant or muscat grapes, herbal tea, earth, or tobacco. Hop growers are breeding so many new and interesting hops with mind-blowing characteristics that the variety is sure to expand in the years to come.

Note: You may taste or smell something from hops in a beer that rubs you the wrong way, but that is simply unavoidable based on growing conditions. Certain harvests of certain hops can come across with onion or garlic notes, while others have an aroma that triggers some people to say they smell cat pee. Think of it like cilantro: some people love it, and some people think it tastes soapy.

Hops and Pairing: You can probably already see the food parallels with hops, such as the amazing synergy with fruits, herbs, and spices. That said, when trying to complement citrus, floral, and grassy notes in hops, taste the dish and beer together before saying it is definitely going to work. We've both been at beer dinners where the "clash of the bitter green grass" flavor happens because the bitterness from the foods and the bitterness from the beers overwhelmed all other parts to the dish. The key is to remember that hops can have volatile chemical compounds that have the possibility of overwhelming a pairing if they are out of balance.

Gwen: Remember to try different hoppy beers to see what works with your favorite foods as well. I really like mushrooms, and I've found when a beer has a hop like Saaz—something really earthy and peppery—it pairs well with mushroom dishes, which tend to have substantial earthiness.

YEAST

Yeast's Role: Yeast may be single-celled microscopic microorganisms, but they are huge when it comes to making beer! Nearly all brewers use yeast in the genus *Saccharomyces* (either the ale yeast strain *S. cerevisiae* or the lager species *S. uvarum*, also known as *S. carlsbergensis*). Yet within these major species, there are thousands of unique strains. To further complicate things, there is an increasing interest in using various strains of the wild yeast

Without yeast, a microorganism powerhouse, there would be no beer!

Brettanomyces as well. In short, all yeasts convert the fermentable sugars in the wort into alcohol and carbon dioxide, along with many other byproducts that significantly contribute to the overall flavor of beer.

Flavor and Aroma Notes: While alcohol and carbonation will have an effect on mouthfeel, the byproducts yeast creates during fermentation are really where yeast contributes to flavor and aroma. Depending on the yeast, it can create flavors such as banana, apple, pear, anise, pepper, bubble gum, Circus Peanuts, clove, lemon, and tropical fruits (pineapple, mango, guava). It can also give beer an earthy, musty, bready, nutty, or even acidic character.

Note: Yeast also contributes the basic taste of umami. If you look closely, you'll find autolyzed yeast in food items such as broths, soy sauce, meat alternatives, vegemite, marmite, and as a replacement for monosodium glutamate in some foods.

Yeast and Pairing: Breads and other baked goods are made with yeast, so there is an easy parallel when yeast is neutral or amplifies bready, doughy notes in beer. Spicy and fruity yeast characteristics, on the other hand, can be used to contrast or complement those same characteristics in a food dish. A successful pairing of banana-centric weizen and a banana dessert can work wonderfully. Use the spicy phenolic notes from a Belgian-style abbey yeast to your advantage with dishes that have clove, ginger, or orange. English ale yeasts that produce higher esters match sweet caramel and nutty notes in grilled meats. Just focus on the dominant flavor characteristics and go with it.

We also need to mention that yeast can be sneaky. It may have subtle characteristics at levels that you cannot detect, but once you pair the beer with a food item, boom, there it is. Characteristics such as green apple, butter, butterscotch, bruised apple, sulfur, nail polish, solvent, goat, Band-Aid, cooked vegetables, paper, cardboard, and sour might be at undetectably low levels in the beer you are tasting or pairing. They are not flaws in the beer, because they are undetectable; however, accidentally accentuating one of these in an undesirable way can be disastrous. We mention these characteristics so if something like this shows up in a pairing you will know where it came from: CSI-like investigation material!

Gwen: Wild yeasts, such as Brettanomyces, *contribute characteristics that are most unusual: earth, cotton candy, coconut, butter, smoke, horse blanket, barnyard, goat, fruit, tropical fruit (pineapple), lemon, sour milk (lactic acid), sour (acetic acid), sweat, cheese, bacon, spice, clove, and even putrid notes. Yes I said putrid . . . it comes from butyric acid that is initially produced by the yeast. I mention this because, lucky for us, when the acid is combined with the alcohol that is produced it becomes an ester, and not just any ester, but ethyl butyrate, which translates in aroma and flavor terms to tropical fruits like pineapple. I can see why some of your noses might have turned a little at the mention of some of the not-so-delicious-sounding descriptors above; however, they can parallel with food. A stinky cheese with its acidic, earthy, funky, and fruity characteristics seem to me to be a perfect parallel. Goat in beer and goat in cheese must equal awesome, right? Earthy root vegetables such as beets are amazing with the complement of earthy from a Brett-fermented beer. Embracing the funk really is fun, especially when food pairing plays a role.*

WATER

Water's Role: Water makes up 85–95 percent of beer, so naturally the chemistry of that water is an enormous contributor to the overall flavor of the beer. Minerals such as calcium, magnesium, sodium, zinc, sulfates, chlorides, potassium, and bicarbonates are going to contribute overall flavors to beer. However, unlike malt, hops, and yeast, water mostly stays out of the way when it comes to having its own dominant flavor or aroma. Instead it tends to work with—or occasionally against—the other ingredients, and you can just keep it in the back of your mind as you deconstruct.

Flavor and Aroma Notes: Water can affect the character of beer through mouthfeel; minerals can also amplify or suppress the effects of malt or hops when the beer is brewing. For example, in addition to recipe differences, there are considerable differences in the water when comparing US West Coast IPAs and English-style IPAs. The former tend to build on neutral water, while the latter often have considerable mineral content from the water.

On the palate, water can also affect the fullness or roundness of a beer, astringency, and perceived bitterness or sweetness. Rarely, water can come through in the finished beer directly, as when water has excessive sulfur, salt, or chlorine.

Gwen: I learned about the flavor effect of using unfiltered tap water from setting up one of my first sensory classes. The basic-taste samples of sweet, sour, salt, bitter, and umami reacted with the chemicals in the unfiltered tap water, and we ended up tasting chlorine in all of the samples.

OTHER INGREDIENTS

Brewers are a creative bunch and increasingly use a variety of specialty ingredients in their recipes. These range from unconventional sugar sources (honey, agave, maple, candi sugar, brown sugar, molasses) and fruits (cherry, blueberry, blackberry, peach, apricot, coconut, cranberry, raspberry, apple) to herbs and spices (coriander, chilies, lavender, lemon balm or grass, licorice, dandelion, heather, citrus peel, ginger, cardamom, cinnamon, vanilla, nutmeg, cocoa, sage, yarrow, spruce tips) and vegetables (pumpkin, rutabaga, rhubarb, cucumber, squash, sweet potato). We've even seen brewers using nuts (hazelnuts, walnuts, peanuts, pecans).

Other Ingredients and Pairing: When a beer contains an unusual ingredient, you might think you can safely pair it with foods containing the same ingredient. This can certainly be the case, from chocolate stouts with chocolate to blueberry-infused porter with blueberry-braised short ribs. A beer brewed with honey? Try it with baklava or a baked ham. Pair a cucumber saison with Greek food for a refreshing combination. And beers brewed with pumpkin and spices can certainly complement pumpkin in a dish, stew, or dessert.

Pairing terminology will help you communicate what you're tasting and smelling.

However, we've found that you can have too much of a good thing. For example, at the Lost Abbey there is a Belgian-style saison that contains ginger. Pairing that gingery beer with a dish containing ginger just doesn't work. We believe it's because the ginger molecules seem to attract each other and combine to produce a very intense flavor that overwhelms the entire pairing. After a bite and a sip, all you taste is ginger. We've found vanilla, clove, coffee, chilies, and other herbs and spices can be dangerous in the same way. If the beer you are trying to pair has an ingredient that is overly dominating, go with emphasizing a different ingredient such as sweet caramel or roast. The only real way to know is to try it and learn.

PAIRING TERMINOLOGY

Throughout this book you'll find plenty of words and concepts you know inside and out, and plenty more you have a working knowledge of. Still, there are specialty terms when it comes to pairing practices. On the following pages, we'll provide a brief, concept-oriented guide to many of the words you'll read (hopefully, you'll soon be using them yourself!).

If you start to feel overwhelmed, just remember it all comes down to this: when you describe beer and when you describe food, those are two different things. When you describe the pairing, that should be its own separate thing as well.

These descriptions should not be "Oh, this is nice." Instead, elevate your pairing description to the description you would give beer or food separately—use your words! Saying "You have to try this: the lemon just jumps out at you from the hops in the beer and the lemon zest in the dish" means you not only shared why you liked the pairing, you also made someone else want to try it. We are going to get into how to do this in later chapters, but the pages that follow will provide words and concepts to describe what happens.

THE BUILDING BLOCKS OF PAIRING

Before we get into how flavor elements work together, we're going to deconstruct food and beer into their components in Chapters 2 and 3. This means we'll look closely at the individual concepts that follow.

Flavor: Flavor is the big one: it's the combined interaction of aromatics, basic taste elements, and physical and chemical mouthfeel perceptions. That means experiencing the total flavor of a beverage or food is going to involve a complex interaction of all of these senses and perceptions.

Aroma: Your nose really knows! Aroma makes up about 80 percent of what we commonly think of as flavor. When we talk about aroma, we're including odors detected through your nose (also known as orthonasal aroma) as well as through your mouth (also known as retronasal aroma). Saying there are thousands of aroma molecules is a bit abstract. So perhaps it's easier to try drinking or eating while plugging your nose initially. As soon as you release your fingers and exhale, you'll immediately get the huge effect aroma has on the overall flavor.

Basic Taste Elements: Chances are you learned about these in school at some point. We're talking about sweet, sour, salty, bitter, and umami (savory). These five elements are what the taste receptor cells on your taste buds sense. These primary tastes are also the building blocks of pairing.

Mouthfeel: *Mouthfeel* is a funny word for a fun concept: it's how a food or beverage feels in your mouth and throat, including the sensation you experience or perceive, whether physical or chemical. In a study done by the Department of Food Science and Technology at the University of California, Davis, it was discovered that mouthfeel sensory impact is as vital to overall flavor classification as odor and basic tastes, particularly when it comes to beer.

You may think there aren't many options, but the more you pay attention, the more you'll realize the vast array of mouthfeels out there for food and drink: crunchy, smooth, harsh, slick, sticky, creamy, viscous, astringent, oily, tingly, prickly, full, heavy, hot, cold, rough, mouth-coating, alkaline, acidic, velvety, powdery, chalky, gritty, metallic, spicy (hot), soft, chewy, thick, thin, sharp, drying . . . the list goes on.

Intensity: Perhaps the most abstract of these basic concepts, intensity comes from many elements in both beer and food, including alcohol, bitterness, acidity, fat, and more. How we each perceive intensity is tied to our personal preferences and our personal perception differences, but more on that later. Intensity is one way to give a qualitative or ranking aspect to flavor, and thus to pairings.

PAIRING IN ACTION

It can be difficult to wrap your mind around how food and beer interact, but it is impossible without learning some new words to describe the experience. This is where the magic happens.

Bridge: Bridges, also referred to as flavor hooks and echoes, are where beer and food meet, ingredient to ingredient, via similar flavors. For example, when you pair a fettuccine Alfredo sprinkled with rosemary and sage with an American IPA that has hop notes of pine and spruce, you have a flavor bridge. The herb flavors of the rosemary and sage are not the exact flavors of the pine and the spruce notes in the beer, but they find and bridge to each other, thereby creating affinities because the flavors are similar.

You can use one ingredient's flavor characteristic to bridge to another and find flavor harmonies (see below). Flavor groups can be used as a starting point to find bridges.

Flavor Groups: Flavor groups are what we call the similar flavors found in both beer and food. Think of them as individual elements that are part of the whole. They're the starting place to find bridges, and eventually harmonies. They can vary wildly, but here are some examples:

- Smoked: bacon, hickory, maple barbecue, wood fire
- Earthy root vegetables: beet, carrot, potato, yam
- Green: grass, hay, herbal, tealike
- Tropical fruit: guava, passion fruit, mango, papaya
- Stone fruit: peach, nectarine, apricot
- Spicy herbs: ginger, mustard, horseradish, cinnamon
- Pepper spice: jalapeño, habanero, serrano, ghost pepper
- Creamy nuts: pistachio, cashew, pine nut, hazelnut

Harmony: Harmony, also referred to as balance, is a synergistic marriage of flavor elements. Whether two flavors complement each other or contrast, they are in harmony if they agree with each other and are pleasing to your palate.

Complement: The Latin word *completum* means "completed," and that is where the word *complement* stems from. When pairing, beer and food that share flavor elements are said to complement each other. These pairings generally strengthen and enhance one another, helping to create that "complete" experience. For example, tropical hop notes in an American IPA complement pineapple salsa on top of grilled chicken.

Contrast: When food and beer elements have opposing flavor attributes, they contrast. Contrasts can either enhance or surpress each other's intensities. In general, contrasts are more tied to basic taste elements and are not as prevalent in aromatic elements.

For example, the bitterness of an IPA contrasts against the sweetness of cheesecake. In this example, the contrasting elements—bitterness and sweetness—lessen each other, allowing flavors including beer's citrus or forest hop aromatics, white fruit ester notes, and biscotti and graham cracker malt notes to shine through brighter. However, when the same bitter beer contrasts with a hot spicy dish, the bitter and spice qualities are emphasized instead.

Cut and Suppress: Cut and supression are a form of contrasting when one characteristic lessens another and it's harder to detect those original characteristics, thus letting other characteristics shine. For example, an American barley wine's bitterness suppresses the impact of fat, richness, and oil in a rich, aged cheddar cheese, which lets you identify flavors and taste elements in the cheddar that would have otherwise been hidden behind the richness.

There are different degrees of cut or supression. It can have a soothing effect, as when a sweet beer soothes capsaicin heat in food. Cutting also occurs from carbonation and acidity, often with an effect that we call "cancel" or "cleanse." For example, a highly carbonated Belgian-style tripel can cancel some of the rich nature of a triple-crème cheese, letting nutty and earthy flavors come out. Likewise, the acidity in a Berliner-style weisse cancels much of the acidity in pickles, so you can better taste the dill and garlic. Throughout the book you will also see us use the terms *calm*, *lessen*, and *diminish*, which also reflect a degree of lessening of individual flavor elements.

Emphasize or Enhance: Emphasize or enhance, also known as potentiation, is when food and beer elements combine to make each part more strongly perceived than it is on its own. For example, salty foods accentuate and bring out residual sugar sweetness in beer, with the combined pairing resulting in emphasized flavor overall. Even a Belgian-style wit, which is not a sweet style, can taste sweeter when paired with something like salted eggs.

Rest: Rests occur when beer or food ingredients provide a break for your senses. A rest can be an intermezzo in the middle of the meal. It's something that resets your palate. Some examples include:

- The pickle next to your corned beef sandwich
- Coleslaw next to a Reuben
- Shaved ginger with sushi rolls
- Parsley as garnish on the side of your plate
- And of course, beer between bites of food.

THE THREE TYPES OF PAIRING

While there are an infinite number of pairings out there, you can likely classify any of them into one of three categories.

Home Run: These pairings are outta-da-park great! Both the food and the beer are enhanced, and the whole is better than the sum of the parts. One plus one doesn't just equal three—it equals five. Some classic examples include Belgian-style dubbel and barbecue,

WHAT'S THE WORD FOR YOU?

Beer Beginners: Beginners are those who are just starting their beer journey. You may not yet be attuned to the nuance of different beers or attributes of beer's different ingredients. This is a great starting place for both learning about beer and how it pairs with food.

Beer Enthusiast: Enthusiasts enjoy different beers on different occasions. You frequently try different styles and brands again and again. You can list beer's main ingredients and are relatively familiar with at least the most popular beer styles. This is also a great place to start to connect the ingredients of beer with what you perceive in food.

Beer Geek: Beer geeks are the gurus of the group, and others often turn to you for advice on what to drink and when. You might even homebrew. You are very familiar with a variety of beer styles and beer brands and what ingredients make up those beers. The only downside to being a beer geek is that you know so much you sometimes need to be reminded to keep an open mind—a key for beer and food pairing!

chocolate stout and chocolate cake, or English-style barley wine and an English Stilton. It's hard to achieve home runs, but they're oh so worth the effort.

Middle of the Road: These pairings are down the middle. They're nothing to write home about but not bad either. These are your common, everyday pairings. The beer did not help the food shine brighter, nor did it lessen the desirability of the food. These do have their place when it comes to pairing, but they are not going to be remembered and talked about later.

Train Wreck: These pairings are what happens when there's a clash of elements from the meeting of food and beer. Yep, the whole tastes less desirable than the individual parts. One plus one equals . . . negative one. Think orange juice and toothpaste, lemon and milk, mint and coke, cottage cheese and lemonade. Still, these can be amazing learning experiences. Also, most people will tell you exactly why they don't like something—especially when they're passionate about it. Use that passion to deconstruct the bad pairing and improve on it next time.

CHAPTER

— 2 —

HOW WE
PERCEIVE

SEEK OUT ANARCHY!

Most of us begin our day with some sort of a routine. And whether you realize it or not, that routine is a sensory routine: the sound of the alarm, the smell of coffee or tea, the feel of a hot shower. These are all triggers that the day has begun and it's time to get going. These sensory triggers are learned and implanted in the brain. They let your brain go on autopilot to some degree to get you out the door.

Of course, learned behavior and routines create scenarios that you don't think about throughout the day, including routines that impact how and what we eat and drink. Most people have set times for breakfast, lunch, and dinner. Almost everyone has go-to choices for what they eat and drink on certain days—some may even eat the same thing for breakfast or lunch every day.

Traditional pairing advice was often based on the "drink this with that" approach. It's a fine system in that it can get you where you're going. Yet it often leads to pairings that fit into your own routine with all its inherent preferences, and you're doing little more than following a script. This sort of prescribed matching has its place. In fact, it's such a great way to get started we do plenty of it in this book as well.

However, we've learned more, and we think you will, too, if you become an anarchist. Don't worry. We're not going to overthrow any governments or tell you to set anything on fire. We're talking about *sensory anarchy*. We're the founders of this new movement, and here are the principles.

1. Disrupting routine is the key to learning more about tasting and about yourself.

One key to pairing and to learning how to taste is eating and drinking things that you might think you don't like. Unless you have an allergy to a given food or beverage, it's best to let those biases go when tasting. We promise that you will find things that you had no idea you actually enjoy.

Even more important is this advice: stop evaluating what you are eating and drinking as good or bad. Sure there are a lot of emotions involved, but you are going to have to realize that as your sensory therapists, we are here to break you of this habit. How crazy are you willing to be? We want you to experiment even more. Expand your horizons!

2. We're all genetically different.

Science has found, and continues to find, that everyone's taste receptors are sensitive to different chemical combinations at different levels. That means there can't be a true one-size-fits-all tasting or pairing methodology. It's all personal. If you don't like the taste of something or of a classic pairing, that's fine! If you love the taste of something your friends don't or if you come up with an amazing pairing that works for you and only you, in our book you're still a winner. (Just keep in mind how unconventional you are when you're serving others.)

Gwen: When I teach sensory classes, I always end up saying, "Congratulations, whatever you're tasting, you are correct!" That's because there are no right or wrong answers when it comes to what you perceive. Pairing and perception are both personal.

Every one of us is different, and we all taste and smell things differently. That's why when you go out to eat, it can be tough to pick a restaurant as a group—never mind how difficult it can be to actually split a whole dinner. There are always a variety of opinions, and that variety gets bigger as the number of people increases. Just think how many people love onions and how many people really dislike onions. That is just one ingredient!

3. Screw tradition.

OK, maybe that's too dramatic. Tradition has a place, and we both love traditional beer styles. However, the culinary world and the brewing world are both in an exciting place. New recipes and new beer types are invented every day. In our opinion, that means tasting—and pairing—needs to go beyond the classic "pair this with that" formulas. We want to equip everyone with a deeper ability to dial into flavors so when you encounter a new dish or a new beer, you have the tools in your tasting toolbox to evaluate them.

You might be asking yourself, *But wait, didn't they already say whatever I taste is right?* We did! However, training and continued exploration will open you up to what you might be missing, break down mental barriers, and broaden your possibilities. It will eventually allow you to help everyone around you participate and become conscious tasters as well. Voila! You are creating a culture that can be shared and expanded on—and this happens even when you don't agree with your neighbor. Who knew that disagreeing could actually be such a positive thing?

TASTING BASICS

Dr. Morton Meilgaard, developer of the beer flavor wheel, defines flavor as "the term used to describe the complex interactions of taste, smell, and chemical irritations of foods in the mouth that add to its mouthfeel."

What?

In nonscientific terms, he's saying flavor is the total impression you gather with all of your senses rather than just taste. In fact, the basic tastes that you perceive with your mouth usually only determine about 20 percent of the total impression of flavor. That's because flavor is a combination of **aroma, taste, and mouthfeel**. The complex interaction of those three elements is collectively sent to your brain so it can register flavor. Your brain then connects these pieces and parts to its amazing collection of words, images, and memories. These stored memory areas are triggers for flavor descriptors.

Triggers are what gives you the aha moment. They're what lead you to say, "I know what this reminds me of," and then connect that thought to the flavor descriptor. You don't have to prepare or overthink this part. You already have the tools you need to figure out how, what, and why. You just need to listen to what your brain has been telling you all along.

In this chapter, we will focus mainly on those three elements. Since it's estimated that aroma accounts for 80 percent or more of total flavor detected, we will start there. And while chances are you're familiar with sweet, sour, salty, bitter, and umami, we'll explore all of them in detail when it comes to taste. Finally, there's the most unfamiliar concept to most people new to professional tasting: mouthfeel. It includes trigeminal (chemical) and tactile (texture) sensations. For example, think of the fizz of carbonation or the coolness of menthol; they're basically the sensations that occur in your mouth and throat.

We have one last thought before we move on to the big three: never forget that flavor starts with your eyes. That's right, your eyes. What you see is the first step toward determining how you feel about what may or may not make its way to your mouth. Those visual cues of texture and color are precursors to your sense of taste.

Time and time again studies have proven that people have preconceptions about an item's flavor based solely on the appearance of that item. For example, in an article published in *Appetite*, the researchers concluded that whether the food was raw or cooked, ultimately it was the overall appearance that guided the expectations and preferences of the consumer. Another study from this same publication concluded that the color of the plate that food was served on had an influence on the consumer's expectations of the flavor of the food. Aside from the research, just think of your own experience. Have you ever heard someone say something like, "I don't like the look of that, so I'm not going to try it"? This sort of evaluation can make sense, especially when your brain is protecting you from ingesting something toxic or rancid, but it's not always helpful.

Gwen: I love unsweetened soy green-tea lattes from my local coffee shop. However, one time I was at a new coffee shop, and I wasn't paying close attention until my drink came out. This particular place used a matcha mix instead of tea leaves, and they served the tea chilled rather than hot. Now the appearance of this tea in its clear cup, the milky green color of the Grinch, was absolutely not what I was expecting. My eyes judged this particular concoction as unappetizing. Still, I ignored my judging eyes and tried it anyway. It wasn't my favorite drink; it wasn't going to replace my favorite green-tea latte. But still, it was delicious and a great new sensory experience. In fact, the next time I got my "regular" from the local shop, I decided to change it up and ordered a matcha latte, making it more earthy and less sweet, but still hot. You know what? I loved it!

AROMA

Your taste buds and receptors distinguish five basic tastes. However, your olfactory system distinguishes thousands of different volatile chemical compounds. Yes, the amazing abilities of your olfactory system are responsible for aroma detection, and ultimately what flavor you perceive. And since we all experience aroma before taste, we are going to discuss it first.

As far as we're concerned, there are two ways that aromas are going to influence our perception of overall flavor. Aroma can be detected when odors originate from breathing in through your nose. This first method of perceiving aroma is called **orthonasal aroma**. (See Figure 1 for details.) When aromas are strong enough to enter your nostrils before you even take a bite of food or a sip of drink, they can have a profound effect on the overall flavor once you put the food in your mouth. However, aroma

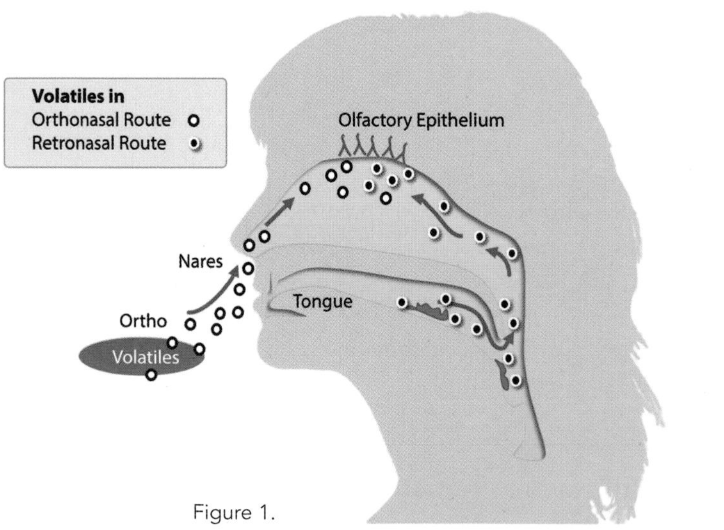

Volatiles in
Orthonasal Route   O
Retronasal Route   ⦾

Olfactory Epithelium

Nares

Tongue

Ortho

Volatiles

Figure 1.

is also detected when you breathe out from your mouth and nose. This is called **retronasal aroma**. Retronasal olfaction is occasionally a sense by itself, but the majority of retronasal aromas combine with other mouth senses, such as basic tastes and mouthfeel. No matter which way you detect the aroma, signals send messages to the brain that tell you what you're eating or drinking.

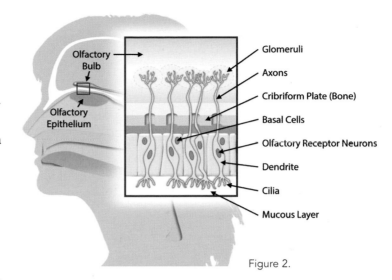

Figure 2.

Let's take a brief look at the process. Odor molecules come in different shapes and sizes. When an odor molecule binds to an odor receptor cell (itself made up of fifty million receptor neurons), electrical signals are sent to the olfactory nerve. This collection of signals is organized into aroma messages and sent on to the olfactory bulb. (See Figure 2 for details.) Throughout your life, olfactory receptors are continuously regenerating and reestablishing connections with the olfactory bulb. Your senses continue to learn new aromas your whole life (all the more reason to keep trying new things).

The olfactory bulb itself begins in the limbic system of your brain. Why is this important? Well, in addition to the limbic system's role in smells (olfactory regulation), this system also controls emotion, behavior, motivation, memory, and autonomic behavior. That's why it can be the case that when you like or dislike a smell, you can trace it back to a long-term memory. It's all the same section of your brain.

That's a lot of science, but it can get even more technical than that. Let's simplify it: volatile molecules are released from everything we eat and drink. These molecules are then evaluated by the brain, and the same area of the brain that evaluates aroma information is also responsible for your emotions, learning, language, and decision-making processes. See the connection? Aromas are read by your olfactory system, which then returns visual images that can also trigger an experience or memory. That's a lot of information from just a smell. These memories, and the experiences you have with them, can lead to a sense of flavor without anything having actually touched your mouth.

SENSORY VOCABULARY AND VARIATION

This is a great place to start decoding and building your own sensory vocabulary. If you pay close attention, you'll quickly realize that when your brain receives an aroma message, it triggers a visual image of something. That visual might be a memory of a person, place, event, or something in the past that you ate or drank. You just need to learn to focus on what that image is, and then you will be able to narrow down a term for what you have smelled. Even better, you should then be able to deconstruct what is in what you just smelled by breaking it into its component pieces.

For example, let's say the smell of something baking wafts into the air. You immediately smile because you're reminded of your grandmother's house at the holidays. What is it exactly

What flavor elements remind you of *your* grandma's cookies?

that made you think of that aroma? It must have been those special cookies that she always baked. Once you get the image of the cookies, now you can think about what the ingredients were: what you remember most were butter, nutmeg, and vanilla. Congratulations! You just deconstructed an aroma and gave yourself the aroma descriptors for what you smelled.

You might not get down to the nitty-gritty of all the ingredients, but if you can start to narrow down the aroma to a visual, like grandma's cookies, you will have a starting point and a vocabulary reference. It also can be fun to try this activity with others and hear what memory descriptors aromas conjure up for people. In fact, during one of the sensory classes in the UC San Diego Extension Brewing Certificate program that Gwen teaches, there was a student who could not figure out the aroma in the vial that was passed around in an exercise. He closed his eyes to further visualize what he was being reminded of from this particular aroma. His response was "Puerto Rico," which made everyone giggle. From there, the class had him narrow down what about Puerto Rico this aroma reminded him of. He figured out that it was the empanadas he would buy from a cart on his way home from school growing up. The aroma he couldn't put a word to happen to be clove, which was a dominant seasoning in those empanadas. Now whenever he smells clove, he immediate gets the visual of his childhood after-school reward, and the word *clove* has a visual in his head. Pretty cool, huh?

— *Ray Isle* —

Ray Isle, executive wine editor of *Food & Wine* magazine, is also a friend to beer. At the annual Food & Wine Classic, an amazing event bringing together food-world stars and the public, Isle shared a number scale he applies to pairings, whether they're with wine or beer.

Can you give us a quick overview of your famous pairing scale?

The pairing scale I use (inspired by cheese guru Max McCalman, who uses a similar scale for cheese and wine pairings) is essentially very simple. It goes from +2 to –2. The best pairings are +2, when both the wine or beer and the food are distinctly improved by the pairing. Those are pairings that make you sit back and think, "Wow— that tastes amazing." A +1 is when one of the two is improved. Most pairings, though, are 0s, where neither the food nor the wine is particularly affected by the matchup, neither is good nor bad. Essentially your palate responds by thinking, "OK, fine, whatever." In a –1, either the food or the wine tastes worse. And a –2 is a disaster; both things taste awful. A big tannic red and a really oily fish like mackerel is a great example. Your mouth will taste like you licked a roll of pennies.

How often do you find foods reach the top end and how often are they the bottom end?

The distribution is pretty much a bell curve. There are very few +2s and –2s, more +1s and –1s, and a whole lot of 0s; the tasting world is full of benign neutrality. At least that's true of wine. At baseline it's a beverage that works very pleasantly with a very wide range of foods—much more than cola, milk, or orange juice, for example.

Do you think the wine world is embracing beer as an ally in pairing?

I think the restaurant wine world certainly is. The wine world as a whole, that's harder to say—I don't think a lot of tasting rooms in Napa are going to start pouring beers alongside their cabernets anytime soon.

What pairing attributes do you like most about beer?

I like the fact that it's not wine, honestly. It's interesting to me to think about pairings for a beverage that has a very different flavor spectrum. With the exception of certain esoteric categories (sour beers, etc.), you aren't working with the same tart acidity that you are with wine, and you generally aren't working with overt fruit flavors either. On the flip side, you typically do have bitterness to play with, and I love bitterness—it's a very underrated flavor characteristic. Plus beer is texturally very different from wine; it feels different in your mouth. We tend to think of texture as a food characteristic, but it's something to consider in beverages as well.

Researchers have found that up to 30 percent of human olfactory receptors can differ between any two individuals. This is significant, and here's why. Every person has around four hundred odor receptors, so a 30 percent differential equals quite a bit of variation in olfactory perceptions. These kinds of variations certainly can have an effect on people's likes or dislikes for certain volatile compounds, and hence anticipated flavor. Whereas you might love cilantro, your friend might have a strong dislike of this herb. Much of it comes down to our genetic variations.

CONSCIOUS SMELLING

There is a technique that we use called "consciously smelling." It's all about being in the moment and remaining fully aware of what you are doing and feeling. It's about making the effort to listen to yourself and what you are experiencing. Sounds Zenlike, right?

Conscious smelling begins with a quick sniff, which helps you focus. Also, as opposed to a deep inhalation, a small sniff will quickly tell you if something is extremely pungent or acrid in aroma, and hopefully prevent premature olfactory burnout. Think about it as if you're testing the temperature of something that might be hot before just picking it up. If you hold your hand near it or just touch it quickly, you're less likely to burn yourself than if you grab it and hold on tight. In fact, just as physical burns scar, you can receive olfactory scarring as well. When certain volatile compounds bind to odor receptors, they can scar if the compound is particularly pungent or too intense, leaving a mark that indicates there was injury. Just think about smelling vinegar or ammonia. That's some potent stuff! The good news is, with some exceptions such as injury or genetics, your olfactory receptors regenerate every sixty days throughout your whole life.

After assessing that the item isn't going to hurt or damage your olfactory system, you are ready to proceed with your aroma adventure. Don't skip the "drive-by" step just because you know what the item is. You are also priming your system for what is to come, and let's face it, some of us are a bit more sensitive to certain aromas. Preventing burnout prior to starting will make your adventure more fun. If you have a beverage, swirl it to release the volatile aromas. Carbonation and heat will also help to release them (think of lime-flavored seltzer water compared to water with lime), so you may not need to swirl as much if it's bubbly or hot (see page 54 for more). Now take a couple of sniffs through your nose with your mouth closed. You can close your eyes, too, if it helps you to visualize what you're smelling. What image pops into your brain? Was it a memory of a person or a place, or another food or beverage?

This is where the phrase "it smells so good I can just taste it" comes from. As discussed, aroma can build up until a particular threshold is reached and a signal is fired off to the brain's limbic system. This is where some crazy triggers happen. Your brain will send signals that will give you an image of what you might be smelling, as well as what that image might taste like, and then an emotional response. Think about the smell of brownies: the image of a brownie comes to mind before you have even seen what this particular brownie looks like. Your mouth might start to salivate, and you may even smile in anticipation. The aroma primes not just your mouth, but your perception of the entire experience of flavor that's about to occur.

All right, time for the last step. This time, take one big long sniff and exhale through your mouth. You have just experienced orthonasal and retronasal aromas as a conscious aroma experience. This experience did not even involve putting anything into your mouth. It was all about the aromatic volatile compounds and how big a part they play when it comes to the overall flavor.

You will need to be aware of how much you do this because you can and will experience olfactory burnout. Since everyone is different and aroma intensities vary based on what you're tasting, the burnout speed will vary. Even when smelling clean laundry, where burnout may not ever happen, you can become accustomed, or acclimated, to the aroma, and then you're not consciously smelling it. The same thing happens when you walk into your house at the end of a long day and are hit with the glorious smell of that slow-cooker meal that you started in the morning. A few minutes later you can no longer smell it because your senses have acclimated.

TASTE

OK, you've sniffed and smelled as much as you can possibly bear. It's time to take a sip, or a bite, and move on to taste!

We have five basic tastes that are detected in the mouth by your taste receptors, which we will just call taste buds. Those five are sweet, sour, salty, bitter, and umami. When you think about eating and drinking, you wouldn't think we'd experience just five basics tastes, though. That's because when we have something in our mouths, whether solid or liquid, we are experiencing a combination of things (the aroma and mouthfeel are also playing their role). (See Figure 3 for details.)

Think of taste elements like the primary colors. Just like the color blue is blue and you do not get it by mixing other colors, you do not get basic tastes through a combination of other elements. Just like blue is blue, sweet is sweet. Tastes do not come

VOLATILE COMPOUNDS

Volatile compounds are molecules that have an ability to become a gas or vaporize—and are thus considered volatile. As temperatures and humidity increase, so does a compound's volatility. Since we just talked about brownies, think of a hot brownie as opposed to a room-temperature brownie. That hot brownie's aromatics permeate the entire kitchen because the compounds are much more volatile. If the brownie were at room temperature, you might not smell the chocolate, butter, and sugar until you brought it directly beneath your nose. A hot, humid day will emphasize aromas that would normally be suppressed by a cold, dry environment like your refrigerator. (Anyone who has left food in a hot car on a summer day can confirm this.)

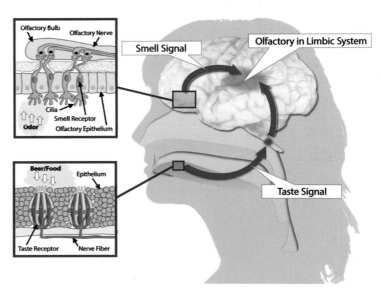

Figure 3.

as the result of mixing, whereas aroma can. Another thing that separates taste from aroma is that we sense the basic tastes on our tongue, soft palate, upper throats, and epiglottis. Tastes are not sensed with our olfactory system. That means that you cannot actually smell sweet, sour, salty, bitter, or umami.

Chances are you already know your own palate somewhat in terms of these basic tastes. Maybe you would describe yourself as a sweet person, or maybe you just love those bitter IPAs. Even if it's not top of mind, you can probably decode your own preferences. Perhaps you add sugar and cream to your coffee, which cuts the bitterness. Or you might find that you use a little more salt than most of your friends.

Recognizing these five basic tastes and being able to pick them out of the sensory picture is one of the most valuable tools you can acquire when it comes to tasting beer and food. It sounds simple, but getting the sensory noise out of the picture is fairly hard.

TASTING EXERCISES

Time to practice! For starting out, we recommend picking a very simple item that will be easy to deconstruct, perhaps an orange or glass of lemonade at room temperature. (By eating or drinking something that is at room temperature, you are eliminating temperature as a variable that might distract you.)

Begin by plugging your nose and taking a bite or a sip. Chew the orange and let it really coat your mouth, or allow the lemonade to warm and coat your mouth. Go ahead

GEEK OUT

PAPILLAE

This illustration shows small bumps, called papillae. These are where your taste buds, each of which contains taste receptor cells, are located. (The taste receptor cells are exactly what their name implies: receptors for the basic tastes.) This tiny world is located not only on the tongue, but on your palate, cheeks, upper throat, and epiglottis. Now you can see how basic tastes are perceived, but not connected with the olfactory system directly.

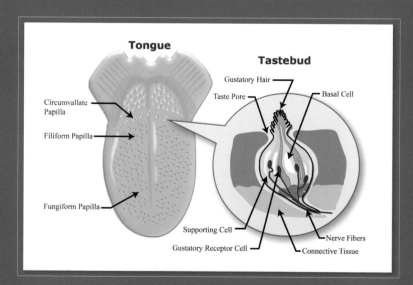

and swallow, but don't unplug your nose. What do you experience without orthonasal or retronasal aromas? If you did not cheat, you should have experienced only the basic tastes of sweet, sour, and bitter, and maybe just a hint of umami, depending on the fruit's ripeness or the ingredients in the lemonade. Go further, though: What is the order in which you taste them? How intense is each one of these basic tastes?

Note: Although when you smell, you may smell elements you would call sweet, you are really experiencing the deconstruction of an element. Take honey or maple syrup, for example. They each have an aroma that you might naturally associate with sweet. However, their aromas could conceivably be accompanied with any of the other basic tastes, depending on the food or drink. So if you smell honey and you describe something as honey sweet instead of just sweet, you have already increased your sensory vocabulary.

Now try it again, but this time release your fingers from your nose as you swallow and exhale. Voila! This should have changed your whole flavor experience, because now you are actually experiencing the aroma along with the basic tastes. What visual descriptors popped into your mind as you exhaled? How are they similar or different from before?

Another fun experiment along the same lines can be done with jelly beans. We recommend trying the following, which we often do at workshops: First, pour out ten jelly beans. Now close your eyes, plug your nose, and eat one jelly bean. Notice how it's only sweet and maybe sour. Now unplug your nose. Whoa! Was that buttered popcorn? This step is a great way to try tasting blind, where even visual data will not cloud your sense of taste.

Now pick a specific color of jelly bean. Repeat the same process as before. In this step, the tasting is not truly blind: you'll come into it with some expectation of flavor and aroma. Still, color does not always correlate to your expectations, so you can get quite a surprise if you taste before you open up to the aroma. Green might be pear or green apple when you were expecting lime. Red could be pomegranate, strawberry, or cinnamon.

In between tastings, don't forget to cleanse your palate and clear your olfactory system. Once you burn out, you will have to take a time-out and step away in order to reset. When it comes to resetting your palate, water and unsalted crackers work wonders. (What sounds like a prison diet actually has the opposite effect; it frees your palate and allows it to continue on your tasting adventure.) Cleansing your olfactory system can be the simple act of tilting your head and smelling your shoulder or your arm. Since

Sweet is one of the five basic tastes, but there are many different ways you'll perceive it.

you're accustomed to your own odor, by smelling yourself you are resetting your system to what you are used to.

THE SWEETEST THING

Sweet is almost always thought of as pleasant. The word *sweet* even imparts positive connotations that reach beyond flavor. Sweet, especially pure carbohydrate sweet, sends the signal to your brain that energy is on its way to your body, so your brain registers sweet as a reward. Sweet also signals nutrition. Fruit, for instance, is sweet when ripe (with a high sugar content), but bitter or sour when unripe. Whereas bitter compounds are added to prevent you from ingesting things, sugar is often added to help the medicine go down.

Where and how you detect sweet can vary in degrees as well as stages. When you taste something, sweet can be detected at the very beginning, somewhere in the middle, or in the finish or aftertaste, all the while competing with the other basic tastes your brain identifies and catalogs. (One of the reasons many people don't care for alternative sweeteners is their tendency to linger in the finish. Additionally, most don't have the depth, complexity, and roundness of sweetness that natural sugars do.) There are hundreds of compounds that taste sweet. How sweet is perceived varies from compound to compound, and when describing sweet, people tend to include the aroma that accompanies the basic taste.

What do you think of when you think of sweet? Sugar may be your first answer. But let's take a step beyond that: What about brown sugar or maple syrup? What does honey sweet taste like versus a citrus sweet such as orange juice? If you start thinking about sweet, you may very well start tying together seemingly unrelated foods. For example, the sweet in chocolate is much different from the sweet you get from an apple, but you'll find it's similar to the sweet quality of butter. In pairing, you may notice that sweet can cut sweet, tannins, bitter, roasted characteristics, capsaicin spicy heat, acidity, and salt.

SALIVATING FOR SOUR

Sure, the classic sour face may be puckered, but sour is a taste that will increase your salivation and make your mouth water. This happens because the acidic quality of sour irritates nerves in your mouth and sends a signal to increase salivation. The higher the concentration of acid, the more saliva you will produce. The body uses saliva to dilute and buffer the acid that is in your mouth, which helps protect the lining of the mouth, throat, and even the stomach from the destructive qualities of acid.

Sour and acidity are nature's warnings that something is rancid or spoiled, but sour isn't nearly as disliked by the masses as bitter. When it comes to sour as a taste, it's helpful to start thinking about which acids might be in play. The big ones are citric acid (lemon-like), lactic acid (sour milk), and acetic acid (vinegar). Test your palate with condiments. Try a careful tasting of your favorite ketchup, mustard, and salad dressings, which are all full of sour vinegar notes. You could also try pickled veggies for a big hit of acetic acid. Fruit juices, jams, and of course anything made with citrus (such as fresh lemonade) are a good place to search for citric acid. Cheeses, sour cream, and yogurt are great places to taste lactic acid, and surprisingly, so is chocolate! Other acids that we don't commonly think of are malic (green apple, grapes, rhubarb), tartaric (grapes, banana, apricot, and tamarind), and gluconic (honey, pineapple, cantaloupe).

You can see with all the acids that come into play with sour, that not all sours will be described the same way. Sour and acid can cut and balance other sources of sour and acid. Sour and sweet contrast each other to create balance, such as a honey mustard or good old sweet-and-sour sauce. Sour will cut through fat, calm salt, and can contrast tannins as well.

THE ZEN OF SALT

We won't get into the biology, but salt is so important to your existence that your body

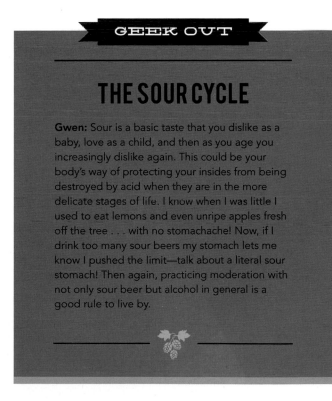

GEEK OUT

THE SOUR CYCLE

Gwen: Sour is a basic taste that you dislike as a baby, love as a child, and then as you age you increasingly dislike again. This could be your body's way of protecting your insides from being destroyed by acid when they are in the more delicate stages of life. I know when I was little I used to eat lemons and even unripe apples fresh off the tree . . . with no stomachache! Now, if I drink too many sour beers my stomach lets me know I pushed the limit—talk about a literal sour stomach! Then again, practicing moderation with not only sour beer but alcohol in general is a good rule to live by.

Salt is a basic taste that can cause a variety of interactions.

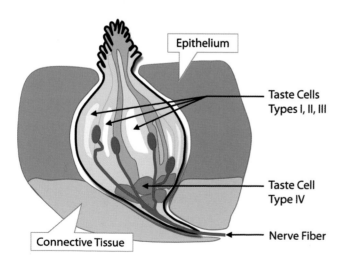

Details of the different types of taste receptor cells found in every taste bud.

naturally craves it (though it typically craves more than we actually need). Yet when it comes to the perception of food and drink, we're more concerned with what salt does on the palate—and it's not always what you'd expect.

So what does salt taste like? A quick dip into the ocean where you're pummeled by a wave can force you to get the taste. Or maybe you've mixed a glass of saltwater to gargle with for an irritation in your mouth. Even if you think you know just what salt tastes like, a great calibration exercise is to sprinkle some salt straight onto a plate, lick your pinky, dip it in, and taste. Now try to smell just the salt on the plate. You can't! This is another example to reinforce that the basic tastes are not aromatic.

Just like beer, not all salts are created equal. There's kosher salt, sea salt (of many origins), flake salt, smoked salt, seasoned salt, and Himalayan salt, among others. Since we are busy questioning everything, we challenge you to evaluate the quality and source of *all* the ingredients you use, including your condiments and spices—and yes, even your salt.

If something is rather bland, just a pinch of salt makes a world of difference—think about a salted cracker versus an unsalted one. At higher levels, however, salt can not only be detected but can be quite unpleasant. Still, whether you prefer sweet or savory by nature, salt can be on your side. How? The correct amount of salt can suppress bitter and sour acidic notes and thus enhance your perception of sweet. On the other hand, salt in combination with umami will enhance the overall savoriness of a food. Salt is also known to increase or heighten the impressions of astringency and tannins.

The classic food for showing how salt works in surprising ways is grapefruit. Ready to play along at home? Just slice up a grapefruit and add a pinch of salt to one piece and a pinch of sugar to another. Now taste them both and see how the basic tastes have changed. You would expect the piece with sugar to be sweeter, but actually it is the one with salt that has

NaCl

There is one bit of salt science we should mention because it explains what's happening under the surface. In table salt, positively charged sodium (Na+) is attached to negatively charged chlorine (Cl-). Salt will move from higher concentration to lower concentration through the process of osmosis. As the result of this chemical reaction, water will move out of cells. This can also be referred to as "salting out." If you have ever salted a piece of fruit, you know that water droplets bead on the flesh of the fruit, which can give the perception of increased crispness.

Heat can also increase this reaction because it accelerates the evaporation of water. When water molecules are pulled to the surface, the protein molecules in the food band together and precipitate. So when you use a salt rub on meat prior to cooking it, the moisture is pulled from the inside to the outside and can give you a crisp outside layer. Salt and heat also increase the aromas released by the food because they are pulled into the air in a more concentrated form.

Too much salt tastewise can be useful for drying out some foods—think of curing meat. The lack of moisture makes the environment less desirable for bacteria. Excessive salt dehydrates the items it comes in contact with—like the reactions that occur when using salt for curing meat.

"Salting in" is when the salt concentration in food is increased by suspending the food in a liquid such as a marinade, brine, or pickling solution. The higher concentration of salt will move from the solution into the food cells, but because the food is surrounded by water as well as salt, water will also move into the cells. This helps the food gain moisture overall. If you want to experiment with this, just cut an apple into slices. Place half of the slices on a plate and salt them. Place the other half of the apple slices in a bowl of salted water. Wait thirty minutes, then taste both.

an increased perception of sweet. The salt suppresses the bitter, which in turn suppresses sour and allows the sweet to be enhanced.

Here's another taste test: tomorrow morning when you brew your coffee, take a sip of it black then add a pinch of salt. Now take another sip. You will find that adding salt to coffee tends to cut the bitterness, which allows other flavors to be accentuated and creates a more balanced, mellow, and nuanced cup. In some countries, people use water that has a higher salt content than distilled water to brew their coffee so this effect occurs naturally. In other countries, it's common practice to add a pinch of salt before brewing the coffee. Maybe now you'll make it a new custom in your house.

BITTER BY NATURE

Bitter is nature's way of telling us that something might be poisonous or toxic. That's why as we humans have evolved, bitter has become the most sensitive of the basic tastes. To this day, bitter compounds are often added to drugs, chemicals, pesticides, and more as a taste-based deterrent. Babies will reject anything bitter that is placed into their mouths, and if you've had a puppy you may know about using bitter sprays to prevent chewing and biting.

Since bitter can be detected by most people at a very low threshold, a small amount goes a long way, and too much bitter can quickly become overwhelming. Yet bitter tastes can be complex, and even pleasant. When you have something that is extremely salty or sweet, a bit of bitter will add balance. Bitter can also cut bitter and umami; think about how a bitter vegetable such as kale cuts the umami of bacon. Bitter also cuts through fats and oils (think bacon again), which will come in very handy when we start talking about pairings. Last but not least, bitter contrasts and enhances capsaicin heat. This can be a pleasant or unpleasant combination, depending on your preference level for spice.

According to research done by the National Institutes of Health, 25 percent of the populations is considered taste tolerant to bitter compounds, meaning their palates are not very sensitive to bitter compared to the average palate. These are the people who are more likely to take their coffee black. They also would be more likely to enjoy an aggressive IPA or bitter veggies such as Brussels sprouts, dandelion greens, arugula, or kale. On the opposite end of the spectrum, 25 percent of the population is considered taste intolerant to bitter compounds. These are the folks who may never appreciate a good IPA. That leaves 50 percent of the population somewhere in between; they can go either way. As far as tasting and pairing goes, this tells us that no two people are going to perceive bitter in food and beverages the exact same way, and that bitter is perhaps the most divisive basic taste.

Bitterness intensities vary quite a bit. When in balance, bitter can be restrained or moderate. When out of balance, it can be perceived as drying, harsh, and astringent. (This is why astringency, which is a mouthfeel, is sometimes confused with bitterness.)

UMAMI = DELICIOUS TASTE

Umami has to be the most difficult-to-describe basic taste. It's meaty, savory, brothy, causes salivation, and lingers in the mouth. Officially identified in 1908 by a Japanese scientist, umami is tasted by your receptors as the amino acid glutamate. MSG (or monosodium glutamate) has umami. Perhaps it's easiest to pinpoint what it tastes like through examples:

Umami is the most recently documented basic taste.

- **Tomatoes:** Glutamic acid is what gives ripe tomatoes their savory quality. In other words, they're bursting with umami! This is probably why so many recipes that are meaty incorporate ripe tomatoes. Just think of chili, stew, or spaghetti sauce and how those tomatoes work with meats to make something that's super savory.
- **Yeast:** When yeast cells self-destruct, a process called autolysis, the cell walls break down into basic components that contain free glutamic acid. That's why meat alternatives for vegans and vegetarians often rely on yeast for that savory quality they'd otherwise lack. Powdered yeast is also found in packaged foods, like chips, to boost the addictive flavors.
- **Cheese:** Cheese, which is high in protein, is another big umami food. As cheese ages, the protein molecules begin to break down and decrease in size. The smaller the protein molecule, the higher the umami taste. So it makes sense that aged cheeses, such as Parmesan, are highest in umami. This is also true with ripe vegetables compared to unripe; it takes time for the umami to develop.
- **Fish sauce/anchovies:** The fermentation of fish with sea salt yields amino acids that include glutamic acids, and the salt emphasizes the autolysis richness of umami,

much like yeast cell, when they self-destruct. It might not sound appetizing to discuss microbes fermenting fish, but the flavors they produce balance and add excitement to many dishes.

As you can see from that list, there are certain processes that either create umami or amplify it. In general, heating, fermentation, aging, ripening, drying, and curing all reduce the size of protein molecules and increase the umami taste in foods and beverages. Three quick umami facts before we move on:

1. Beers can have low levels of umami from yeast. Often this comes out more when beers are aged.
2. Salt enhances the perceived savoriness, which means it can be used to quickly boost umami when umami is already present.
3. Umami can emphasize the perception of sour and acidity, and it can complement not just salt, but fat, sweet, and bitter. Adding a dash of soy sauce to sweet-and-sour soup, a sprinkle of cheese to tomato sauce, or caramelizing mushrooms are all examples of these kinds of umami interactions.

Are ready for some hands-on training? Grab a bottle of ketchup. First, with your mouth shut, smell the ketchup. Soak up all its aroma. Next, plug your nose with your fingers and place a drop of ketchup on your tongue but do not release your fingers. Let the ketchup coat your mouth and think about what basic tastes you're experiencing. You should register salt,

GEEK OUT

THE SICK EFFECT

People with colds often say food and beverages don't taste good or don't taste right. That's partly because you're not getting the full aroma you're used to from foods or beverages. However, your immune system is cranked up, and this can change your basic taste cravings as well. For example:

- Sweet is a signal for energy and hence a pleasant taste when sick.
- Sour can be the signal for rancid or spoiled foods. Since your defenses are up, most sour things won't sound appetizing.
- Salt, on the other hand, is craved even more than usual when you're sick because salt is vital to overall well-being.
- Remember how bitter is considered a sign of something toxic? When you're sick, even the bitterness of coffee is one of those things that become unappealing.
- Umami is tricky to decode, but brothy soups can certainly be craved when sick, but avoid soups containing tomato because of the sour/acid component.

Everyone's different, of course. So next time you're under the weather, look on the bright side and learn a little something about your own palate.

sweet, sour, and savory, and possibly some bitter. Now, as you are swallowing, release your fingers from your nose and exhale to get the retronasal aroma. As you likely noticed, ketchup not only involves all the basic tastes you know, but it also gives you a hit of umami in the form of glutamic acid. If you try it again and think about those ripe, cooked tomatoes that are used in ketchup, when you deconstruct the aroma and flavor you can probably pick out the mouthwatering, savory effect they have. That is umami at work as a basic taste. If you are still struggling to wrap your head around it, try another tasting, but this time with an aged cheese like Parmesan or Asiago.

ADDITIONAL FLAVOR: FAT

Besides the accepted basic tastes, there are additional flavor elements. While research is not yet to the point where they can officially be added to our basic tastes list, there are two in particular that are very important when pairing, so we want to discuss them here: fat and alcohol.

Let's start with fat. Also known as lipids, fats are molecules composed of fatty acids (hydrogen and carbon atoms). When metabolized, these molecules can provide energy, be used as cell membrane building blocks, or be stored for future energy. The structure of the fatty acid determines the type of fat: solid or liquid, animal or vegetable, saturated or unsaturated (and then mono- and polyunsaturated).

Saturated fats, such as butter or coconut oil, are solid at room temperature because they are "saturated," or covered in hydrogen atoms. Unsaturated fats, including olive oil or fish oil, are liquid at room temperature and have pairs of hydrogen atoms missing from their chains. Both plants and animals contain a mixed amount of saturated and unsaturated fats. Animals, with the exception

continued on page 46

CHARLIE PAPAZIAN'S TAKE ON UMAMI

Who is Charlie, you may ask? Well, he's the father of homebrewing in the United States, founder of the Great American Beer Festival, and president of the Brewers Association. Directly or indirectly, Charlie has influenced more beer people around the world than just about anyone else. And he's not just into homebrewing and beer, he's also into food. He's extremely well traveled, and thus his friends are always gleaning insight from his beer and food adventures. He's also fascinated with the topic of umami, the fifth basic taste.

Charlie: I've recently discovered that for me, food and craft beer pairings are not about the marriage, nor the independent characteristics of food and beer. Pairings are about the child—the final, resulting experience.

It's all about something called umami, a fifth taste sensation we all experience but are usually unaware of. Combining different elements of umami creates enhanced flavor experiences. Pairing acidic foods and beverages with umami proteins also intensifies flavor experiences. This is one of the keys to understanding how beer flavors interact with food to create the pleasure of umami. Simply speaking, when enjoying meat, seafood, and mushrooms (foods high in umami), we should accent those foods with salt, sour/acidity, and bitter flavors. Craft beer offers two out of three: sour/acidity and bitterness. Want to try it for yourself? Give one of these a taste:

- Parmigiano-Reggiano and porter
- Spanish sardines and IPA
- Aged prosciutto and pilsener
- Grilled shitake mushrooms and American pale ale

— Dr. Nicole Garneau —

Nicole Garneau is the chair of the Health Sciences Department and curator of human health at the Denver Museum of Nature & Science, and she is leading the way on research tied to how we taste—including taking a look at bitterness as a basic taste and dispelling the supertaster myth. Her work documenting how the sixth basic taste could be fat (omega-6 fatty acids) may very well evolve how we view the basic tastes. On top of that, she loves beer!

What is going on behind the scenes in research tied to flavor?

Flavor is a complicated beast. It is the brain taking in all the information it can from the environment and then making a decision to help us survive: eat/drink more, or stop, or maybe even spit it out. We use our peripheral nervous system (in other words, our senses) to detect these clues about foodstuffs—Is it nutritious? Is it poisonous?—and those clues are sent to the brain for perception, identification if possible, and then they are used to recall past experiences. Finally, the brain makes a decision on what to tell the body to do. The cutting-edge research is really about cross-modal interactions, how one sense or input can affect

another. We've got a pretty good understanding of the role of genetics and are beginning to understand that other factors like age play a big role, but we're only now starting to really get a handle on how our experiential differences and emotions can also alter our perception response.

What are the obstacles to better understanding complex flavor mixtures?

Real food and drink are not usually made up of only one or two tastes and odors, yet most of the research on mixtures is binary (it looks at two flavor compounds). At the end of the day, we can't necessarily generalize what happens in a binary mixture to what happens in a complex mixture. Studies show that in complex mixtures we can identify, on average, only up to three individual tastes and smells. Researchers hypothesize that this might be due to short-term memory and processing capacity, and that your brain just can't identify everything above threshold in such a short period of time. In addition, at the molecular level, things aren't so straightforward. Physical interactions between the molecules can occur and there may be competition for receptor binding in your taste buds, both of which can lead to suppression of flavor. So although a molecule exists in your pairing, the signal recognizing the molecule may never make it to your brain, and therefore you may not perceive it. As an industry moving forward, to really understand pairings we will need to recruit an interdisciplinary group of neuroscientists, molecular biologists, geneticists, and other experts to delineate this complex process.

How does that relate to beer?

In all the time I've spent digging into the science of beer, there is one thing that has not changed: the complexity of beer flavor and the added complication when you add in food pairings.

The craft beer industry is growing and evolving rapidly. This is great . . . and also tricky, because the science can't keep up. In terms of sensory science, much of what we know about flavor in beer is based on outdated data about lagers and other pale-roast varieties. In the case of the flavor wheel, the data is nearly forty years old! We know much less about the flavor components of the wide range of beer styles that exist than you would think based on the number of tasting and beer pairing events out there. When it comes to pairing, unfortunately our understanding is not much better in the world of traditional chemoreception science. There is a significant amount of data from scientific papers that are reporting on bitter in mixture studies, however most are on the study of caffeine, propylthiouracil (PROP), phenylthiocarbamide (PTC), and quinine, *not* bittering molecules from hops. Moreover, while we do generalize data from one bittering agent to all bittering agents, the fact is there are forty commonly recognized genes that account for a confirmed twenty-five receptors for bitter—and the receptors known for hop-derived bitter molecules are not the same receptors that quinine, PTC, and PROP bind to. So in reality, it is difficult to generalize, although it's the best we can do at this point. The good news is that through the efforts of the American Society of Brewing Chemists, we have started to pool our collective resources as a community to develop and answer the scientific questions. Plain and simple, as an industry we need to invest more thought, effort, and resources into scientific experiments to fully understand beer itself if we are ever going to understand beer pairings.

How will the research you are doing today evolve how we think about beer and food?

We are pushing the boundaries of taste in our lab and challenging the central dogmas in the field. Our first study sought to replicate supertaster data, and we were all surprised when our data definitively refuted the conclusions of the original study. What a lot of folks don't realize is that the scientific definition of *supertasters* is people highly sensitive to the bitter taste from the chemicals PROP and PCT, bitter molecules commonly used in taste research that are related to foods like broccoli and kale. Supertasting has nothing to do with any other tastes or sensations, but somewhere along the way the use of the superlative *super-* allowed people to overgeneralize that supertasters are super at all tasting. While our data confirm that genetics is the key predictor in the ability to taste bitter, we found genetics were not responsible for supertasting. In an effort to explain this phenomenon, previously published works have attributed supertasting to a high number of papillae (bumps) on the tongue. We were surprised by what we found when they tried to reproduce this effect. No matter how we looked at the data, we couldn't replicate this long-held assumption that a high number of papillae equals supertasting. We published this study in the open access journal *Frontiers in Integrative Neuroscience*, and it has since fueled our confidence to challenge and explore the unreached areas of taste. We are working to prove that fat is the sixth taste and are in talks with microbiologists to study the role of the oral microbiome in how we perceive food and drink. It is an exciting time for understanding flavor and a great time for beer sensory science to become a driver in the future of chemoreception studies.

Photo Credit: Tara Hubner, Denver Museum of Nature and Science

continued from page 43

of some seafood, have a large percentage of saturated fats, whereas plants typically contain a larger percentage of unsaturated fats. When you saturate the molecules of polyunsaturated fats with hydrogen, a process known as hydrogenating, these liquid oils (fats) become solid at room temperature. Margarine is a good example of this process.

When it comes to pairing, the intensity of the fat in a dish can overwhelm other elements. Beer is fat free, so use the magical ingredients of hops, carbonation, and alcohol to cut through the fattiest of foods and enhance your enjoyment of the entire pairing. Cheeseburger with bacon? Hoppy IPA it is! Cleanse your palate of a fatty mouthcoating from a blue cheese or Gouda with a higher alcohol beer like a barley wine. Or, since avocados are satisfying but fatty, try pairing them with the high carbonation of a Belgian-style saison.

In food, beyond nutrients, fat is essential for flavor. Barb Stuckey's *Taste What You're Missing* does a fantastic job of describing how fat stretches, carries, and thus highlights the flavor of the other ingredients around it. So in food and pairing, don't shy from fat, as it is your friend for flavor—just don't have it be all that your dish is about.

ADDITIONAL FLAVOR: ALCOHOL

Oh alcohol, how we love thee. Yet alcohol offers more than just a buzz. As a main component of beer, it's a huge factor in pairing. It increases the body of beer and is associated with mouthfeel and specific flavors of its own.

Like all flavors elements, alcohol can be your friend or your foe when considered in the context of pairing. In beer, alcohol is primarily the chemical compound ethanol. It is a byproduct of yeast in the fermentation process and is the chemical that causes intoxication if consumed in excess.

Ethanol in its pure form is a volatile and flammable solvent. In beer, those solvent properties allow the alcohol in beer to cut through fat in foods, which helps keep the food from barreling over the beer. Those solvent properties are also responsible for increasing volatile spice heat, like capsaicin in peppers, ginger, or cinnamon. This is why higher-alcohol beverages clash with spicy food. Lucky for us, malt's residual sugars lessen that heat. Since most spirits and wine have higher alcohol by volume and lower residual sugar, many beers provide a better match.

A few other things to keep in mind regarding alcohol:

- Always consider alcohol by volume (ABV). Foods higher in fat are rich and heavy, and thus more intense, so serve them with a higher ABV beer to match that intensity. On the other hand, milder dishes, such as shellfish, are lower in intensity and call for a lower ABV beer.
- When it comes to sweet foods, alcohol can really bring balance to the pairing. If you have a sweet piece of chocolate cake with buttercream icing, bring in a higher-alcohol beer like an American imperial stout for complete bliss.
- Alcohol intensity can be heightened by salt, so watch your beer's ABV with a salty dish or you could end up with a train wreck of *fusel* proportions (*fusel* is the German word for "bad liquor").

MOUTHFEEL

While aroma and taste are often top of mind—likely because they're more easily understood—the importance of mouthfeel on flavor cannot be overstated. What a sensation feels like in your mouth and/or throat makes up the final piece of flavor.

In a nutshell, it involves the physical (also referred to as tactile) mouthfeel, which includes texture, and the chemical (also referred to as trigeminal) mouthfeel, which includes temperature and sensations. Let's begin with the **physical** aspect of texture and how profound an effect that has on the overall flavor perception of food.

To experience a blind texture-based tasting yourself, try the classic Halloween game where you fill mystery buckets with creepy treats. Make sure to label the buckets with various body parts to match the textures of each food: peeled grapes or cocktail onions are eyeballs, dried apricots are ears, leather fruit rolls can be tongues, cotton candy is matted hair, candy corn are teeth . . . the possibilities are only limited by your imagination. After people reach in, have them close their eyes and eat what they just touched. Because of the messages their brains have already received, that mouthfeel is going to be fairly disturbing at first. Once people get rid of those emotional thoughts, the true mouthfeel comes into focus. And on the upside, everyone who played will now have a whole new image in their memory banks for those foods.

Gwen: Training flavor panels begins with products that are composed of simple ingredients: mayonnaise, for example. Mayonnaise deconstructed involves oils (vegetable, canola, olive, safflower), eggs (whole, yokes, and whites), and various spices such as onion and garlic. The panelists register basic tastes of sweet, salt, and sour. (Mayonnaise is also rich in umami. Bonus!) When you think about tasting oil and egg all on their own, you think a lot about mouthfeel. Descriptions might include sensations such as oily, mouthcoat, chalky, powdery, and slick.

Let's move on to **chemical** mouthfeel, which includes temperature, touch, and sound reactions. These sensations have descriptors such as full bodied, effervescent, astringent, flat, crispy, crunchy, mouth coating, cold, hot, creamy, spicy heat, herbal cool, and alcohol burn. This still may sound abstract, but really you're quite used to these sensations: think about coolness from mint, menthol, eucalyptus, and camphor or that sense of heat you get from chili peppers, ginger, black pepper, and some kinds of herbs. Of course, alcohol is a big sensation in beer as well, and there are two other big ones: temperature and carbonation.

Temperature is an often-overlooked part of chemical mouthfeel. Sure, ice cream feels cold, coffee feels hot, and so on. But temperature is even more important than you might think. It has the ability to suppress aromas and mask basic tastes, and it also has the ability to amplify them. For example, sweetness is one of the basics tastes that can be greatly suppressed by cold temperatures. Think of ice cream again: increasing the temperature changes the ice cream from an amazingly delicious dessert to a bowl of glop too sweet to be enjoyable. The same thing happens with liquids such as beer. Cold will suppress the overall flavor. Sometimes that's good, and sometimes it's not.

The fizzy feel of carbonation is an important one too. Sure, beer is bubbly, but there's a surprising range. Think of the following scenarios:

TRP CHANNELS

Ion channels are a type of protein that regulates the movement of ions across the membranes of cells. They have to be the correct ion in both shape and size to fit into the channels. It's a round peg into a round hole type of thing. When it comes to temperature, the ion channels are referred to as thermo-TRP channels. TRP is an acronym for transient receptor potential.

It was recently discovered that these ion channels can be activated by specific compounds and can send messages to the brain that indicate temperature sensations have occurred. Trigeminal mouthfeel sensations that are not from an actual temperature change are referred to as false cold or false heat reactions. For example, when you eat something minty, your brain is tricked by the menthol chemicals that bind to the thermo-TRP channel (TRP-M8) to give the impression of cold.

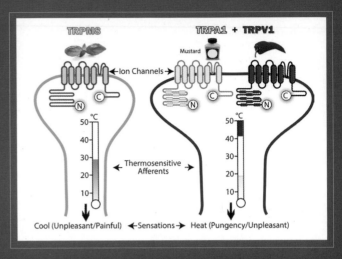

This seems like a great time for an experiment. Eat something minty, like a peppermint. Now drink something cold, like ice water. Since your sensory neurons are still activated and are thinking cold, when you introduce an actual cold item, it will seem even colder. Maybe this is why hot mint tea always seems to cool off faster than other teas. Spiciness from capsaicin and ethanol activates a different thermos-TRP ion channel (TRP-V1). Not only is this channel activated by hot peppers found in Mexican, Thai, Indian, and Szechuan dishes, good old black pepper also does the trick. The activating capsaicin chemical is also found in very small amounts in oregano, cinnamon, and cilantro.

- **Normal carbonation (CO_2):** When carbon dioxide dissolves and is suspended under pressure in a liquid, it is known as carbonation. Once that pressure is released, small bubbles are produced from the chemical reaction that gives an effervescent fizz to the liquid.
- **Nitrogenated:** A beer on a nitrogen tap can be a beautiful thing. Just picture the classic cascading bubbles in an Irish-style dry tout or English-style milk stout—doesn't it make your mouth water? The next time you order one, pay attention to the way nitrogen affects the feel of the beer in your mouth. A nitrogenized beer has smaller bubbles than the same beer with CO_2 and will give the beer a smoother, softer mouthfeel.
- **Cask:** Beer on cask has very little carbonation, and the temperature is typically warmer than beer on tap. Taken together, this change in character often elicits a love-it-or-hate-it reaction, even among beer nerds.
- **Flat or still:** When you expect a beer to have carbonation only to find it's flat for some reason, it can really affect your perception of the beverage. Chances are, if you take a sip of flat beer you're going to quickly make a determination if you should pour the rest out or embrace it while you finish it.

Although mouthfeel is fun to learn about and think about in isolation, contemplating it as a piece of the flavor puzzle is key. Start thinking about mouthfeel as you're considering aroma and the basic tastes. How is mouthfeel affecting your perception together with those elements? This all brings us to our final thought . . .

FLAVOR IS A FUSION

We have spent many years training, teaching, and enlightening people about the pleasures of sensory exploration. When teaching, and certainly when writing, we have discovered that there will always be parts of the learning experience we just can't convey—you will have to do plenty of hands-on (or should we say mouths-on?) exploration on your own.

Still, it's safe to say that good sensory training starts with the basics we've outlined here. When it comes to everything you do in life, you have to start simple and then build to the more complicated. Beer and food pairing is no different. By breaking aroma, taste, and mouthfeel out into pieces and appreciating each aspect individually, you will build a foundation so you can then move on to understand the why, what, and how of tasting and of pairing. Until you are able to separate the pieces of flavor, it is going to be very difficult for you to explain why your pairings work or don't work. You must learn to simplify.

Yet at some point, it all needs to come together. Flavor is the sum of the parts you've just learned about; it's a fusion of aroma, taste, and mouthfeel. Moving forward, we're going to expand on these foundations of perception. We'll address how flavors work together in different ways and also what happens when flavors clash. As you come along with us, keep your mind and palate open, not only to the full experience but to all the component pieces and parts. If something doesn't make sense or isn't working for you for some reason, come back to this chapter as you think about why. It could be a particular aroma, but it could also have to do with mouthfeel. These will be the first part of your tasting equation and pairing mental library. Soon you'll find you're automatically integrating this sensory training into your daily life!

CHAPTER
— 3 —

TASTING
BEER

Now that we've covered how we perceive in general, it's time to move on to the good stuff: tasting beer. The beautiful thing about beer is that each one is different in its own special way. Some may be dramatically different, like a Belgian-style lambic or gueuze compared to a smoked porter. However, even within a style, such as American India pale ale, there is a wide range of aromas, basic taste elements, and different mouthfeels.

At the heart of this chapter, we will deconstruct what we're drinking. This will give you a greater understanding of how beer works with food and help you decode the "why" of pairings that work (and pairings that don't work). It will not only make you more knowledgeable about pairing, it could very well make you a better chef as well. By increasing and expanding your understanding of beer, you'll open all kinds of sensory doors. Like the viewer of an impressionist painting, you'll step toward the painting and start examining individual brushstrokes of color.

As you taste with friends or family, you will also begin to understand the way flavor comes across to others, notably when they agree or disagree with your likes and dislikes. Paying attention to these similarities and differences will make you an even more powerful master of tasting, and eventually of pairing. When you can present multiple pairings over the course of a meal with everyone's preferences in mind, you will be the best host ever!

At the heart of thinking about others' preferences as well as your own is a central truth: there are no right and wrong answers when it comes to taste. If you've ever read an old book or taken a class where there are clear instructions telling you what you "should" be smelling or tasting, it's time to toss that advice right out the window. We're all unique individuals, and this translates to our individual food and beverage preferences, which in turn affect flavor. As we've previously pointed out, both pairing and perception (what we sense) is personal. Just like our taste in fashion, art, food, movies, and more is unique, so, too, is flavor.

Gwen: For example, my mother loves onions and will eat one like an apple. That makes me gag! My own strong dislike of onions affects how I perceive some hoppy beers, since some crops of particular hops can give off an onion-like aroma—how gross! But hand that beer to my mom, and she'd think the bouquet is downright pleasant. Taking that even further, if a beer with a few onion notes were paired with a dish containing onions, my mom would be in heaven while I wouldn't touch the stuff. All that is to say that personal preference can lead to a situation where you have the same dish and beer, but two different people who read them completely differently. (A simple switch of beer may make the oniony dish palatable to me and the combination a home run.)

HOW TO TASTE BEER

SET UP FOR SUCCESS

When you're tasting beer—we mean really, seriously tasting beer and not just socially sampling—you have to start by preparing for your tasting. Make sure you have exactly what you need on hand: clean glasses, water, plain crackers, pen, and paper. Just as important, make sure to avoid bringing certain things to the table. Wait, what shouldn't be at the tasting station? Anything that smells, of course. If you have scented lotion or even a strong soapy

Sampling in smaller quantities will allow you to evaluate a variety of beer styles in one sitting.

smell on your hands, that can affect the tasting. So can your writing utensil, of all things: just give a freshly sharpened pencil a whiff, or a pen with a large rubber grip. You don't want those notes in your beer! Bring to the table only your unscented self and clean, simple pens.

The temperature of the beer will also alter your tasting experience. Not all beer styles are created equal, yet most are served at standard refrigerator and kegerator temperatures: a chilly 38 degrees Fahrenheit. You will find aromatic nuances (such as hop aroma and yeasty esters) are easier to detect as the beer warms up. When tasting at home, simply remove all the beers from the fridge ten minutes before serving, or even longer for beers that are more than 8 percent ABV. If you don't have that option and the beer feels too cold in the glass, cup your glass in your hands. Your body heat will help it warm up faster.

When it comes to what you're drinking out of, it's helpful to have a set of small taster-size glasses. About two to three ounces of beer is all each person needs for a tasting, though you should look for glasses that are slightly larger than that, as you need room to swirl the beer.

Even when we are out at breweries, we love, love, love taster-size beers. Yes, we know we have been saying to be open to possibilities and new flavors; however, if you truly do not like something, then the experience will become counterproductive if you force down a full pint. Also, if you're trying to taste a few beers in one trip—for the purposes of deconstruction, of

Appreciating beer often starts with its visual attributes.

course—it's best to evaluate just a few ounces at a time. With that slightly tipsy feeling comes slightly fuzzy senses!

POUR AND EXAMINE

OK, now you're just about ready to pour your beer. Make sure your glassware is clean, pop the top, and fill the glass—but not to the brim. Remember, although you might not be judging beer, you are going to be using the same techniques as a judge. That means you need room to swirl the beer and release the aroma, helping the carbonation carry volatile compounds up and out of the glass toward your nose.

Now examine the beer. First you're looking at the color, which can be anywhere form pale straw to gold, amber, copper, brown, or black.

Next, examine the collar of foam (also known as the head) on top of the beer before it dissipates. Is it thick and creamy, a thing of beauty? Or is it thin to nonexistent? Continue to observe the foam for a moment. Does the foam linger longer than sixty seconds, or does it quickly collapse? Do the bubbles look mousse-like and stable, or do they look more like whisked milk and appear thin and fragile? Generally, thick, creamy, long-lasting foam is a hallmark of many German and Belgian beer styles as well as strongly hopped styles such as IPAs. American lagers, on the other hand, tend to have smaller, thinner, and less long-lasting heads.

Last, is your beer cloudy or clear? Is there a slight haze, or you can see through it? Cloudiness can be a sign of suspended hops or yeast and is certainly a sign that the beer is unfiltered. Crystal-clear beer may be filtered, or it may simply be a style where the yeast and hops drop out and leave the beer relatively clear, as with pilseners and other pale lagers.

SMELL

With the visual inspection complete, swirl the beer gently to help release those volatile aroma compounds. Another trick to coax out aroma is to use the palm of your hand to trap volatile aromas, and then let them escape with your nose right over the glass.

Although you cannot smell basic tastes, you can follow the visual clues from your brain.

Now we recommend taking either three short sniffs or one long one. Then do the reverse. Continue to sniff and change the position of your nose: in the glass, just above the glass, and several inches away from the glass. See what changes.

You'll find aromatics can be quite complex and layered. Try to pick out the individual elements and the order they appear in your brain. Remember, you do not actually smell sweet, sour, salty, bitter, or umami (those are the basic tastes that we sense via our tongue and soft palate). If those descriptors come to mind, try to dig deeper and give what you smell a more descriptive term.

Let's say that the first aroma you smell is what you think of as sour. Press pause and focus on what image that "sour" smell brings to mind. Is it lemon or sour cream or red wine vinegar? Use any memories that spring to mind to your advantage and break it down even further.

After you have some notes on the basics, move on to specific beer ingredients. You already know that beer is made up of malt, hops, yeast, and water. Deconstruct the beer a bit for each one of those elements (see pages 12–19 for more on each).

Aroma will continue later in the tasting, after you take a sip, thanks to retronasal aroma. However, these initial notes set the tone for the first sip and will foreshadow a beer's flavor.

TAKE A SIP

Ah yes, it's finally time: go ahead and take a sip. No, wait! Not just any sip. Sip just enough to whet your whistle. It will prime your mouth and get both your mind and palate in the game. Now slowly sip again and pay close attention to the order of the elements as they appear to you.

At this point, a good first step is to seek out the basic tastes, then move on to beer

A beer's aromatics ignite visual sensory images and prime you for what's to come.

A proper beer tasting means you'll evaluate aromatics, basic tastes, and mouthfeel for the full flavor picture.

ingredients—the same way you did when analyzing aroma. Going beyond the most basic elements and breaking flavor down to more descriptive terms will give you valuable information. It will help you decode why you like what you like, and it will also come in handy when it comes to pairing beer with food.

As you swallow one of your sips, exhale through your nose. This action provides a combination of retronasal aromas and tastes from the mouth and throat. Many people find this can emphasize certain elements that were not previously detected.

Next, consider the body and the physical feel of the beer on your tongue. These are both the sense of mouthfeel. Just as your fingertips sense and feel textures, so do your tongue and soft palate. Examples of descriptors might be a mouthcoat (wow, this beer is sticky), thick, thin, sharp, smooth, astringent, powdery, cooling, spicy (think of the heat you get from peppers, ginger, or even mustard seeds), or alcohol-warming. Be sure to make note of the carbonation if it is particularly effervescent or very low. If you're still unsure of how one mouthfeel might be different from another, try a Belgian-style blonde ale next to an imperial stout. You'll instantly get the difference.

The final component you want to think about is the aftertaste, also known as the finish of the beer. About thirty seconds after swallowing, what flavors remain? Are they crisp and clean? Or is there bitterness, warming alcohol, or cloying sweetness? Which flavors linger, and which do not?

EVALUATE INTENSITY

Now that you have notes describing the individual elements of your beer, it's time to smell and taste your beer yet again, except this time you'll think about the intensity of each one of those elements and the duration of time that those aromas and flavors last.

For intensity, you could use words or numbers to quantify what you mean; however, we recommend one of two 7-point scales. By using a numerical scale, you are making your deconstruction of the beer or the food more objective than subjective. (Though subjectivity is always going to be a part of the evaluation because your brain is sending you flavor images based on your experiences and memories.) Still, we like saying something is between 1 and 7 points rather than "somewhat" or "really" intense. Let's start with the easier option, the one that runs by full points, and look at how it works for beer.

7-POINT SCALE

DESCRIPTION AND/OR INTENSITY

Color	Clear	1 2 3 4 5 6 7	Dark
CO$_2$	Slight	1 2 3 4 5 6 7	Strong
Balance	Blended	1 2 3 4 5 6 7	Disjointed
AROMA			
Intensity	Slight	1 2 3 4 5 6 7	Strong
TASTE			
Sweet	Slight	1 2 3 4 5 6 7	Strong
Sour	Slight	1 2 3 4 5 6 7	Strong
Bitter	Slight	1 2 3 4 5 6 7	Strong
Mouthfeel	Slight	1 2 3 4 5 6 7	Strong
Aftertaste	Slight	1 2 3 4 5 6 7	Strong
OTHER			
(Off-notes)	None	1 2 3 4 5 6 7	Many

It's pretty straightforward, right? It can be used for any beer, and it will yield some useful information. However, we both prefer a more detailed 7-point scale that's broken down into half-step increments to give even greater detail. While this might be a bit of overkill for some of you, we wanted to include the information and the scale that follows for anyone interested.

7-POINT SCALE

INTENSITY	SCALE IN 1/2 INCREMENTS	SCALE AS WHOLE NUMBERS
Threshold	0	1
Very Slight	½	2
Slight	1	3
Slight to Moderate	1½	4
Moderate	2	5
Moderate to Strong	2½	6
Strong	3	7

So there's the basic scale, but how do you put it into practice? You might notice that the intensity threshold is equal to zero. That is because *threshold* means the lowest level of detection. It's that level of intensity where you think to yourself, "I kind of get this, but I wouldn't notice it if I weren't looking for it."

To look at the rest, what follows is an example of how one of the sensory classes Gwen teaches for the UC San Diego Extension Brewing Certification program deconstructed and assigned intensities to aromas and flavors of an American pale ale. When the term *other* is used, it indicates that there were elements detected but at extreme threshold levels, and they were detected by less than half of the participants. While majority rules overall, some individuals may be extremely sensitive to certain elements, so it's important to make sure that what they are smelling and tasting is noted and recorded. The generally undetected aroma and flavor elements have the possibility of showing up to everyone once they are paired with food. Recording these also gives validation to all participants.

AMERICAN PALE ALE PROFILE

The order of the elements was determined after everyone's assessment and descriptors were recorded. There were various opinions on the order; however, this particular order was determined by the majority. Each semester Gwen's classes do this exercise several times, evaluating the same beer as a previous class as well as completely different beers. Each semester the results are different because the students are different and thus detect components at different intensities than the previous class. Many times, the same elements are interpreted differently.

An example of this would be one person using the descriptor "maple," someone else saying "pancake syrup," and a third person calling the flavor "butterscotch." Everyone is tasting the same element but with subtle variations in the sensory images, intensity, and order their brains perceive.

Variations are also going to occur based on when and where you purchase a beer, because age, storage, and many other variables will come into play with how the elements are going

AROMA			FLAVOR	
MALT Toasted, Biscuit	2		CO$_2$ Tingle	1–1½
HOPS Perfume, Pine, Citrus	1½–2		SWEET Caramel, Citrus	½–1
SWEET Caramel, Citrus/Orange	1		MALT Toasted, Grain, Roast	1½–2
SOUR Malt, Citrus/Lemon	½–1		HOPS Green, Citrus	2
YEAST Bread	½		ALCOHOL	1½
			SOUR Malt, Tart	½–1
RESINOUS (Bitter)	½		YEAST Bread, Fruit	½
			BITTER Citrus Peel, Pine	1–1½
			AFTERTASTE Drying, Yeast Mouthcoat, Astringent	½–1
OTHER: Husky/Musty, Sulfur, Alcohol/Fusel, Green Tea			OTHER: Diacetyl, Musty, Lemon, Fusel	

to be perceived. Additionally, when you are profiling a specific style of beer, there can be large differences depending on the brewery and the recipe it uses.

Ready for your homework? Go to the grocery or liquor store and purchase a build-your-own six-pack assortment. Try to keep your selections on the simple side with nothing too exotic or strong.

When it's time to taste the beers, open them, pour them into glasses (leave swirling room), and begin the individual descriptive evaluation for each one. Pick those bad boys apart! Use the scales on pages 57–59 or the tasting sheet on page 60.

If you want some extra credit, after you have completed your homework, grab a condiment from your refrigerator or pantry and pair it with every one of those beers. Olives, capers, jelly, peanut butter, salad dressing, ketchup, chocolate sauce . . . anything goes! Make note of what flavors the condiments have, and see if you can describe how the individual elements of the food change with each beer.

CRAFTBEER.COM
Tasting Sheet

Beer Style / Brand / Name: _____

Circle what is detected in each section below.

Appearance

Color (SRM): Very Light (1-1.5) / Straw (2-3) / Pale (4) / Gold (5-6) / Light Amber (7) / Amber (8) / Medium Amber (9) / Copper/Garnet (10-12) / Light Brown (13-15) / Brown/Reddish Brown/Chestnut Brown (16-17) / Dark Brown (18-24) / Very Dark (25-39) / Black (40+)

| 2 | 3 | 4 | 6 | 9 | 12 | 15 | 20 | 30 | 40+ |

Clarity: Brilliant / Clear / Slight Haze / Hazy / Opaque

Collar of Foam & Head Retention/Texture: None / Poor (Up To 15 Seconds) / Moderate (15 To 60 Seconds) / Good (More Than 60 Seconds)

Texture: Thin / Interrupted / Foamy / Fluffy / Rocky / Mousse-Like

Carbonation (Visual): None / Slow- / Medium- / Fast-Rising Bubbles

Aroma

Alcohol: Not Detectible / Mild / Noticeable / Harsh

Hops: Citrus / Fruity / Floral / Green / Herbal / Onion-Garlic / Pine / Resinous / Spruce / Sweaty / Spicy / Tropical / Woody / Other_____

Malt: Bread Flour / Grainy / Biscuit / Bready / Toast / Caramel / Pruny / Roast / Chocolate / Coffee / Smoky / Acrid / Other_____

Esters: Apple / Apricot / Banana / Blackcurrant / Cherry / Fig / Grapefruit / Kiwi / Peach / Pear / Pineapple / Plum / Raisin / Raspberry / Strawberry / Other _____ / None

Phenol: Clove / Cinnamon / Vanilla / Smoky / White Pepper / Other _____ / None

Other: _____

Flavor And Aftertaste

Alcohol: Not Detectible / Mild / Noticeable / Harsh

Hop Flavor: Citrus / Fruity / Floral / Green / Herbal / Onion-Garlic / Pine / Resinous / Spruce / Sweaty / Spicy / Tropical / Woody / Other _____ / None

Hop Bitterness: Restrained / Moderate / Aggressive / Harsh

Malt Flavor: Bread Flour / Grainy / Biscuit / Bready / Toast / Caramel / Pruny / Roast / Chocolate / Coffee / Smoky / Acrid / Other _____

Malt Sweetness: Low / Medium / High / Cloying

Other: _____

Palate

Astringency: Low / Medium / High

Body: Drying / Soft / Mouth-Coating / Sticky

Palate Carbonation: Low / Medium / High

Length/Finish: Short (Up To 15 Seconds) / Medium (15 To 60 Seconds) / Long (More Than 60 Seconds)

Oxidative/Aged Qualities

Almond / Blackcurrant / E-2-Nonenal (Papery/Cardboard) / Honey / Metallic / Sherry / Sweat Socks / Other _____ / None
Desirable / Undesirable

Balance and Drinkability

Desirable / Undesirable

Style

Appropriate / Out of Style

- **Pairing Notes:** _____

- **Other Comments:** _____

CraftBeer.com
Presented by the Brewers Association

BA BREWERS ASSOCIATION

March 2015

GLASSWARE FOR BEER

There is so much discussion of glassware and so many opinions on what—if anything—glassware does in regard to the aroma and overall flavor of beer.

First off, why drink your beer out of a glass instead of straight from the can or bottle? We'll be the first to say that there are some places—camping, the beach, and so on—where drinking from a can or bottle is not only fine, it suits the occasion. However, chances are if you've ever drunk the same beer from a bottle and from a glass, you know that in most cases the beer in the glass is worth two in the bottle. Drinking straight from a bottle or can is like painting with sunglasses on: it mutes the experience. Test it out and you'll see.

When your beer is a package with a small opening, you're simply not able to perceive as much. Since so much of what we taste is aroma rather than basic taste elements, drinking from a bottle or can means you'll miss out on a lot of complexity. Esters and phenols from the yeast, as well as hop aroma from essential oils, will not come through as strongly. Additionally, when beer is poured into a glass it expels some of its CO_2, heightening aromatics by carrying them up and out of the glass.

Now that we've established that yes, beer is better in a glass than straight from a bottle, we're ready to move on to whether specific types of glasses make a difference. Sure, we'll admit there are some times when the glass at hand is the best glass—even when it's, perish the thought, plastic. (What would a day at the ballpark or stadium be without that overpriced plastic cup of beer?) But let's get real. In your own home, who actually wants a plastic cup instead of a glass?

Wine, which by tradition is nearly always enjoyed out of a specific glass, is not so different from craft beer. Different beers benefit from slightly different glasses. We believe certain glassware can improve aroma and flavor depending on the glass shape. But even if you want to dispute that, there's no disputing that the type of glass you pour a beer into sends a message about the beer. For example, an imperial pint glass implies beers you'd expect to be at least somewhat sessionable and easy to drink. However, a snifter sends a message that there's a strong beer inside, something to savor and sip slowly.

Note: Speaking of pint glasses, ditch the shaker pint glass if you can. Sure, it's the most common beer glass used today, but that shaker glass was originally created to *shake* cocktails. Yep, the shaker pint was created so mixologists could do the mixed-drink boogie. The reason it has stuck around is because it is also very durable and stackable, which saves space behind the bar, where things are often crowded into a small space. However, the shaker pint does not highlight the flavor of beer in as pleasing a way as many other types of glassware. Try it for yourself. The next time you're out, order an American IPA in a shaker pint and one in a Belgian-style tulip glass. Have a friend hold the glasses while you sniff and then taste. That way you are tasting blind and cannot tell easily which glass is being used. Chances are you'll find increased aroma, at the very least, in the tulip glass.

GLASSWARE TYPES

These suggestions are based on today's variety of beer glassware and focus on function instead of being too tied to tradition. In regard to glassware function, the main variables are the shape of the glass and the size of the glass (i.e., the number of ounces it holds).

Shaker Pint Glass: As we just mentioned, we are not fans of the shaker pint glass. Aromatics tend to get lost rather than trapped because of the design. Instead, we recommend

If you get into glassware, you'll find there are just about as many types of beer glasses as there are styles of beer.

an English nonic pint, a German Willie Becker (a less rounded nonic pint), a Belgian-style tulip, or even an Italian-style Teku glass.

Belgian-Style Tulip: The tulip is good for a variety of beer styles such as American amber lager, pale ales, IPAs, Belgian-style dubbels, and more. The concave nature of this glass heightens and concentrates aromatics. Also, the base allows you to hold the glass without fully cupping it, so you won't heat up the beer inside too quickly. The rim of the glass, also called the lip, flares outward. This gives a lift for flavor and helps direct the beer toward the tip of the tongue. Bonus: it's also a great resting place for your lips.

Italian-Style Teku Glass: This glass shares many similar features with the Belgian-style tulip, but it has less of a bowl-shaped midsection. This more angular vessel is also taller than the tulip and has a wider lip that serves as a seductive resting place for the mouth. It was designed with the goal of emphasizing beer's aromatics through the glass' curvature.

Rocks Glass: This is a great all-purpose glass for beer dinners or sample flights at the local brewery since you are serving smaller amounts (three to four ounces) of beer. It's also a good choice for medium-high alcohol beers where concentrating the alcohol is not the goal. Medium to medium-high alcohol beers can stand to be served warmer, thus having a glass with no foot and stem is not a problem. It won't matter that cupping the glass with your hands leads to faster beverage warming. Since the carbonation of these beers is often less than lower-ABV beers, a big collar of foam is not as essential either, which is good because foam will collapse quickly in these glasses due to their straight, untapered shape. Rocks glasses are durable and easy to hold as well.

GEEK OUT

THE BEER CLEAN GLASS

Julia: One of my favorite statements is "Beer lovers should not be forced to consume the evidence of any vessel's previous affairs, no matter how intimate we like to get with our craft beer."

Red flag alert! If you see a beer glass with bubbles sticking to the sides of the glass, that indicates spots where detergent, oil, and or other remnants of food linger because they were not cleaned from the glass. Send a beer served in a glass like this back from where it came. At home, there are other tests you can use to see if your glasses are 100 percent clean, including the sheeting test (does the water poured out of a clean glass sheet evenly?) or the salt test. To do the salt test, fully wet the inside of your glass, then pour out the water. Generously shake salt on the inside of the glass. Wherever the salt sticks, the glass is beer clean, and where salt does not stick, it's still dirty.

Although fine bars and restaurants have a dedicated dishwasher for glassware (often with temperatures so high detergent is not necessary), at home using a detergent that is not fat- or oil-based is key. Drying glassware upside down so the air can circulate is ideal; don't use a rag to wipe down the glass because it can leave lint behind. In your own dishwasher, using a rinse aid that removes detergent and ensures the glass does not spot as the water dries can be effective too.

Right before you serve the beer, give the interior of your glass a quick rinse with water. This rinse primes the glass temperature, which helps retain foam when you pour the beer and removes any residual dust or lint.

— Stephen Beaumont —

Stephen Beaumont is a beer expert who has charmed tens of thousands of people into not only trying but also into *getting* that beer and food are a natural match. In 1995 he wrote *A Taste for Beer*, which had a full chapter devoted to pairing, and in 1997, which was still considered the early days for the flavorful beer revolution, he authored *Stephen Beaumont's Brewpub Cookbook*. His book *The Beer & Food Companion* was published in 2015. Needless to say, he was an early instructor on the world's emerging beer and food scene.

You state bars spend more time, effort, money, and physical space on wine and spirit glassware compared to beer glassware. Why do you think this is the case?

I believe it relates to what the big breweries have done to beer since Prohibition. By reducing the number of beer styles on the market, and diluting the flavors of those that do exist, they left us with little reason to treat beer as anything but a second-class beverage, far behind wine and cocktails. It's no coincidence that as the craft beer boom provides ever-increasing variety and highly sophisticated flavors, specialty beer glasses are coming back into style.

Many bars only stock a common pint glass but have a variety of wine and spirit glasses in numerous shapes and sizes. Do you see that changing?

This is changing, however slowly, and the reason it's changing now and will continue to advance in the future is consumer demand. When bar and restaurant owners realize that they're losing customers to the place down the street that stocks stylish, clean, unfrozen glassware, they'll appreciate the need to do the same themselves.

What is your ideal scenario for how beer is presented in establishments that care about beer?

First, there is not a shaker pint sleeve in the house—that glass is a well-known pet peeve of mine—and what glasses are used are kept clean of detergent residue and out of the deep freeze. Obviously, no bar can carry every possible glass, but it would be nice to have enough variety that I'm not being served a hefeweizen in a straight-sided pint glass or a Trappist ale in a chunky mug.

Photo Credit: Jay Brooks

Goblet or Chalice: Sometimes referred to as a schooner, this is a fine glass for beers such as dubbels, quadrupels, and Berliner-style weisse. Each of these beers has lower head retention, which is good because the open, bulbous, round nature of the glass (think of the glass as a half circle) does not support foam well. Carbonation and thus aromatics leave the glass quickly, with the chance for lots of air circulation when you swirl the glass. Nucleation points (strategically etched craters in the bottom of the glass) help induce a more robust collar of foam by giving carbonation a place to gather and group until the bubbles finally have enough collective mass to leave the etching site and flee toward the top of the beer.

Snifter: Barrel-aged beers, American imperial stouts, English-style old ales, and American and British barley wines are wonderful matches for a snifter. It's a great glass when you want to really concentrate aroma as opposed to when you want aroma to leave the glass quickly. The round, inward curvature forces alcohol and aromatics to linger longer in the glass. Snifters also have a stem that attaches to a base also called the foot, providing a stable point to hold the glass if you don't want to cup it.

Small Pilsener: This is a perfect match for any German-style lager, English-style ale, and American ale that is 4 to 6 percent ABV. There are both footed and stemmed versions (called pokals) and pilseners with just a base. These glasses have a V shape and are specifically designed to support a long-lasting, stable collar of foam, which allows a fresh beer to showcase its aromatics.

HOW TO POUR BEER

If you're a nerd like we are, one of the most enticing, seducing, and intriguing moments you experience with beer is when it's poured into the glass. This entire act sets the stage for the glory of beer enjoyment that is about to unfold.

When pouring a beer, there are three things to strive for:

1. Help coax out the carbonation.
2. Create a collar of foam.
3. Don't overpour the beer so that it ends up swelling out of the glass.

There are a variety of documented beer-pouring techniques, but no one way is right. Hey, does anyone tell you how to best peel an onion or eat corn on the cob? Different strokes for different folks.

Still, the *Brewers Association Draught Quality Manual*'s recommendation is to serve most beer styles with a one-inch collar of foam. To achieve this, the association's suggested pouring technique is to hold the bottle or can with one hand and pour it into the glass, held at a forty-five-degree angle, with the other. About one-half of your way through the pour, start to straighten up the glass. Stop pouring before the beer reaches the top of the glass to ensure you leave room for the foam.

Before you pour, check to see if your beer has been bottled conditioned, which means it likely has yeast sediment at the bottom of the bottle. Some brewers intend for the yeast to be roused into the beer prior to serving, so be sure to check the label to see if that's the case. If there are no instructions indicated on the label, be careful not to disturb the yeast; leave it on the bottom of the bottle. When handling and storing, keep the bottle or can more upright than horizontal. Then pour slowly to prevent mixing the yeast into the beer.

PAIRING
PRACTICES

Gwen: My eye-opening experience with pairing happened while visiting a winery in Temecula years and years ago. My friends and I had arrived at the winery around 10:00 a.m. to begin our day of tastings. Two older gentlemen were sitting in the tasting room with giant pieces of chocolate cake and glasses of wine. I couldn't resist saying something, so I said, "That looks like an amazing breakfast!" One of the men took me seriously and asked if I had ever had chocolate cake with a glass of Moscato. I quietly replied I had not. The gentleman proceeded to get me a piece of chocolate cake and a glass of Moscato and told me to sit down and enjoy.

That pairing forever changed my way of eating and drinking. I was determined to never miss out on interactions of that magnitude again. Oh, and it turns out the gentleman who changed my way of thinking was Vince Cilurzo, the father of Vinnie Cilurzo of Russian River Brewing. What a small world!

***Julia:** What led to my pairing passion was not a lightning bolt moment but instead a slow and steady progression. I can trace it all back to when I was a little kid with a soap collection. When my parents traveled, they'd bring me different soaps to add to my collection. I'd spend hours taking them out of the box or wrapper and enjoying their different aromas and textures. I also had a perfume collection that left me forever chasing down glorious new fragrances. Eventually I built a sort of natural first-aid kit with exotic salves, liquids, and lotions. For me, the fun was in combining different ingredients to find new aroma combinations. In my teens, I started to play a game with myself where I'd guess what was for dinner based on what I could smell from my room upstairs while my mom cooked in our kitchen below. I slowly but surely became just as interested in the flavors of food, and then drinks. Putting new flavors together the way I used to experiment mixing my own salves, lotions, and perfumes is very enjoyable to me. I guess I've always been after that new, exciting combination!*

Whether your interest in pairing comes from an aha moment or whether it comes from years of gradually building interest, we're glad you're here. In this chapter, we're going to address the steps of pairing in order. However, there's a reason pairing is Chapter 4 and not Chapter 1. Knowing the basics of flavor and how to taste are important, and it's advantageous to learn them on their own before diving in here. So without further ado, here are our basic steps to pairing and the outline for this chapter.

PAIRING IN A NUTSHELL

1. Consider your beer and food elements separately.
2. Find flavor harmonies.
3. Think about potential interactions.
4. Carefully match overall intensities.
5. Perform a test tasting (and describe what stands out).
6. Tweak and modify the pairing.

CONSIDER BEER AND FOOD ELEMENTS SEPARATELY

Key Concepts: Perception and Deconstruction

As you read this chapter, there's one big thought you should never lose track of: remain aware of what the beer and the food bring to the table (and to our mouths!) on their own. Remember when we spent a whole chapter on perception? We did that because tasting beer or food—really analyzing it—gives you an important base of knowledge. If for some reason you skipped Chapter 2, turn back now! For the most successful pairings, we've found it's essential to get a mental handle on what you're tasting. Only then can you move on to detecting interactions and the interplay of beer to food and food to beer.

We're stressing the importance of looking at the individual elements because when it comes to pairing, the equation is large. You're figuring out the sum of the separate parts for beer and for food. Identifying those individual elements, the pieces, is vital to creating the perfect pairing, the whole. The result is stacked and layered. You'll perceive a completely new flavor with the combination of multiple elements. That's the reason why pairing can really blow your senses away!

Still, you should also keep in mind that all-important concept from the end of Chapter 2: *flavor is a fusion*. Although we spend a lot of time deconstructing, flavor is never just what we taste, what we smell, or the mouthfeel or intensity of what we are eating or drinking. Flavor is all of these things put together—it is one experience. Below are the elements, the individual pieces, you should examine when you deconstruct both beer and food:

1. Intensity (as it relates to individual flavor components; we will discuss overall intensity on page 75)
2. Aroma elements
3. Basic taste elements (sweet, salty, sour, bitter, umami)
4. Additional taste elements (fat, alcohol)
5. Mouthfeel (body, aftertaste, temperature, texture, etc.)

FIND FLAVOR HARMONIES

Key Concepts: Complements and Bridges

While you might get lucky searching for contrasting taste elements, it's much easier to search for places where beer and food flavors will work together, the intersections where they complement each other. This could be as simple as matching the exact same

Find flavor harmonies between beer and food.

flavors. For example, a chocolate-laden porter will likely have some harmony with a medium-intense chocolate bar (say 60 percent cacao content).

Yet you can also stretch it a bit further once you're comfortable. Think about the chocolaty Porter again, but now think of pairing it with foods that have similar or complementary flavors. How about spicy chicken with a mole sauce that has smoky and chocolate notes of its own? What about chocolate peanut butter pie, which will make those chocolate and nutty characteristics jump out at you? Either way, knowing you like spice with chocolate or peanut butter with chocolate will set you on a path toward a rewarding pairing.

At the core of the process is just this sort of introspection. Ask yourself what flavors are in both the beer and the food, and start there. What sensory images do you see? Then move outward to find **complements**, those elements that match each other. To do this, it helps to think of flavors in groups of commonality. For example:

- Brown sugar, butter, caramel, maple syrup, vanilla, coconut, toffee
- Chocolate of varying cacao contents, truffles, cocoa powder
- Cinnamon, cumin, pepper, cardamom, ginger, clove
- Date, fig, raisin, plum, prune
- Fruits:
  - Pineapple, tangerine, clementine, Valencia orange, blood orange, grapefruit, passion fruit, lemon, lime
  - Mango, papaya, guava, lychee, banana, kiwi
  - Strawberry, raspberry, blackberry, loganberry, cranberry, chokecherry, pomegranate, currant, gooseberry
  - Apple, pear, star fruit, apricot, peach, rose hip
  - Honeydew, cantaloupe, watermelon, tomato
- Malt vinegar, balsamic vinegar, rice vinegar, red wine vinegar, white vinegar, apple cider vinegar
- Mint, dill, basil, endive, coriander, fennel, parsley, lemongrass, bay leaf, oregano
- Rosemary, juniper, pine, spruce
- Walnut, almond, pecan

These lists are just to get you started. The important thing to realize is that connections happen over **bridges**, where beer and food meet ingredient to ingredient via similar flavors. For example, pear flavors from the yeast in some Belgian-style saisons can bridge to apples from an apple pie. The pear esters in the beer will find their way to the apples in the pie, resulting in a harmonious experience of like flavors. By considering similar flavors and aromas in groups, you can start bridging deconstructed elements of beers and foods.

THINK ABOUT POTENTIAL INTERACTIONS

Key Concepts: Complement, Contrast, Cut
Once you have a beer and a food you think might work together, it's time to consider how they'll interact. An interaction is what happens when aromas, taste elements, mouthfeel, and intensities connect and combine to create a new flavor experience.

Flavor interactions can be as simple as the lactic acid elements of a Berliner-style weisse beer interacting with the vinegar acid elements of sauerkraut. In this case, the like acidic elements lessen one another so that the other flavors, such as the beer's wheat malt and the sauerkraut's caraway and onion, shine brighter. Or think Thanksgiving, where a sweet potato pie might contrast with the bold hop bitterness of an IPA. After a sip of that IPA, you'll find you can better taste the spices and creamy butter elements in the pie because bitter cuts the sweetness of the sugar and sweet potatoes.

Texture interactions are just as fascinating—in fact, chefs practice this all the time. Think of the contrasting crunch of your coleslaw next to tender and succulent barbecue ribs or the crisp snap of romaine lettuce complemented by the even more extreme crunch of croutons. Beer also provides contrast in texture. Carbonation and alcohol play a big role with chemical sensations and texture interactions between beer and food. For example, pair a bright and robustly carbonated 7 percent Belgian-style tripel against rich, fatty meat such as cured, aged country ham. The carbonation bubbles and a medium-intense alcohol contrast with the fat of the meat in a way that downplays its rich, gamey characteristics and lets the more pleasing meaty flavors shine.

The interactions of flavor elements in beer and food can result in home-run pairings.

Interactions can also be more advanced, like pairing a German-style pilsner with a classic Margherita pizza, where the refreshing carbonation and medium-bold bitterness of the German pils interact with the rich, creamy mozzarella cheese. On top of that, the pungent basil acts as a rest, and the toasted bread crust of the pizza harmonizes with the graham cracker flavors of the pilsener malt. You've got numerous interactions going on here.

Another fascinating phenomena tied to interactions is they are commutative (similar to math in how 6 × 7 gives you the same answer as 7 × 6). So when sweet is cut by bitter, as when a beer with a lot of malty residual sugar is balanced by the bitterness of hops, the same happens in reverse. Sweet also diminishes bitter. Keeping this in mind when you pair helps position the interplay between flavors and textures in both your beer and food. In the IPA and sweet potato pie example, the bitter of the hops is cut by the sweetness of the pie.

Interactions can also cause problems that derail a pairing, turning it into a dreaded train

POTENTIAL INTERACTIONS

Ah, interactions: the interplay of different elements. Kinda like life, right? Interactions come from aromatic-based elements, basic tastes (sweet, sour, salt, bitter, and umami), fat, and alcohol, and can even include mouthfeel elements such as temperature, texture, and sensation. While it's complicated, when you dial in and really consciously taste and deconstruct, you just might notice a few patterns when it comes to how specific elements interact. (Though when multiple interactions happen at the same time, throw any assumptions to the wind.) The charts that follow will help you begin to identify some of the potential and individual interactions you may find.

Beer Taste	Interact with	Associated Element	Interactions	Additional Comments
SWEET **Sweet-Centric Beer Examples** For sweeter beer styles, try examples with higher residual sugar such as American-style wheat wine, German-style doppelbock, Scotch ale/wee heavy, American- and British-style barley wine, English-style old ale, American imperial porter, Baltic-style porter, English-style sweet stout, imperial stout, German-style weizenbock.	+ Sweet	Sugar	Complement / Cut	Like cuts like
	+ Sour	Acid	Contrast / Cut	Increases salivation
	+ Salt	Mineral	Contrast / Cut	
	+ Bitter	Roast	Contrast / Cut	
	+ Umami	Savory	Complement / Emphasize	
	+ Chemosensory Irritants	Capsaicin, ginger, mustard, peppermint, menthol	Cut	Sweet cuts heat
	+ Tannins	Astringency	Complement or contrast; cut or emphasize	Intensity dependent
	+ Fat	Oil	Cut	
	+ Alcohol	Warming	Complement or contrast; cut or emphasize	Intensity dependent

Beer Taste	Interact with	Associated Element	Interactions	Additional Comments
SOUR **Sour-Centric Beer Examples** American sour ales, American Brett beers (which sometimes are acidic-centric—see beer styles section), Belgian-style Flanders, Belgian-style lambic, gueuze and fruit lambic, Belgian-style saison (some are acidic-centric—see beer styles section), Belgian-style wit and barrel-aged beer.	+ Sweet	Sugar	Complement or contrast	Intensity dependent
	+ Sour	Acid	Complement / Cut	Like cuts like; increase salivation
	+ Salt	Mineral	Contrast / Cut	
	+ Bitter	Roast	Contrast / Cut	
	+ Umami	Savory	Contrast / Emphasize	
	+ Chemosensory Irritants	Capsaicin, ginger, mustard, peppermint, menthol	Complement or contrast; cut or emphasize	Intensity dependent
	+ Tannins	Astringency	Complement	Intensity dependent
	+ Fat	Oil	Contrast / Cuts	
	+ Alcohol	Warming	Complement or contrast; cut or emphasize	Intensity dependent

Beer Taste

SALT

Salt-Centric Beer Examples
Salt is not usually a dominant taste in beers, but the beverage can have low-level sodium from the brewing water. Sometimes salinity can be detected in beer, but it's rare. American cream ale, barrel-aged sours, and German-style Gose are style examples in which salt can be perceived.

Interact with	Associated Element	Interactions	Additional Comments
+ Sweet	Sugar	= Contrast / Emphasize	
+ Sour	Acid	= Contrast / Cut	Increases salivation
+ Salt	Mineral	= Complement / Cut	Like cuts like
+ Bitter	Roast	= Cut / Emphasize	Cumulative and intensity dependent
+ Umami	Savory	= Complement/ Emphasize	
+ Chemosensory Irritants	Capsaicin, ginger, mustard, peppermint, menthol	= Complement or contrast; cut or emphasize	
+ Tannins	Astringency	= Contrast / Emphasize	
+ Fat	Oil	= Complement or contrast; cut or emphasize	Intensity dependent (e.g., salted fish)
+ Alcohol	Warming	= Complement or contrast; cut or emphasize	Intensity dependent

Beer Taste

BITTER

Bitter-Centric Beer Examples
German- and Bohemian-style pilsener, German-style alt, English-style pale ale/ESB, American pale ale, American amber ale, American brown ale, Baltic-style porter, Irish-style dry stout, American stout, American imperial stout, American- and English-style IPA, imperial India Pale Ale, American- and English-style barley wine.

Interact with	Associated Element	Interactions	Additional Comments
+ Sweet	Sugar	= Contrast / Cut	
+ Sour	Acid	= Complement or contrast	Intensity dependent
+ Salt	Mineral	= Cut / Emphasize	Cumulative and intensity dependent
+ Bitter	Roast	= Complements / Cut	Like cuts like
+ Umami	Savory	= Contrast / Cut	
+ Chemosensory Irritants	Capsaicin, ginger, mustard, peppermint, menthol	= Contrast / Emphasize	Intensity dependent
+ Tannins	Astringency	= Contrast / Emphasize	
+ Fat	Oil	= Cut	
+ Alcohol	Warming	= Complement or contrast; cut or emphasize	Intensity dependent

Beer Taste

UMAMI

Umami-Centric Beer Examples
Low levels of umami in beer can be detected from the yeast as well as age. Look for umami in bottle-conditioned, yeast-centric, cellared/aged beer, including American-style wheat, American imperial stout, barrel-aged beer, Belgian-style quadruple, French-style Bière de Garde, American- and British-style barley wine, and German-style doppelbock.

Interact with	Associated Element	Interactions	Additional Comments
+ Sweet	Sugar	= Complement	
+ Sour	Acid	= Contrast / Emphasize	Increases salivation
+ Salt	Mineral	= Complement	
+ Bitter	Roast	= Cut	
+ Umami	Savory	= Cut or Emphasize	Too much umami—cumulative effect
+ Chemosensory Irritants	Capsaicin, ginger, mustard, peppermint, menthol	= Complement or contrast	Intensity dependent
+ Tannins	Astringency	= Complement or contrast; cut or emphasize	Intensity dependent
+ Fat	Oil	= Complement / Cut	
+ Alcohol	Warming	= Complement	

CHEMICAL INTERACTIONS

Chemical interactions might sound like something out of your high-school textbooks. However, you actually experience them more than you realize. Here are a few examples:

- The protein molecules in dairy products, called casein, are fat-loving and bind to capsaicin molecules, which are fat-soluble, allowing the painful spicy heat from things like hot peppers to be washed away. That's why milk is a go-to beverage when you eat something that's too spicy.
- Wine is known to be *horrible* paired with artichoke because of its interaction with the chemical compound cynarin contained in artichoke. This organic acid can make whatever beverage it is paired with taste sweet, and the residual sugars in wine come off as cloyingly oversweet. (We'd encourage you to try a Belgian-style saison, German-style Kölsch, or American wheat and steamed artichoke with tarragon dipping sauce instead.)
- Sodium lauryl sulphate in toothpaste is a foaming agent that has the aftereffect of making orange juice taste bitter. This chemical compound interacts with your taste receptors and masks the sweetness of the toothpaste but then emphasizes the sourness and bitterness of your orange juice. Yuck!
- Salmon and hoppy beers commonly clash. The fish's omega-3 oil molecules quickly become unstable when they come into contact with hops. This oxidation of the fatty acids makes the salmon taste metallic.

wreck. Ever try lemonade with mint cookies? What about red wine and artichokes (see left)? Or, for a beer example, try an aggressively bitter IPA with simple, undressed salmon. Identifying train wrecks can be as educational and palate-expanding as finding home runs, though, so don't despair if it happens to you.

COMPLEMENT, CONTRAST, CUT

It has long been taught that there are three things that happen at the same time in every pairing. Dubbed "the three Cs," they are complement, contrast, and cut. Sometimes what you get from a pairing will lean more toward complement or contrast, depending on what interactions occur. With beer pairing, cut occurs in the presence of carbonation, bitterness, and acidity. However, the important thing to remember is that no one pairing will simply be just one of these things. Here's our approach:

Complements happen when similar flavors in the beer and food find each other. For example, strawberries on top of a green salad could complement raspberries in a fruited lambic. However, in terms of what you perceive in totality from a pairing, it's not a sure bet that complements are the dominant interplay one will notice. If the salad is also topped with green onions, for example, the onions could overwhelm the complementing fruits and make the lambic a middle-of-the-road pairing, or worse.

Contrast is tied to the main basic taste elements (sweet, sour, salty, bitter, umami) as well as fat and alcohol. When elements contrast they can accentuate (heighten the taste elements interacting with one another, such as salt and sweet) or cut, and thus allow other flavors to be noticed more. Contrasting interactions can be good or bad, and are often the main reason a pairing feels either balanced or off. Your home run, middle-of-the-road, and train wreck pairings often hang in the balance based on contrasting interactions.

Cut as an interaction is beautifully displayed when the carbonation, bitterness, and acidity in beer wash away the heavy or oily richness in food. It's one of the many reasons beer is such a great companion with so many cheeses. The characteristics of carbonation alone will convince you that beer can help food taste better. It allows you to perceive flavors in each bite more evenly and thoroughly. Garrett Oliver, Brooklyn Brewery's brewmaster, is famous for teaching beer lovers about this effect: carbonation acts as scrubbing bubbles on the tongue, getting your mouth ready for the next bite by lifting fats, oils, and the rich side of food up off the tongue and thus helping the next bite reach a fresher palate. This is an invaluable tool when you are drinking and eating.

Julia: Complement, contrast, *and* cut *are the words we use today, but ongoing research may soon change some or all of these descriptive terms. For example, some say the word* cut *should change to* cleanse, *as it describes the physical act of refreshing the palate.*

CAREFULLY MATCH OVERALL INTENSITIES

Intensity is tied to how strong specific flavors from both food and beer come across. It is also tied to how much you like or dislike those flavors. For pairing, it's advantageous when that the overall intensities of the beer and food match.

For beer, intensity comes from many places, but the key sources are the levels of acidity, alcohol, bitterness, residual sugar, sensations (such as carbonation and temperature), roast and smoke character, and yeast-derived elements such as esters and phenols. With today's craft brewers continuing to push the boundaries, the intensity scale for beer is ever broadening. (See scale on pages 57–58.) Outside-the-box ingredients from today's small brewers and resurrected Old World beer recipes feature all sorts of things that affect intensity: spices, chili, flowers, and even legumes such as split pea.

When it comes to food, the intensity sources are even more diverse, including acidity, bitterness, cooking methods, spices, fat, mouthfeel sensations (for example, capsaicin heat and temperature), and more. Foods that are typically low in intensity include salads, many sandwiches, and some soups—basically, foods that have low to no acidity, less fat, and are milder in flavor. Foods that are higher in intensity tend to have a variety of complex flavors, and they have added fat or acid content and increased spice. There are thousands of food ingredients and dishes with a staggering diversity in intensity.

For pairing beer and food, the goal is almost always to have the overall beer and food intensities match. You don't want any one element to barrel over all the others. To do this in a fairly precise way, we use a scale (as on pages 57–58) to help gauge how weak or strong individual flavor elements seem. When conducting your test tasting (see page 60), sample both beer and food, and use the scale to get a baseline on what dominant flavor elements exist and how strong they seem to you. This is a good place for you to start observing how your personal pairing preferences are different from others' personal pairing preferences. What you think is strong or intense may not be to someone else.

If you find you've landed on a good intensity match right away, good for you! However, you may also find either the beer or food is too intense for the other component. When that's the case, you can switch either the beer or food component to one further up or down the intensity scale, depending on your own personal pairing preference.

Let's look at an example for matching intensities. Start by picturing a classic burger right off the grill, served on a bun with no condiments or toppings. (Perhaps you're camping for this example and don't have access to all the trimmings.) There is definitely some intensity from both the fat of the beef and the charred flavors from the grill, but the intensity is not as strong compared to a burger with all the toppings. This plain grilled burger is a great intensity match for a classic American pale ale (APA), since that beer has medium-intense bitterness (up to forty

GEEK OUT

BEER OVER WINE

Wine is famous for pairing, largely because of its acidity, which calms salt so other flavors shine brighter. It also cuts through the fat in many foods and has some great flavor harmony potential. However, put beer on the table and it goes where no fermented grape can go. Beer also has varying acidity, depending on the beer style, plus it has unsurpassed flavor harmony potential. Its roasty styles can go with grilled, roasted, and smoked food. It has additional flavor echoes from hops' floral, herbal, and citrus notes, as well as fruity yeast esters. Its bitterness from both roasted malt and hops counters sugar and fat. Its residual sugar ranges play well with spicy (capsaicin) hot foods as sweet calms heat. And of course, the carbonation scrubs the tongue and gets it ready for the next bite.

While you may never convince die-hard wine drinkers that beer is superior when it comes to pairing with food, you can at least open their eyes to pairing with beer some of the time—especially when a particular food isn't so wine-friendly. Here are a few suggestions:

- Sourdough bread changes the pH balance of wine, making it an unpleasant pairing. However, you'll find sourdough is brilliant with beers like Belgian-style saisons.
- Salad greens with elements of bitterness (for example, arugula) are generally not so good with wines. Throw in a sharp vinaigrette, and it gets even tougher. Yet beers like Belgian-style wits pair beautifully.
- Eating pretzels with wine just doesn't feel natural. Go for a malt-forward beer style instead, such as a pale ale, amber, brown, or a bock.
- Veggie burgers, or even just vegetarian dishes featuring aromatics such as onions, chives, and leeks, are hard to pair with wine because of their pungency. Yet the residual sugar of onion-family vegetables, especially when cooked, works so very well with multiple beer styles including American wheat, Belgian-style blonde, and Belgian-style pale ales, just to name a few.
- Spicy foods from Ethiopian to Indian can be tough matches for wine because of the complexity of spices. Ethiopian spices include *berbere* (a customized combination of red chili, garlic, salt, and paprika), *niter kibbeh* spiced butter, and so much more. Indian spices include aniseed, black cardamom, cinnamon, cumin, fenugreek (celery-like with maple), turmeric (bitter and earthy), and a variety of mustard seeds. Thank you, beer, for your complexity! Try styles that have similar flavor families to what you are pairing with, including Belgian-style saison, Belgian-style wit, English-style oatmeal stout, herb and spiced beers, winter ales, and beyond. This is where you have to experiment to confirm.
- Thanksgiving dinner can be hard for wine because of all the different foods. However, you'll find a Belgian-style tripel or Belgian-style pale strong ale is wonderfully versatile. The tripel's pilsner malt flavors match the white meat flavor of turkey beautifully. These beers' white fruit esters help keep your palate fresh during the meal, and the high carbonation cleanses your palate for the next bite of rich potatoes and gravy.

IBUs) and medium-low residual sugar. Maybe you packed in a six-pack of Sierra Nevada Pale Ale and cooled it down in the stream next to your campsite. Sounds perfect!

Now pretend you're no longer camping. You're grilling back at home with a fully stocked fridge. Picture that same grilled burger with mayonnaise on the bun, Maytag blue cheese slathered on top, some red onion slivers, and a fresh-cut tomato slice. Each one of these additions pumps up the intensity and umami savoriness of the burger except the onion, which brings additional intensity from its acidity. It's time to step up from APA and try a Robust Porter or American IPA instead. The porter will have incredible flavor harmonies with both the grilled beef burger and marbled blue cheese, and it has increased intensity from the specialty malts (strong chocolate and low coffee roast flavor). Compared to the APA, the IPA brings more alcohol, more hop flavor, increased bitterness, and additional residual sugars. It will also harmonize with the burger bun and blue cheese. So while it still comes down to preference—would you rather have a robust porter or an IPA?—both of those options are more closely matched with the burger's intensity than the APA. Maybe you don't like blue cheese or onion on your burger (your personal preference), but whatever you add atop your grilled masterpiece will have an impact on the overall intensity of your pairing. All the same principles still apply for your beer pairing choices.

PERFORM A TEST TASTING

Even if you're a beer expert, guessing what beers and foods work together will only get you so far (but it sure is fun to try!). Taking the time to try a variety of beers with a variety of foods will always result in the best pairings. In addition to ensuring success, a test tasting gives you additional experience without the pressure of pleasing guests in the context of a

AN INTENSE GABF

Julia: I remember a big intensity match "aha" as the organizer of the Great American Beer Festival (GABF) media luncheon. This luncheon has huge importance to the Brewers Association, which is the national nonprofit trade association for the majority of breweries in the United States. Two hundred people attend this luncheon, where we not only strive to share news, information, statistics, and story ideas with the journalists, but we also put beer pairing center stage by serving a world-class luncheon that strategically pairs GABF award-winning beers with a variety of foods.

During the test tasting for one of the first luncheons I organized, we wanted to serve a s'more dessert featuring marshmallows from Lucy Saunder's book *The Best of American Beer and Food*. The chef for the luncheon prepared a test version of the dessert to sample. I kept digging into the cooler to try to find something that would pair in a pleasing fashion while I took small bites of the s'more.

We worked our way through most of the beers, trying to find flavor matches, but nothing seemed to match. This dessert was dense and rich, sweet, and this was no ordinary s'more; it was *intense!* We tried an American strong ale, a robust porter, and a Belgian-style tripel, but none of them seemed to work. The flavors in the beer kept getting washed away. I finally realized I needed to find a perfect intensity match in addition to a beer that had flavor harmonies with the dessert.

With this realization in mind I pulled out a bottle of Avery Brewing Company's The Reverend. This beer is a Belgian-style quadrupel. Some key components of this beer include its alcohol level (10 percent ABV) and the fact that Belgian candi sugar is used (adding browned and burnt sugar flavors, including notes of molasses). Finally, the clouds parted and our taste buds began to sing. What we had discovered was a beer that not only echoed the flavors in the s'mores but matched their intensity as well.

dinner party or official event. You and your fellow tasters can take your time and truly evaluate how things are working together (or not). Without test tastings, you cannot tweak, refine, or even truly know what the end result of different pairings might look like. The whole thing should be fun in a different way than a big pairing event you might be planning for. Think of your final pairing as a play, and think of the test tastings as a private rehearsal. What follows are some thoughts based on the three ways you might approach an evening of pairings.

Predetermined Beer(s): This could be as easy as pairing what you're eating at dinner on a few different nights with the beer or beers you want to drink. You'll find you not only learn about what foods work and don't work with the beer, you'll have new tasting notes on the beer as well. For this type of tasting:

- It's helpful to know the basics of the beer you are tasting: style, flavor profile, alcohol level.
- While tasting the beer, make note of the residual sugar, acidity, intensity, and dominant flavor characteristics.
- Sound out what food items might have flavor harmonies and intensity matches with this beer.

Even last-minute additions to food, such as burger toppings, increase the intensity and impact. Be careful when you match intensities.

HEDONICS

Hedonics is another concept that plays into intensity. Simply put, hedonics is the likeability factor, and it affects our individual perception on how strong or weak something comes across. You might think to yourself that an element is too sour, but your friend might think it's perfect. Remember, we each have different degrees or measures of intensity, different degrees of how much we like or dislike varying intensities, and different genes.

The crazy part of this concept is that flavor is not something that can be nailed down with rules that work for everyone. Our perception of intensity, one part of flavor, varies based on our personal experience and personal preferences. Take hot sauce, for example. The Scoville scale measures the amount of the chemical compound capsaicin that causes the heat of peppers. This scale goes from 0 to over 16 million (pure capsaicin). Tabasco has an estimated 2,500–5,000 Scoville heat units. To many, that is just about right. After all, Tabasco wouldn't exist if millions didn't love the stuff! However, you'll no doubt meet many people who think Tabasco is just crazy hot and something best avoided.

Predetermined Food(s): Just as you can pair a couple of different meals with the same beer, you can pair the same meal with a couple of different beers. Don't feel you have to do this all in one sitting. Try two beers that you think might work, and let them battle it out over dinner. You might also find that several beers would be appropriate instead of just one. For this type of tasting:

- Start conceptually, before you're in the kitchen. Brainstorm which beers could work with the dish you're going to cook.
- Have your beers ready to serve.
- If you find a beer that closely works with the dish but is not quite a home run pairing, think about ways you might tweak the dish get closer to a perfect match. Since you can't change the beer recipe, change the food recipe a bit.

Totally Open Slate and Multi-Course Pairings: When the options are wide open or when you're planning a whole dinner, start with what you're excited to try and narrow down the possibilities from there. For this type of tasting:

- Decide if you want a theme for the meal (see Chapter 8), and then build food menu and beer options based on this theme.
- Talk out the food and beer options and their possible flavor profiles with family or friends. Break down and deconstruct all your pairing options and groups. Everyone wins because everyone's opinions count!
- Taste your way through some of the beer options to begin to sound out if you like the direction of these beers. Think about food options and the possible order in which you'd want to serve the beers. At this point you might encourage your guests to pick their personal preferences and make this a completely interactive pairing.
- Eventually, you'll need to prepare the dishes and try them with the beers. Take notes so you can use what you deconstruct for future pairings.

DESCRIBE WHAT STANDS OUT

Now you're at the part where you have to describe the pairing. Each person might start by establishing what flavors he or she perceives in both the beer and food. Different people might not dial into the same flavors. Still, everyone can learn and get excited about where their own personal sensory perceptions and understandings take them. And remember, you can find similarities if you know where to look. For example, your mental picture of white peach flavor might be another person's apricot. Yet these two descriptors are close; in fact, you could even group them as stone fruits. Or, your toffee might be another's caramel. Again, those are pretty close. All of a sudden you are both on the same page because you can relate to each other's mental images.

Pay attention to how present and past experiences relate to your perception. Are you tired? Then you'll likely sense less of what you taste. If you've never had fennel, then you might not notice its background presence in a specific dish, even though it's there and noticeable to others. Is the room noisy to the point that you are distracted? Or did you eat something recently that is affecting how you perceive everything? (Spices, watermelon, cucumber, and other foods that you don't digest easily are distractions.) Each of these variables will influence what you perceive and ultimately describe in your pairings.

Julia: Trying to describe what you perceive can be as difficult as explaining color to a blind person. Unless the other person has reference, how can they see what you are talking about? If a person has never seen a specific color, then how can we expect them to know what it is? An effective pairing description technique to get around this is to describe something in relation to something else. For example, an Irish-style dry stout (which has more roast than chocolate notes and a strong base note of bitterness) and Black Forest ham (which is very salty) mimic the classic flavors of franks and beans. Saying the pairing evokes that dish can help other tasters paint a mental image. This works for beer, too. You could say a barrel-aged barley wine evokes sweetened iced tea (no lemon!). If you deconstruct iced tea, you've got the flavors of the black tea (which mimic malt), tannins from the tea leaves (which mimic the astringency from wood- or oak-aged barley wine and hops), and the residual sugar that sweetens the tea (which mimics barley wine's high residual sugar). Try it out! Tell people what a specific pairing reminds you of, and then encourage them to relate pairings to what they are reminded of as well.

Now assess the overall picture: is the pairing a home run, middle-of-the-road pairing, or train wreck pairing? Remember that what is a home run for you might not be a home run for everyone else. If there's disagreement, figure out what's working and what's not. The more you practice verbalizing what you experience, the easier it will become.

TWEAK AND MODIFY THE PAIRING

Say you've got a pairing that isn't working. Now what? Use those notes you just took and create a picture of the interactions that are occurring and the resulting aroma, taste, aftertaste, and palate sensations of the pairing. Then you can decide whether you should tweak the dish or switch out the beer.

In pairing, it's generally much easier to modify the food rather than the beer. After all, unless you brewed it, the variables you can change in a beer are mostly limited to temperature (you can always serve a beer warmer or colder), carbonation (you can let a beer sit out and lessen its carbonation, but this is not advised even though it's a variable), and blending (you can take your current beer and blend it with another to lessen the bitterness; up the residual sugar, acidity, or alcohol; advance the flavor; and more).

Altering the food is usually easier, and it has greater potential for changing your flavor interactions. You can greatly alter the beer and food interaction just by changing cooking or preparation methods, or you can tweak food slightly by adding a pinch of salt, squeezing on a twist of lime or lemon (acid addition), throwing in a sprig of parsley (to rest your senses), hitting it with a shot of cream (fat addition), giving it a splash of soy sauce (umami and salt addition), or spiking it with anise or a bit of vanilla (flavor additions). All of these are food correction techniques, but by applying them to the food, you are modifying the entire pairing.

Common issues in pairing feedback we see often include:

1. The pairing was not quite right, but you served it anyway.
Solution: The test tasting! Test taste and then tweak before guests arrive.

2. The pairing is not an intensity match.
Solution: If the food is too rich and big for the beer, then go for a beer that's bigger in alcohol,

A squeeze of lemon is a quick and easy way to modify a dish and tweak your pairing.

higher in residual sugar, or bolder in taste elements. If the beer is too big and burly for your food, then make the dish richer by adding oil, butter, or fat. Sometimes, however, the easiest solution is to switch out the beer.

3. The pairing seems kinda meh and middle of the road.

Solution: Seek out more flavor harmonies and bridges between the beer and food. Listen to your brain and go with the flavor image it is sending you. What ingredient do you want to focus on? Consider what flavors could be added to the dish that would not alter it in a negative way, and make sure similar complementary flavors exist in the beer. Maybe a hint of cinnamon in the dish would really pair well with the sweet malt in the beer? Use this as an opportunity to pair with the other beers at the table, too. Everyone gets to participate and comment.

4. You've got an amazing beer, but the food needs to be balanced.

Solution: Drink the beer to help balance out the dish, up the acid content of the food itself (with a squeeze of lemon) to brighten it, or see some of the other tweaks on page 83. Simplify, don't complicate when you are tweaking.

5. The food has so much going on and so many flavors that it's difficult to know what beer would work best with it.

Solution: We find the best pairings are with dishes that have clean and distinctive flavors that aren't too busy and muddled. They simply leave some room for the beer to play a role. Pairings can't always be home runs, but you can avoid train wrecks this way.

JULIA'S CLASSIC FOOD TWEAKS

You already have a good idea of how adjustments can bring balance or focus in your pairings, but here are some of my favorites.

WHAT	SERVED WITH	INTERACTION
Squeeze of lemon	Fresh seafood	The acidity from the lemon juice cuts and tames salt as well as any fishy flavors. Of course, it also brings lemony citrus flavors to the dish.
Spring of parsley	Wide variety of foods	Parsley is a natural breath freshener. It also provides a rest for the palate, short-circuiting the brain for a nanosecond by saying, "Just pay attention to me!" Parsley does not commonly marry with other flavors; it delivers its own fresh herbal notes that stand alone.
Pickle	Corned beef sandwich	This is a deli classic for a reason. Pickles contain a lot of salt along with vinegar acidity, plus flavors of cucumber, garlic, onion, peppercorns, and more. Corned beef, which is also brined like the pickle, likely has peppercorns and a whole lotta salt, too. Yet the salt and acid from the pickle contrast with the salt and fat in the corned beef. Plus, the pepper flavors interact and find each other for harmony.
Salt	Everything!	Salt is sacred. It is used in both food and beer to enhance flavors, so use it to adjust anything and everything.
Fresh cracked pepper	Many foods	Sprinkles of black pepper lend a sharp spice to each bite of food. The interaction here is increasing flavor.
Herbs and spices	Just about everything is fair game	Herbs and spices, from dried garlic and chili powder to cinnamon and nutmeg, increase flavor and quickly change dishes in a variety of ways. Some beers can be spiced as well.
Freshly grated Parmesan cheese	Fresh pasta	When the waiter, or you, grates cheese over your pasta, the goal is to up the umami and increase the seductive savory and salty nature of the dish.
Soy sauce	Anything! (It's my favorite condiment.)	Soy sauce is a vehicle for not only salt but umami as well. It interacts with whatever you add it to. I sprinkle it over rice, add it to beans, and even sneak it into baked dishes that need a rich boost. If you use a light hand, it can even be a secret ingredient.

— Robert J. Harrington —

Robert Harrington is a PhD, MBA, and professor of hospitality and wine business management at Washington State University, Tri-Cities Campus, Richland, Washington. He's also the author of *Food and Wine Pairing*—a book worth its weight in gold to any foodie.

You've come up with twelve amazing pairing relationships in your work with wine. Could you use the same relationships for beer?

Beer has several characteristics that make it similar to and different from wine. Beer certainly has taste components, texture, and flavor elements, but some of these differ from those in wine. For example, the beer taste components of sweetness and acidity in general have less variability than in wine. But the taste component of bitterness has much more variability in beer and is more pronounced. Also, in contrast to wine, all beers have carbonation, which is true of only a minority of wines.

What is your systematic approach to pairing, and how can it help those who work with beer?

It considers twelve main relationships of food and drink elements that when profiled create a predicted level of match that is highly correlated to match levels when tasted together. This systematic process is intended to allow you to identify good to great food and drink matches to maximize your or your guests' experience.

Beer and food pairing can be done using the same systematic process but with some thought to key differences. The basic process starts by looking at the beverage and food characteristics of sweetness, acidity, saltiness, and bitterness levels. Low to moderate levels of these characteristics in food provide the most flexibility of moving to higher levels of match with a variety of wine or (in this case) beer styles.

The second category assesses texture or body in food and beverage. For wine, these are typically alcohol level, tannin, and overall mouthfeel. For beer, alcohol level and overall mouthfeel are important, but the overall sense of body can be greatly affected by the type of beer (wheat beer, ale, stout, etc.) as well as the carbonation. In particular, nitrogenized beers have a much fuller and creamier mouthfeel that will impact body-to-body relationships with food.

The final element category is flavor that is driven by in-mouth smells. These include the flavor type, intensity, and persistency. Flavor type can range from spicy to flowery to fruity, as well as many others. As with body, intensity and persistency relate to matching the beverage complexity with the food complexity; this is generally perceived as creating greater harmony, liking, and overall match than when food overpowers the beverage or vice versa.

Which of the twelve relationships is the one you've seen the most "aha" moments from?

While the body-to-body concept and watching out for higher levels of sweetness, sourness, and spiciness in food are important aspects, the ones that seem to create the most "aha" moments are those associated with flavor elements (these can be complementary or contrasting flavors and assist in adding a more interesting layering of complexity). For instance, last semester we embarked on a student research project pairing beer and chocolate. This process developed out of brainstorming on beer styles, chocolate styles, flavor layering, and asking, "What seasonal beer flavors can be used to suggest chocolate flavors that can create synergies when beer and chocolate are consumed together?" Interestingly, the two highest ratings were a dark chocolate truffle "explosion" (candied habanero and Pop Rocks) paired with an amber lager and a white chocolate truffle with toffee and espresso flavors paired with a Euro-style dark lager.

Photo Credit: Russell Cothren, University of Arkansas

CHAPTER

5

PALATE TRIPS

What is a palate trip? It's our way of trying different foods with different beers with thought and intention behind the experience. But that dry description leaves out the heart of what palate trips are all about: the beauty, the spontaneity, the freedom!

Palate trips are an adventure. Sure, you may have a road map, but it's a loose guide and you're encouraged to take the dirt paths rather than the main road. Your tour guide is a little bit unhinged, and he isn't exactly sure how you'll get where you're going next. If there's a hill that looks interesting, he'll say, "Let's go ahead and climb it right now!"

A palate trip is all about experimenting with foods and beers—those you've tried before, sure, but also ones you wouldn't normally try. It can be based on impulse buys at the grocery store or on trying new menu items at your favorite restaurant. It's about letting down your guard, putting aside any prejudice, and embracing pairing passion. Go ahead: forget the rules. Forget what anyone told you is "right." Try something simply because it's fun! Unless you're allergic to something, just eat (or drink) it.

The goal of this chapter is to get you off and running, inventing palate trips for you and your friends. But what kind of teachers would we be if we didn't provide plenty of examples of palate trips first? For each palate trip on the pages that follow, we will provide you with a food shopping list, as well as a beer style list. Particular beer examples are just that, examples, and not all are available nationwide. Still, hopefully they will help you identify something from your local brewery that will work.

We will provide you with some brief notes on what you might expect to experience or what interactions you might want to focus on, but these are also just to get you off and running. If you use trips for tasting parties with family or friends, remember that everyone's palate is different. Nobody is wrong if they taste or smell something differently, or if they like or dislike a particular pairing. Oh, and whether you're tasting in a group or on your own, don't forget to take notes. Otherwise, you will certainly forget some of the specific interactions (and not just because you're having a couple beers!). Memory is a great tool, but so is your pen.

We can't wait to see what palate trips our readers invent. Maybe you want to go to Mexico, so you spend a night pairing only Mexican food elements. Or maybe it's summer and you're on a barbecue kick, so you keep it all American. Either way, you're buckling up for a sensory road trip. Pick up your map: it's palate trip time!

PALATE TRIP #1: YOUR FIRST TRIP

For your first palate trip, we want to demonstrate a bit of everything when it comes to beer and food interactions. Moving clockwise, begin at the top by smelling and tasting the American IPA. Think about what flavor images come to mind. Next, eat some sweetened dried mango, focusing again on the flavor images. Before swallowing the food, take another sip of the American IPA to get the interaction between the beer and the fruit. The sweet of the mango probably cut the bitterness of the hops and complemented the sweetness of the malt, right?

Using the same procedure of beer, food, then beer and food at the same time, move on to how that same beer (the IPA) interacts with a sour pickle. You might find some interactions are going to be home runs, while others might be train wrecks. You are on your first trip, after

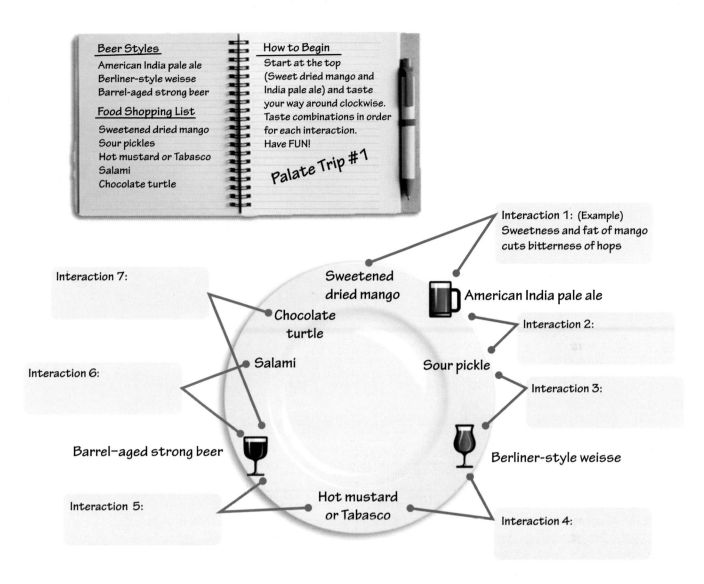

Beer Styles

American India pale ale
Berliner-style weisse
Barrel-aged strong beer

Food Shopping List

Sweetened dried mango
Sour pickles
Hot mustard or Tabasco
Salami
Chocolate turtle

How to Begin

Start at the top
(Sweet dried mango and
India pale ale) and taste
your way around clockwise.
Taste combinations in order
for each interaction.
Have FUN!

Palate Trip #1

Interaction 1: (Example)
Sweetness and fat of mango
cuts bitterness of hops

Interaction 7:

Interaction 6:

Interaction 5:

Interaction 2:

Interaction 3:

Interaction 4:

Sweetened dried mango

American India pale ale

Chocolate turtle

Salami

Sour pickle

Barrel-aged strong beer

Berliner-style weisse

Hot mustard or Tabasco

all. If you found IPA and sour pickle weren't great together, try to pick out what it is you didn't care for.

As you switch beers to a Berliner-style weisse, stick with the sour pickle and you'll find sour negating sour. An interesting combination! But when the Berliner is paired with spicy hot mustard or a drop of Tabasco, you'll probably find that all elements involved are out of balance and a great example of a train wreck.

The third beer is a barrel-aged strong beer, but stick with the spicy hot interaction at first: tease out the interaction of alcohol and capsaicin heat. Cool that down with the addition of rich, salt-laden salami, still with the barrel-aged strong beer, and you'll find that the fat cuts through the heat and the high alcohol from the beer cuts through the fat. Now let's finish up this palate trip with your favorite chocolate and that barrel-aged beer for a harmonious combination of chocolate, nuts, and sweet caramel in both beer and food.

As you go back through the palate, talk with your tasting buddies. Everyone is sure to pick out different elements. Have fun!

BEER RECOMMENDATIONS

American IPA: As you have learned, not all IPAs are created equal. For this pairing, look for an IPA that has aroma notes of citrus, such as grapefruit, and/or tropical fruits to complement the mango. (This is also a good trip to try two very different IPAs.) Examples: Ballast Point Sculpin IPA, Firestone Walker Union Jack IPA, Bell's Two Hearted Ale, Port Brewing Mongo IPA, and Flying Dog Snake Dog IPA.

Berliner-Style Weisse: Almost any Berliner you find should have wheaty maltiness and a lactic, tart, lemon-like acidity. Examples: The Bruery Hottenroth, Saint Arnold Boiler Room, New Glarus Thumbprint, and Bear Republic Tartare.

Barrel-Aged Strong Beer: Try to find one with tannin wood characteristics and a high level of alcohol warming. Darker roasted, chocolate malt characteristics should come out as well. Examples: The Lost Abbey Deliverance, Stone Bourbon Barrel-Aged Imperial Russian Stout, FiftyFifty Eclipse Barrel-Aged Imperial Stout, Heavy Seas Oak-Aged Peg Leg Imperial Stout, Great Divide Oak-Aged Yeti Imperial Stout, Weyerbacher Heresy Imperial Stout, and Left Hand Wake Up Dead Barrel-Aged Imperial Stout.

PALATE TRIP #2:
VISITING BELGIUM WITH ALL THE COMFORTS OF HOME

We believe Belgian beers are inspired, and after you taste a few you're sure to see why. There is a complexity with these beers, and the great thing is the complexity only increases when they are paired with food. Some would also say there is a romance that comes with drinking and pairing Belgians beers. Sounds even more intriguing now, doesn't it?

Beginning at the top, you'll start with flavor of the French-style Bière de Garde. As you smell and taste the corn chips, think about how the corn chip flavor could stand in for anything that contains the characteristics of toasted corn: masa in tamales or cornmeal polenta. Moving clockwise, try the same beer with the chili-dusted pineapple, which incorporates spice, tart, and sweet into the pairing picture.

Now try the same pineapple again, but with saison, thinking about how the yeast, malt, spicy, and fruity characteristics are similar, but different as well. Your next stop is the smoked barbecue nuts. You might notice that the barbecue nut pairing with the saison is a bit of a clash—a lesson in what doesn't work as well. But then, it's a quick about-face: the Belgian dubbel and nuts are a home run combination for most people.

For the final food, you have the sea salt butterscotch caramels. You'll try them first with the Belgian-style dubbel, then the Belgian-style quadrupel. Look for two different intensities of sweet and salt as well as other flavor elements.

What did you learn from this trip? After you've completed your tour, be sure to take a different route and try all the food items with all the beers to experience even more pairing interactions.

BEER RECOMMENDATIONS

French-Style Bière de Garde: This beer should have sweet, toasted malt flavors along with earthy and fruity beer elements. Examples: Jolly Pumpkin Bière de Mars, Stillwater Cellar Door,

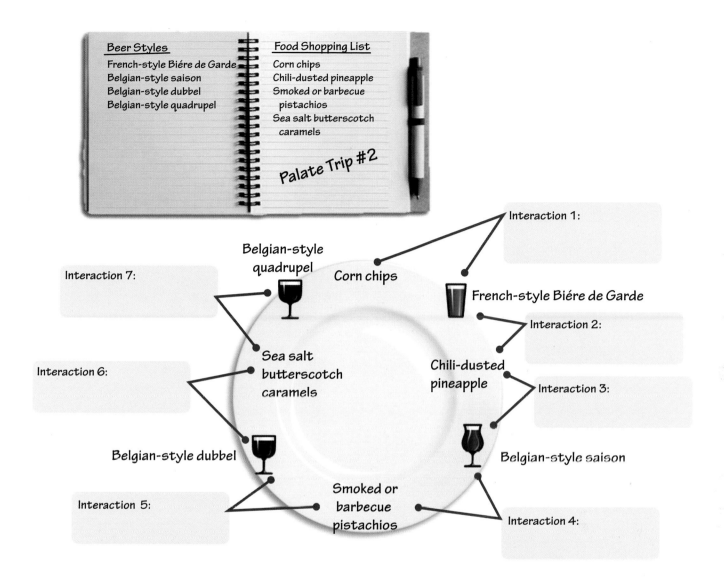

Beer Styles
French-style Biére de Garde
Belgian-style saison
Belgian-style dubbel
Belgian-style quadrupel

Food Shopping List
Corn chips
Chili-dusted pineapple
Smoked or barbecue
 pistachios
Sea salt butterscotch
 caramels

Palate Trip #2

Interaction 1:

Belgian-style
quadrupel

Corn chips

French-style Biére de Garde

Interaction 7:

Interaction 2:

Sea salt
butterscotch
caramels

Chili-dusted
pineapple

Interaction 3:

Interaction 6:

Belgian-style dubbel

Belgian-style saison

Interaction 5:

Smoked or
barbecue
pistachios

Interaction 4:

Schlafly Bière de Garde, The Lost Abbey Avant Garde, New Belgium Bière de Mars, Stillwater Debutante Bière De Garde.

Belgian-Style Saison: Look for saisons with earthy, musty, fruity, and phenolic aromas with just a bit of biscuity malt for balance. Examples: Crooked Stave Surette Provision Saison, Hill Farmstead Flora, and Jester King Hibernal Dichotomous, The Lost Abbey Red Barn, Brooklyn 1/2 Ale, Firestone Walker Opal, Allagash Saison, Ommegang Crescendo, The Bruery Saison Rue, and Starr Hill Starr Saison.

Belgian-Style Dubbel: Look for a dubbel with sweet caramel, chocolate malt, and fruity and spicy yeast characteristics, like banana and clove, as well as a hint of raisin or plum. Examples: Anderson Valley Brother David's Double Abbey-Style Ale, Captain Lawrence St. Vincent's Dubbel, New Belgium Abbey, Tröegs Jovial Belgian-Style Dubbel, and Devil's Backbone Dark Abby.

Belgian-Style Quadrupel: Find a quad with plenty of malty caramel sweetness accompanied by brown fruits such as dates, figs, and raisins, spicy phenolic yeast characteristics, and warming alcohol. Examples: Brooklyn Quadraceratops, Avery The Reverend, Deschutes The Stoic, Ommegang Three Philosophers, and Schlafly Quadrupel.

PALATE TRIP #3: DRIVING SOLO

This palate trip is where the training wheels come off. We've guided you through the first two, but we want you piloting this one as your own. It's designed to be a friendly round-trip. This means you'll start and end on the same food with different beers, and as you progress through the trip it's all about the journey. We haven't buried any combos that don't work here, so no need to watch out for a train wreck. Instead, you'll find combinations that are middle of the road, and hopefully a few home runs.

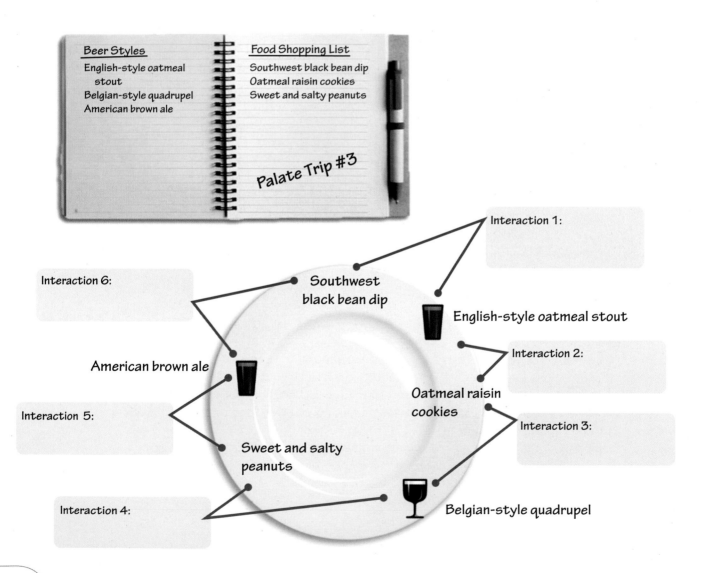

One last note: pay attention to malt interactions on this trip as well as mouthfeel and texture changes. OK, those are your only clues . . . get tasting!

BEER RECOMMENDATIONS

English-Style Oatmeal Stout: These stouts have caramel, coffee, chocolate, and roasted malt elements with a smooth and silky mouthfeel plus sweetness from the oatmeal. Examples: Rogue Ales Shakespeare Oatmeal Stout, Ninkasi Oatis, Odell Gramps Oatmeal Stout, Breckenridge Oatmeal Stout, and Firestone Walker Velvet Merlin.

Belgian-Style Quadrupel: Look for malty caramel sweetness accompanied by brown fruits such as dates, figs, and raisins, spicy phenolic yeast characteristics, and warming alcohol. Examples: Brooklyn Quadraceratops, Avery 5 Monks, The Lost Abbey Judgment Day, New Belgium Cascara Quad, and Ommegang Three Philosophers.

American Brown Ale: Track down a brown that's medium nutty, with hints of caramel and chocolate-sweet malts, earthy dark bread–like characters, and medium hop bitterness. Examples: Big Sky Moose Drool, Shmaltz He'Brew Messiah Nut Brown Ale, Brooklyn Brown Ale, Avery Ellie's Brown Ale, and Dogfish Head Indian Brown Ale.

PALATE TRIP #4: A MOST UNUSUAL KIND OF TRIP

As you look at the food for this trip, we're sure you are thinking that these items seem quite strange. Yet it's often with the weird pairings that you learn the most.

The first stop is a Belgian-style dubbel and sun-dried tomato combo that balances the sweet tomato with the sweet of raisins and molasses as well as a savory, umami-laden finish. The next food with the dubbel is a piece of roasted seaweed; you'll find salty, savory, and maple syrup flavors in this combo, with a nutty sesame aftertaste.

You might find a few similarities as you move to the California common and the roasted seaweed. However, the more exciting combo is when the red pepper hummus and the veggie sweetness interact with the slight caramel malt character of the California common and the contrast of salt.

Say hello to the imperial IPA next, and see how the citrus of hops complements the tart of lemon juice from the hummus and the sweet malt balances the sweet in the vegetables. (Think about the mouthfeel with this pairing, too.) Finally, end with the imperial IPA and a big, bold blue cheese. The higher alcohol and hops cut through the pungent blue vein, and you're left with a less intense, very well-balanced, creamy, funky earthiness. Hope this one was as fun for you as it was for us!

Note: Remember that when a train wreck occurs for you, figure out what elements are out of balance and why. It could be the beer elements or the food elements or even a combination of both. You can use what you learned in regard to other foods as well. For example, sun-dried tomatoes are rarely something that you eat on their own, but they translate well to tomato sauces or even pizza.

BEER RECOMMENDATIONS

Belgian-Style Dubbel: Look for a dubbel with sweet caramel, chocolate malt, and fruity and spicy yeast characteristics such as banana and clove, as well as a hint of raisin or plum.

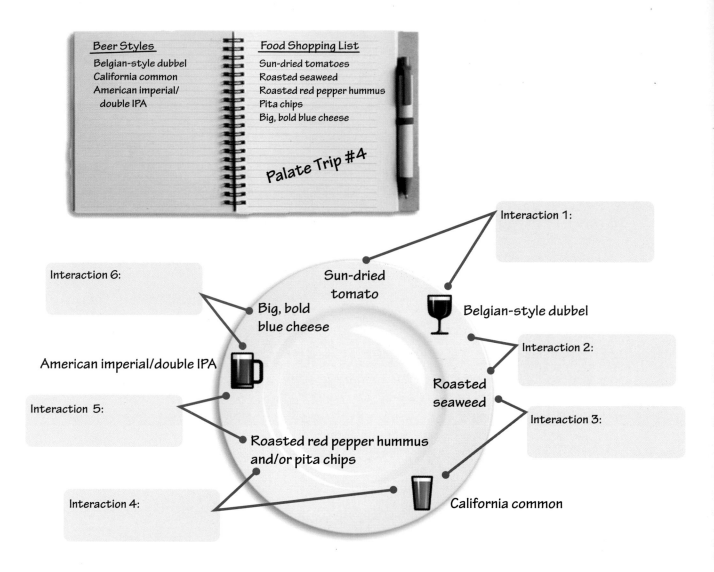

Beer Styles

Belgian-style dubbel
California common
American imperial/
double IPA

Food Shopping List

Sun-dried tomatoes
Roasted seaweed
Roasted red pepper hummus
Pita chips
Big, bold blue cheese

Palate Trip #4

Interaction 1:

Interaction 6:

Interaction 2:

Interaction 3:

Interaction 5:

Interaction 4:

Sun-dried tomato

Belgian-style dubbel

Roasted seaweed

California common

Big, bold blue cheese

American imperial/double IPA

Roasted red pepper hummus and/or pita chips

Examples: Anderson Valley Brother David's Double Abbey-Style Ale, Captain Lawrence St. Vincent's Dubbel, Drop-In Brewing The Selling of Indulgences Belgian-Style Dubbel, Flying Fish Belgian Abbey Dubbel, and The Lost Abbey Lost & Found Abbey Ale.

California Common: In most you'll find caramel, toasted sweet malt with slight fruity hop elements. Examples: Anchor Steam, Steamworks Steam Engine Lager, Flying Dog Old Scratch Amber Lager, and Real Ale Cut California Common.

Imperial IPA: Look for malty, alcohol warming, and dank, piney, citrus hop bitter beer elements. Examples: Russian River Pliny the Elder, Sierra Nevada Hoptimum, Green Flash Imperial, Bell's Hopslam, D.C. Brau On the Wings of Armageddon, Dogfish Head 90 Minute Double IPA, and Port Brewing Mongo.

Even the nice and easy palate trip (see page 96) provides plenty of new flavor combinations.

PALATE TRIP #5: NICE AND EASY

After the weird palate trip, it's time to take the easy route, but that doesn't mean it has to be any less interesting.

   The first pairing starts with hefeweizen and jam, so you can probably imagine that the fruit will be taking center stage. But consider how those characteristics change in both the beer and food when you combine the two. When you move on to the key lime, think about how different the fruity elements are in this pairing as compared with the jam, and how the malt interacts.

   When you taste the IPA with the key lime, what differences stand out for you compared to the hefe? After considering that, continue on your trip with the IPA and the aged cheddar. This is one of those pairings we recommend when people say IPAs aren't their favorite beers, because the combination balances the more extreme elements in both.

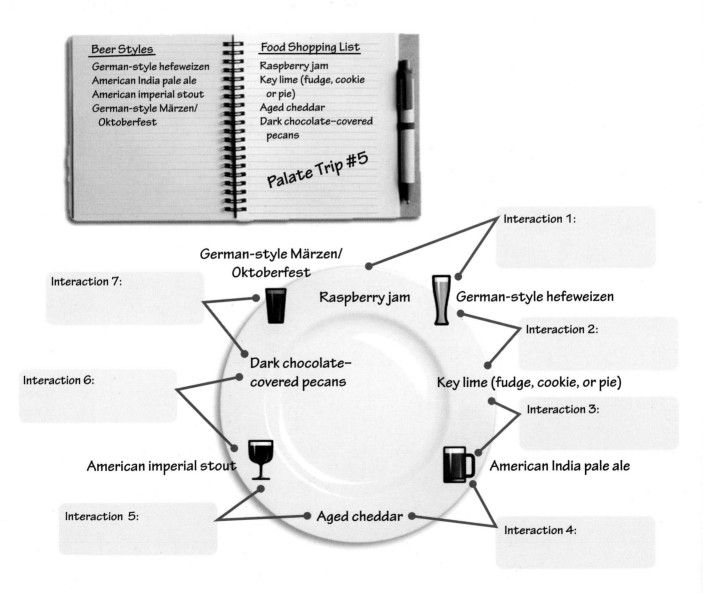

Beer Styles
German-style hefeweizen
American India pale ale
American imperial stout
German-style Märzen/
   Oktoberfest

Food Shopping List
Raspberry jam
Key lime (fudge, cookie
   or pie)
Aged cheddar
Dark chocolate-covered
   pecans

Palate Trip #5

Interaction 1:

German-style Märzen/
Oktoberfest

Interaction 7:

Raspberry jam

German-style hefeweizen

Interaction 2:

Dark chocolate–
covered pecans

Key lime (fudge, cookie, or pie)

Interaction 6:

Interaction 3:

American imperial stout

American India pale ale

Interaction 5:

Aged cheddar

Interaction 4:

When you switch gears to the American imperial stout and aged cheddar, what changes? And which pairing did you like better, the IPA or the imperial stout? Why do you feel that way?

Wrap up the trip with the dark chocolate–covered pecans pairing. While both beer combinations with this food can be simply enjoyable, you should look for the impact of alcohol intensity in particular, since the imperial stout will have a higher alcohol content than the German-style Märzen/Oktoberfest. Also note how roasted and chocolate malts interact differently with the chocolate and nuts than the toasted, sweet malts of the German Märzen.

BEER RECOMMENDATIONS

German-Style Hefeweizen: Look for classic versions of the style with sweet wheat malt and fruity spiciness such as nutmeg, clove, and banana from the yeast. Examples: Harpoon UFO Hefeweizen, Flying Dog In-Heat Wheat, Karbach Weisse Versa Wheat, Tröegs DreamWeaver Wheat, Saint Arnold Weedwacker, and Dry Dock Hefeweizen.

American IPA: Look for dank IPAs with citrus notes and/or a tropical fruit hop element. Examples: Ballast Point Big Eye IPA, Great Divide Titan IPA, Founders Centennial IPA, Bear Republic Racer 5 IPA, and Avery IPA.

American Imperial Stout: Find a stout with big roasted, chocolate, and coffee character and with balanced alcohol warming. Examples: Great Divide Yeti Imperial Stout, Dogfish Head World Wide Stout, Oskar Blues Ten Fidy, Port Brewing Old Viscosity, and Founders Breakfast Stout.

German-Style Märzen/Oktoberfest: Look for Märzens with sweet, toasted bread-like malt characteristics. Examples: Flying Dog Dogtoberfest, SurlyFest, Samuel Adams Octoberfest, Summit Oktoberfest, and Great Lakes Oktoberfest.

PALATE TRIP #6: NOT YOUR AVERAGE PICNIC BASKET

The final trip we planned is definitely down a dirt road, and it's probably going to get you to try some foods that you wouldn't normally think of when it comes to pairing. Remember, even if your mind tells you no, your mother taught you to try everything once, right? If she didn't, you should do it anyway! Still, we realize that there are items in this trip that people have strong opinions about, so we tried to provide some alternate options.

This trip starts with grain and herbs interacting with malt, hops, and yeast. The high carbonation of the Belgian-style pale strong ale, along with the fruity yeast characteristics, can really emphasize the herbal and sweet notes in the breadsticks. When you move to the artichoke heart with the same beer (Belgian-style pale strong ale) and then paired with the American pale ale, pay attention to the tartness and fruity citrus and what, why, and where those flavor characteristics are changing. Was there a decrease or increase in citrus tartness? Look at the intensity of the sweetness from one pairing to the other as well.

Green olives or wasabi almonds both have nutty and salty attributes, so how are those going to play with the American pale ale and the Belgian-style wit? Focus on how sweet malt from the American pale ale interacts differently from the toasted, biscuit-like malt of the Belgian-style wit. If you are using the wasabi almonds, look for the intensity change of spiciness between the two beer pairings.

The final food involves lemon in the form of dessert with Belgian-style wit and American IPA. You can probably guess that the tartness of the lemon will lead to some interesting interactions. But don't forget about the sweetness and bready characteristics. Why and how do those change with the two different beers? Your focus here might be on how the Belgian-style wit is a much softer and more delicate pairing, while the American IPA pairing is refreshing and anything but soft. We hope this trip stirs your sense of adventure!

BEER RECOMMENDATIONS

Belgian-Style Pale Strong Ale: Look for a pale ale with fruity sweet notes, slight phenolic spice, high carbonation, and a drying finish. Examples: Russian River Damnation, North Coast Pranqster, The Lost Abbey Inferno, Brooklyn Local 1, Great Divide Hades, Allagash Confluence Ale, and Ommegang Gnomegang.

 American Pale Ale: Pick a classic pale with caramel malt and medium floral, fruity, or citrus hop elements. Examples: Sierra Nevada Pale Ale, Deschutes Mirror Pond, Oskar Blues Dale's Pale Ale, Boulevard Pale Ale, Ninkasi Quantum, Alaskan Freeride American Pale Ale.

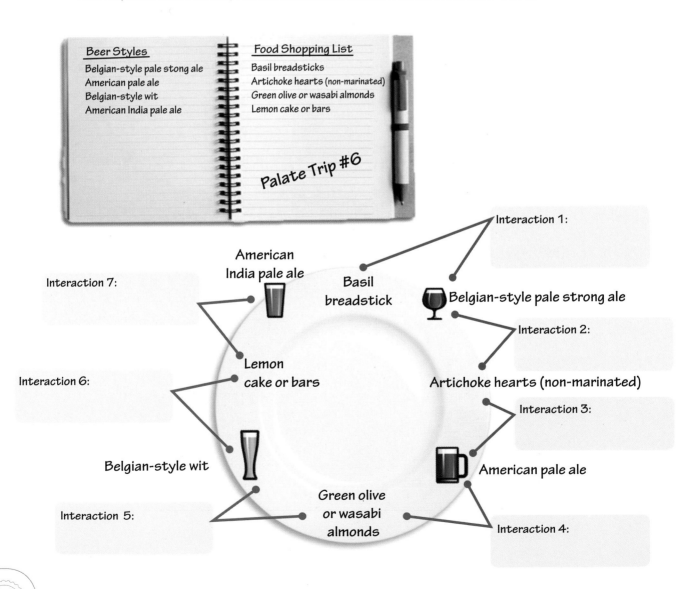

Belgian-Style Wit: Look for creamy malt notes from wheat and oats, spices such as coriander and orange peel, and tangy acidic beer elements. Examples: Allagash White, Saint Archer White Ale, Harpoon UFO White, New Belgium Mothership Wit, Drop-In Katarina Wit, and Funkwerks White.

American IPA: Find an IPA with big hop aroma: you want tropical, floral, dank, and/or citrus hop elements. Examples: AleSmith IPA, Lagunitas IPA, Firestone Walker Union Jack, Odell IPA, SweetWater IPA, Alpine Duet IPA, Smuttynose Finestkind IPA, and Cigar City Jai Alai IPA.

DESIGN YOUR OWN PALATE TRIP

Although this may be the end of the chapter's palate trip adventures, we invite you to continue the journey on your own. The next time you're at the store, start planning your next palate trip. For example, I bet that cinnamon and cranberry goat cheese you noticed would pair excellently with a Brett saison. Those peanut butter pretzels, on the other hand, would go great with that amber ale already in your fridge. And dried fruit and nuts? You'll never look at them the same way again!

If you want to plan out the trips the way we did, here's a blank sheet that you can copy and fill out for your own palate trips.

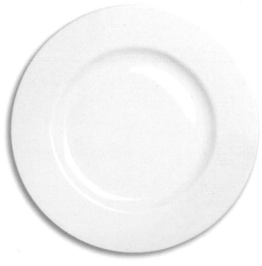

CHAPTER

- 6 -

PAIRING BY BEER STYLE

ABOUT BEER STYLES

Style guidelines exist to give beer lovers a methodology to describe, compare, and contrast different beers in existing categories. Are guidelines needed to enjoy beer? Of course not, but guidelines are helpful when it comes to beer education and figuring out how similar ingredients and brewing techniques from different brewers result in beers with shared profiles. Styles give you a baseline and a preview of the sensory picture. They let you open a bottle or order a pint with an idea of what attributes you may perceive.

The styles in this chapter are selected from among the nearly eighty common styles being made in the United States at the time of writing, based on CraftBeer.com style guidelines. Brewers continue to push the boundaries, and new beers are being created every day. There will never be an absolute when it comes to beer styles, but that just adds to the fun of beer and pairing. Needless to say, these are exciting times for beer lovers.

WHAT DO THE NUMBERS MEAN?

In this chapter you'll find there are a variety of specialty terms, including numbers that will help you place a beer in context for things such as alcohol level or bitterness. You may recognize some or even all of these terms. If so, good for you! If not, peruse the following before moving on to the styles.

Original Gravity (OG): The specific gravity of wort (unfermented beer) before fermentation.
- To get a little more technical, OG is a measure of the total amount of solids that are dissolved in the wort as compared to the density of water, which is conventionally given as 1.000 at 60 degrees Fahrenheit.
- In practice, OG gives you a clue about the alcohol intensity. In general, as OG goes up, so does the strength of the beer. This is why you'll sometimes see strong beers listed as "high gravity" beers.

Final Gravity (FG): The specific gravity of beer as measured when fermentation is complete (when all desired fermentable sugars have been converted to alcohol and carbon dioxide gas).
- After wort is fermented, most of the sugars that made up the OG have been converted, so you'll see FG numbers that are quite a bit lower than OG numbers. FG will never be higher than OG.
- In practice, this number gives you an idea of how much residual sugar (sweetness) is left in the beer. A beer with a FG of 1.006 will typically come across as much drier than a beer with a FG of 1.014.

Apparent Attenuation: A measure of the extent of fermentation wort has undergone in the process of becoming beer. Formula: AA = [(OG − FG) / (OG − 1)] x 100.
- Apparent attenuation reflects the amount of malt sugar that is converted to alcohol during fermentation. The result is expressed as a percentage and equals 65–80 percent for most beers.
- Above 80 percent is very high attenuation with little residual sugar. Below 60 percent is low attenuation with more residual sugar remaining.

Alcohol by Volume (ABV): A measurement of the alcohol content in terms of the percentage volume of alcohol per volume of beer.

- Ranges: Not detectible, mild, noticeable, harsh, hot. In the United States, nonalcoholic beer is under 0.5 percent ABV, an average beer is in the range of 4.8–7.2 percent ABV, and a high ABV can even reach up to 15 percent. (Some beers can go even higher than that with specialty ingredients or techniques.)

International Bitterness Units (IBUs): A measure of the beer's bitterness, usually based on milligrams of isomerized alpha acids (from hops) in one liter of beer. Can range from 0 (no bitterness) to above 100 IBUs, depending on the style. The levels can be described as low, moderate, aggressive, or harsh. Examples of ranges would be Berliner-style weisse at low (3–6 IBUs), American amber lager at moderate (18–30 IBUs), an American pale ale at aggressive (30–50 IBUs), and imperial IPA at harsh (65–100 IBUs).

- 1 bitterness unit = 1 milligram of isomerized hop alpha acids in one liter of beer.
- Most people cannot perceive bitterness above a specific level of IBUs (said to be 80 IBUs by some sources).
- If you want to go even further and analyze the sweetness of malt or gravity units (GU) to bitterness ratio or bitterness units (BU), consider BU:GU ratio. This is a concept from Ray Daniels, creator of the Cicerone Certification Program.
  - 0.5 is perceived as balanced, under 0.5 is perceived as sweeter, and over 0.5 is perceived as more bitter.
  - Formula: Divide IBU by the last two digits of original gravity (remove the 1.0) to give relative bitterness. A low bitterness ratio usually correlates to lower bitter beers, such as hefeweizen, whereas a higher bitterness ratio usually correlates with higher bitter beers, such as American pale ales. It needs to be noted here that this bitterness ratio does not take into consideration malts being used and their effect on flavor. For example, an imperial stout might have a very high bitterness ratio, but the malt roast and sweetness will be perceived over the hop bitterness. Always go with what your taste buds tell you.
  - Example: a pale ale with 37 IBUs and an OG of 1.052 is 37/52 = 0.71 BU:GU.

Color/Standard Reference Method (SRM): Although not related directly to flavor, color is very important to our perception of flavor. Beer derives most of its color contributions from malts and grains, whether they are heated, and how they are heated. Using a spectrophotometer, brewers determine how much light can pass through one centimeter of beer at 430 nm. That is how the chart below determines color. All you have to do is hold the chart up to your beer to determine what color (SRM) your beer is.

- Very light (1–1.5), straw (2–3), pale (4), gold (5–6), light amber (7), amber (8), medium amber (9), copper/garnet (10–12), light brown (13–15), brown/reddish brown/chestnut brown (16–17), dark brown (18–24), very dark (25–39), black (40+)

SRM BEER STYLE COLOR CHART

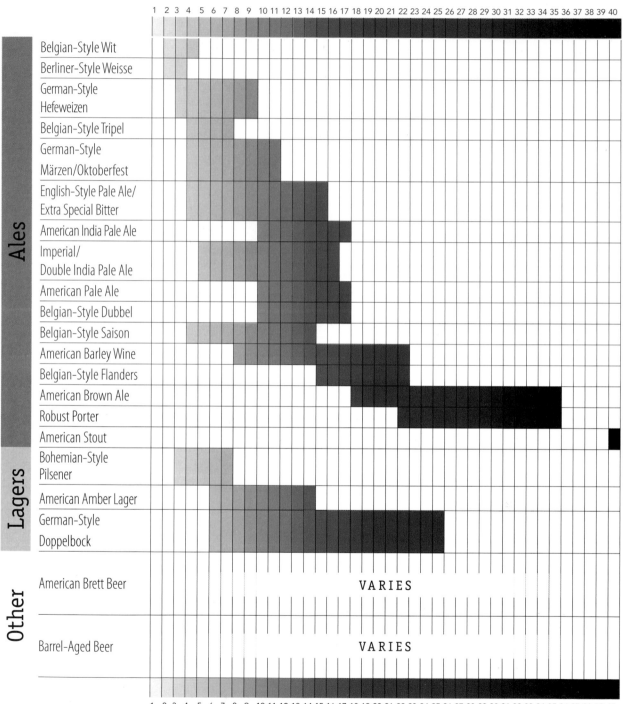

Ales

- Belgian-Style Wit
- Berliner-Style Weisse
- German-Style Hefeweizen
- Belgian-Style Tripel
- German-Style Märzen/Oktoberfest
- English-Style Pale Ale/ Extra Special Bitter
- American India Pale Ale
- Imperial/ Double India Pale Ale
- American Pale Ale
- Belgian-Style Dubbel
- Belgian-Style Saison
- American Barley Wine
- Belgian-Style Flanders
- American Brown Ale
- Robust Porter
- American Stout

Lagers

- Bohemian-Style Pilsener
- American Amber Lager
- German-Style Doppelbock

Other

- American Brett Beer — VARIES
- Barrel-Aged Beer — VARIES

ABOUT THE PAIRINGS

Before we go into the specific pairings by beer style, remember pairing and perception are personal. Since we perceive flavors differently, what is bitter to some may not be bitter to others. A home run pairing for us may not hit it out of the ballpark for you. Or, a pairing that works for you may not work for your best friend. Don't take it personally. Instead, embrace and learn from everyone's flavor personalities.

In this chapter you'll find both general recommendations and specific dishes to try with each beer. They include tried-and-true beer pairings such as Belgian-style wit and mussels, American amber lager and nachos, and American IPA and beef chili. They also include outside-the-box pairings such as Berliner-style weisse and eggs Florentine, German-style Märzen/Oktoberfest and beef Stroganoff, Bohemian-style pilsener and salmon sushi, and Belgian-style Flanders and lentil soup.

Yet all the foods listed are meant to be easy enough for you to cook at home or common enough to order out. The goal of this chapter is the same as the goal for the book: we want to get you off and running in the right direction more than we want to dictate what's right and wrong. We encourage you to try out these pairings and tweak them to your heart's content. Solicit feedback from everyone you know—most importantly, yourself! Parsing out what you like, what you dislike, and *why* is where the real fun happens.

BELGIAN-STYLE WIT
ABOUT THE STYLE

Belgian-style wits are brewed using unmalted wheat (and sometimes oats) as well as malted barley. However, what most people notice first is the spicing, traditionally coriander and orange peel. Wits may also have a low background base note of lactic acidity. A style that dates back hundreds of years, wit fell into relative obscurity until it was revived by Belgian brewer Pierre Celis in the 1960s. This style is currently enjoying quite a renaissance, especially in the American market.

Quantitative Style Statistics
- OG: 1.044–1.050
- FG: 1.006–1.010
- Apparent Attenuation: 80–86 percent
- ABV: 4.8–5.6 percent
- IBU: 10–17
- Color/SRM: 2–4 (straw to pale)

US Commercial Examples: Allagash White, Avery White Rascal, Boulevard Zōn, Harpoon UFO White, Anchorage Whiteout Wit

Country of Origin: Belgium

Beer Sensory Notes
- Intensity: Low
- Malt: Pilsener, flaked wheat, unmalted wheat, and occasionally oats and malted barley
- Hops: German noble
- Yeast: Ale

BELGIAN-STYLE WIT

THE STYLE AND FOOD

There's a reason we're starting the chapter here: wits are one of the easiest beers to pair with a wide variety of foods. Just keep in mind that the wit has low intensity, which means it is easily overpowered by super-flavorful dishes. Mild shellfish almost always works, as do dishes that run with wit's hit of lemon and spices. For example, try lobster and avocado salad; beet and goat cheese salad; ricotta crostini with black olives, lemon zest, and mint; lemon risotto; or cedar-smoked salmon.

Try This First: Mussels

Teddy Folkman, executive chef of the Belgian beer bar Granville Moore's in Washington, DC, defeated Food Network chef Bobby Flay in a throwdown with his signature mussels, which include bacon, shallots, a creamy blue cheese, spinach, white wine (dry Chardonnay), lemon juice, and pepper. The dish is served with a French baguette, to sop up the delicious steaming liquid, and *frites*.

Unlike many of the combinations in this chapter, this pairing is not a perfect intensity match. Flavors of butter, bacon, shallots, and the cheese set up a medium-high intensity backdrop for the mussels. Even though the coriander and orange citrus notes of the wit shine brighter with the mussels and serve as a seasoning for the dish, the mussels overpower the mild wit. Yet each wisp of wit helps refresh the palate with carbonation and brighten up the mussels with very low-level lactic acidity. The saltine cracker flavor from the pilsener malt and white bread flavor from the unmalted wheat work extremely well with the butter, shallots, bread, and fried potatoes. The coriander also latches on to the spinach, helping highlight both green and spice, respectively.

At home, just about any steamed mussel recipe with a splash of wit, butter, salt, and herbs should get you started on an excellent dish to pair with wit. However, you can go even further on a flavor exploration with mussels and beer. Take inspiration from Schlafly Brewery out of Saint Louis, Missouri, which hosts a yearly festival with mussel preparation choices including Kölsch and bacon, spicy red curry, and chili verde, along with the classic white wine, butter, and garlic version.

GERMAN-STYLE HEFEWEIZEN
ABOUT THE STYLE

Weizen means "wheat" and *hefe* means "yeast," so it should be no surprise that German-style hefeweizens are yeasty and wheaty in character. Typically you'll find they're straw to amber in color and made with at least 50 percent malted wheat. Sometimes called weissbeer, the aroma and flavor come largely from the yeast and are decidedly fruity (banana) and phenolic (clove, white pepper, vanilla, and even smoke). This is commonly a very highly carbonated style with a long-lasting collar of foam.

If you find you're a fan of hefeweizens, there are multiple variations of the style to explore. Filtered versions are known as kristalweizen, and darker versions are referred to as dunkels, with a stronger, bock-like version called weizenbock.

Quantitative Style Statistics
- OG: 1.047–1.056
- FG: 1.008–1.016
- Apparent Attenuation: 71–83 percent
- ABV: 4.9–5.6 percent
- IBU: 10–15
- Color/SRM: 3–9 (straw to medium amber)

US Commercial Examples: CB & Potts Big Horn Hefeweizen, Harpoon UFO Hefeweizen, Schlafly Hefeweizen, Flying Dog In-Heat Wheat, Spoetzel Shiner Hefeweizen

Country of Origin: Germany

Beer Sensory Notes
- Intensity: Low
- Malt: Pilsener, malted wheat
- Hops: German noble
- Yeast: Ale

THE STYLE AND FOOD

Slightly sweet and fruity, spicy, citrusy, tart, yeasty, creamy, and spritzy high carbonation provide a lot of beer elements to work with for pairing. Lighter fruit dishes and shellfish, along with citrus vinegar dressings, work very well, and earthy foods such as goat cheese and beets can pair with the spicy notes. Also try a hefe with herbal foods that have olives, rosemary, or mint, as well as smoked fish. Don't forget fruity desserts!

Try This First: Fresh Tomatoes or Carrot, Tomato, and Basil Soup

Tomato and hefeweizen create an umami-filled pairing all on their own. If you can get your hands on a fresh in-season tomato, try it! You'll find this combination actually makes you salivate as you are eating it.

If you want to take things further, or if fresh tomatoes simply aren't in season, try the hefe with tomato soup. But we're not talking about a glob of condensed canned soup here. We're talking homemade tomato soup, the kind from childhood, but with pureed carrots. Why add the carrot? You'll find they not only add a full, creamy mouthfeel but also amp up the overall sweetness of the soup while cutting some of the acidity from the tomato.

For the pairing, sweet fruity and spice elements from the beer, such as clove and banana, complement the sweet of the carrot while cutting through the acid of the tomato. Earthy notes from the carrot balance with the toasted breadiness of the hefeweizen. If you really want to kick this pairing to the highest level, add a grilled sourdough and goat cheese sandwich. It may seem like a lot of flavor, but we feel it all comes together perfectly. The sourdough acts like a wedge of lemon to the hefeweizen, and the bread and goat cheese flavors bridge to the beer's pilsener and wheat malt. The high carbonation of the hefe lifts the dairy fat of the goat cheese off the tongue and refreshes the palate.

GERMAN-STYLE HEFEWEIZEN

BERLINER-STYLE WEISSE
ABOUT THE STYLE
Low in alcohol, refreshingly tart, and sometimes served with a flavored syrup such as woodruff or raspberry, this German wheat ale presents a harmony between yeast and lactic acid. These beers are very pale in color and may be cloudy, as they are often unfiltered. Hops are not a feature of this style, but these beers often do showcase esters. Traditional versions often use *Brettanomyces* yeast, but many today are brewed using ale yeast and lactobacillus.

Berliner-style weisse is a style growing in popularity in the United States, where many brewers are adding traditional and exotic fruits to the recipe, resulting in flavorful finishes with striking, colorful hues. These beers are simply incredible when pairing. Bitterness, alcohol, and residual sugar are very low, allowing the beer's acidity, white bread, and graham cracker malt flavors to shine. Carbonation is very high, adding to the refreshment factor this style delivers. Many examples of this style contain little to no hops, and none have significant hop aroma or flavor.

Quantitative Style Statistics
- OG: 1.028–1.032
- FG: 1.004–1.060
- Apparent Attenuation: 81–86 percent
- ABV: 2.8–3.4 percent
- IBU: 3–6
- Color/SRM: 2–4 (straw to pale)

US Commercial Examples: Nodding Head Berliner Weisse, Southampton Berliner Weisse, The Bruery Hottenroth Berliner Weisse, New Glarus Thumbprint Berliner Weisse, Firestone Walker Bretta Weisse

Country of Origin: Germany

Beer Sensory Notes
- Intensity: Low
- Malt: Pilsener, malted wheat
- Hops: German noble
- Yeast: Ale

THE STYLE AND FOOD
This light-bodied, high-carbonation, and low ABV beer combines a clean crispness with acidic tartness. It calls for foods that will play well with the tartness but not overwhelm the balance. Start with fruits that have tartness of their own: raspberries, strawberries, cherries, or kumquats. Now add cheeses, sweet syrups, marmalades or jams, and even chocolate to the plate. Or try matching the tartness of the beer with tart foods such as pickled vegetables or a citrus salad.

Try This First: Poached Eggs or Eggs Florentine with Spinach and Goat Cheese
Eggs have a great deal of umami richness and are one of our favorite sources of daily protein. When it comes to flavor, they are buttery when cooked in a pan with butter, but to describe the flavor of the egg itself is somewhat difficult. Still, there's no need for us to stress over it: you already know what eggs taste like!

BERLINER-STYLE WEISSE

Poached eggs are incredible with wheat beers of all types. And it makes sense if you think about it: butter (eggs) on bread (beer). Berliner weisse has wheat in its base, plus it has a strong lactic acidity that mirrors lemon.

Going further, Florentine is our recommendation here, as spinach lessens the intensity compared to eggs Benedict, which has ham or Canadian bacon instead. The Berliner weisse would also go great with eggs Benedict, but the home run match to us is the less-intense Florentine. The goat cheese brings funk to this otherwise very smooth and silky dish. Since traditional versions of Berliner have *Brettanamyces*, you may find your beer does a firm and impressive handshake with the goat cheese, creating a connection of flavor echoes that circle round and round.

The hollandaise sauce, with its emulsified egg yolk and liquefied butter, is the flashiest thing about this creation. But lemon is used to brighten and lighten the entire dish, and it can find harmony with the lemon-like tartness of Berliners.

With all this happening, the spinach is then left to shine, which is great if you like the flavors of this leafy green. Especially with the added acidity boost from the beer, the spinach creates a rest (see page 22) that stops everything going on in your palate and allows your brain to say, "Hey, I can actually taste the spinach, and I kinda like it!"

BOHEMIAN-STYLE PILSENER
ABOUT THE STYLE

Bohemian-style pilseners have a slightly sweet malt character and a toasted, biscuit-like, bready malt character. Hop bitterness is medium, with a medium-low level of Saaz hop aroma and flavor. This style originated in 1842, with *pilsener* originally indicating an appellation in the Czech Republic. Classic examples of this style used to be conditioned in wooden tanks and have a less-sharp hop bitterness despite the similar IBU ranges to German-style pils. Bohemian-style pilseners can be darker in color and bigger in final gravity that their German counterparts as well. The water content also comes into play, creating distinct differences between the two styles. Bohemians come from very low ion water known to be "soft." German pils beers have water with higher levels of sulfate, which concentrates the bitterness of the Spalt hops.

Quantitative Style Statistics
- OG: 1.044–1.056
- FG: 1.014–1.020
- Apparent Attenuation: 64–68 percent
- ABV: 4.1–5.1 percent
- IBU: 30–45
- Color/SRM: 3–7 (straw to light amber)

US Commercial Examples: Ninkasi Bohemian Pilsner, Dock Street Bohemian Pilsner, Lagunitas Pils, Oskar Blues Mama's Little Yella Pils

Country of Origin: Czech Republic

BOHEMIAN-STYLE PILSENER

Beer Sensory Notes
- Intensity: Medium-low to medium
- Malt: Pilsener, Carapils
- Hops: Czech Saaz
- Yeast: Lager

THE STYLE AND FOOD

This is a beer style with low alcohol intensity, so be careful to not overpower it with food that is too rich or too umami-centric. However, the bitterness level does give it a big enough boost that it can play in the sandbox with medium-intensity food. It's a great beer to pair with Japanese, Chinese, or Thai foods—even Indian foods on the milder side work well. You will notice how the crisp, slight hoppiness of the beer will blend and lift the starches and spices in the food to allow all the flavors in both to shine through.

Try This First: Salmon Sushi with Wasabi Paste and Sliced Ginger

This sultry and silky fish brings some fat to the table, and also umami. Salmon has a unique mouthfeel as well; it's like soft ribbons of silk. Juxtapose this with the sharp impact of wasabi and ginger, which both pack some tingling heat, and you've got taste elements and textures positioned for impact. The slightly moist and starchy rice serves as a nutty-tinged buffer and also as a vehicle of slight acidity because of its vinegar. (The acidity helps mop up some of the soy sauce salinity so other flavors sing more strongly.)

If you pair the sushi with water, you are still left with wasabi sting. If you try it with a beer that is too high in bitterness or alcohol, you'll get a clash—maybe even a train wreck. However, try it with the pilsener and you've got it: enough bitterness to balance the fat and umami so you can better taste the flavor of the fresh salmon. The residual sweetness of this beer style also helps to stave off heat. And while overall this is more of a contrast pairing, the pilsener's graham cracker malt flavor helps embrace the nutty flavor of the rice as well as the wheat and soybean-based soy sauce.

AMERICAN AMBER LAGER
ABOUT THE STYLE

American amber lager is an adaptation of the drier and less hop-centric Vienna-style lager. It's a widely available, sessionable craft beer style that showcases both malt and hops. Amber lagers are medium bodied with a toasty or caramel-like malt character. Hop bitterness can range from very low to medium-high.

Quantitative Style Statistics
- OG: 1.042–1.056
- FG: 1.012–1.018
- Apparent Attenuation: 68–76 percent
- ABV: 4.8–5.4 percent
- IBU: 18–30
- Color/SRM: 6–14 (gold to light brown)

— *Steve Parkes* —

Steve Parkes has a long, award-winning history as a brewer and writer. He is currently the owner of Drop-In Brewery as well as the American Brewers Guild, and is the former brewmaster of Otter Creek and Humboldt Brewing Companies. He has been a regular speaker at the national Craft Brewers Conference and a regular judge at the Great American Beer Festival and World Beer Cup. He has been the technical editor of *Brewpub* magazine, a contributing columnist to *American Brewer* magazine and *All About Beer* magazine, and was a contributor to the *Oxford Companion to Beer*.

Why is pairing beer and food such a passion for you?

I'm interested in ways beer can become a fixture in people's lives. As brewers, we already have the crowd that goes to bars and drinks for pleasure or entertainment. Opening up the public's eyes to the possibility of finding a flavorful beer that can transform their eating experience is far more rewarding than persuading a beer drinker to try another beer.

What do you want people to know about beer's pairing potential?

To me, it's about life's luxuries . . . sure you can eat a meal and derive nutrition from it, but why not turn the evening meal into a sensory experience that you look forward to? A glass of wine with dinner is historically the choice of millions, but beer is far more versatile, and something many more people can afford to drink with regularity.

Beer has been exposed to heat during the manufacturing process, first in the malt kiln and then again in the brewhouse. This brings all the possibilities of Maillard reactions to the table inside your beer glass. Brewer's yeast is added to consume a range of sugars, and when encouraged to actively grow, it creates thousands of flavor compounds in the process. There are hundreds of different yeast strains, all of which bring unique characters to beer, some even remaining behind in the beer to provide flavor directly. There are as many varieties of hops as there are varieties of grapes, and each offers hundreds of complex flavors. Brewers themselves play an active role in creating recipes and coaxing the flavors from the ingredients. (You don't hear winemakers talking about a recipe.) Beer can be yellow or black, sweet or dry, bitter or mild, and every subtle nuance of color and flavor in between, across an enormously wide spectrum.

What top tips do you have for people who pair with beer?

Look for synergy. There are flavor elements in beers that don't exist in wine to the same degree, so try and highlight those: hop bitterness and bitter salad greens, caramel malt character and grilled meats, and so on. Don't forget the side dishes, either. Sometimes a beer flavor highlight can be mimicked in a side dish or a garnish. The cooking method makes the pairing as well; a pan-seared scallop pairs with an amber ale or lager because of the sear, not the scallop.

Also, cheese and beer share a common source ingredient, since barley is a type of grass. Like beer, cheese can be fresh or aged, and some of the same flavors are present in both.

Photo Credit: Christine McKeever

US Commercial Examples: Samuel Adams Boston Lager, Brooklyn Lager, Yuengling Lager, Abita Amber, Great Lakes Eliot Ness Amber Lager, Stevens Point Point Amber Classic
Country of Origin: United States
Beer Sensory Notes
- Intensity: Medium-low
- Malt: Pale malt, Munich, caramel
- Hops: Varies
- Yeast: Lager

THE STYLE AND FOOD

The Samuel Adams website has forty-two different pairing suggestions for Boston Lager. This helps hammer home just how versatile beer can be with food. Toasted and caramelized malt and hop characteristics make this style of beer one of the most versatile pairing partners. Think peanut butter anything, bologna sandwich, burgers, barbecue chicken or beef, spicy Mexican, chili, and cheeses like Gouda, to get started.

Try This First: Classic Nachos

We know what you're thinking: did we run out of ideas? But don't dismiss nachos just yet. They're popular for a reason. And there are as many ways to prepare nachos as there are ways to prepare pizza, pasta, baked potatoes, salad, chili, and barbecue.

Still, in this case let's go with a traditional version offered at hundreds of thousands of bars and restaurants across the world. Start with tortilla chips—try frying or even baking your own—and pile on shaved cheddar cheese, black beans, sliced black olives, and thinly sliced jalapeño peppers (fresh, of course). In the corners, for dipping, generously dollop medium-hot salsa, sour cream, and guacamole.

When you pair these nachos with the amber lager, you'll find the medium-low malt sweetness finds its way to the umami-rich beans and salsa, and the beer's carbonation calms the richness of the cheddar cheese, sour cream, and guacamole. (The malt also helps calm the jalapeño kick.) The beer's bitterness lessens the creamy richness of the sour cream and guacamole, making each bite of nacho even more appetizing. Any fresh hop flavor complements the overall dish, acting as fresh sprinkled herbs. We find most amber lagers further evolve as well, or at least you can tease out more caramel flavor than usual, possibly due to flavor echoes with the fried tortilla chips and the beer's pale and Munich malts.

GERMAN-STYLE MÄRZEN/OKTOBERFEST
ABOUT THE STYLE

A beer rich in malt with a balance of clean hop bitterness. Bread or biscuit-like malt aroma and flavor is common. Originating in Germany, this style used to be seasonally available in the spring (Märzen means "March"), with the fest-style versions tapped in October.

Quantitative Style Statistics
- OG: 1.050–1.060
- FG: 1.012–1.020

- Apparent Attenuation: 67–76 percent
- ABV: 5.1 –6.0 percent
- IBU: 18–25
- Color/SRM: 4–15 (pale to light brown)

US Commercial Examples: Victory Festbier, Spoetzl Shiner Oktoberfest, Karl Strauss Oktoberfest, Gordon Biersch FestBier, Great Lakes Oktoberfest, Sun King Brewing Oktoberfest, seasonal Oktoberfest from your favorite local brewpub

Country of Origin: Germany

Beer Sensory Notes
- Intensity: Medium-low
- Malt: Pilsener, Vienna, Munich
- Hops: German noble hops
- Yeast: Lager

THE STYLE AND FOOD

Oktoberfest is similar to American amber lager but with less hops and a more straightforward Munich malt (toasted bread crust) profile. Still, to us, part of the beauty of the style is its origins: its seasonality. It doesn't get much better than a windy fall day as you pour your local brewery's Oktoberfest from a growler and have something bubbling away on the stove. And while Oktoberfests work with all sorts of hearty dishes, for example chili and barbecue brisket, they also work with Caesar salad, macaroni and cheese, apple or pumpkin pie, and pancakes or waffles.

Try This First: Beef Stroganoff

Bend your geography and pair this German-centric beer with a Russian-born dish. OK, we're actually talking about the American version here. You know the stuff: spiral egg noodles that cradle rich sour cream, butter, and mushroom sauce, maybe even some Parmesan cheese. On top is seared rib-eye steak, packed with melanoidins (see page 205).

This is a pairing where the beer is lower in intensity than the dish, so it serves to refresh the palate more than match the Stroganoff's impact across the board. Still, you'll find flavor matches. The browned steak and mushroom flavors have a nice interplay with the Oktoberfest's caramel malt body. The rich, buttery, and creamy sauce matches the toffee notes found in the beer and is lifted by the moderate carbonation. The finish is downright satisfying.

ENGLISH-STYLE PALE ALE/EXTRA SPECIAL BITTER
ABOUT THE STYLE

This combined style of English pale ales and ESBs covers a range of three styles, ordinary bitter, special bitter, and extra special bitter, or ESB. Each is more full flavored and higher in alcohol and residual sugar than the previous. English pale ales display earthy, herbal English-variety hop character. They have medium to high hop bitterness, and hop flavor and aroma should be noticeable. The yeast strains used in these beers lend a fruitiness to their aromatics and flavor, referred to as esters. The residual malt and defining sweetness of this richly flavored, full-bodied beer is medium to medium-high. ESB is known for its balance and the interplay between malt and hop bitterness.

ENGLISH-STYLE PALE ALE/
EXTRA SPECIAL BITTER

Quantitative Style Statistics
- OG: 1.040–1.056
- FG: 1.008–1.016
- Apparent Attenuation: 71–80 percent
- ABV: 4.4–5.3 percent
- IBU: 20–40
- Color/SRM: 5–12 (gold to copper)

US Commercial Examples: Odell 5 Barrel Pale Ale, Shipyard Old Thumper, Summit Extra Pale Ale, Great Divide Denver Pale Ale, Great Lakes Devil's Pale Ale

Country of Origin: United Kingdom

Beer Sensory Notes
- Intensity: Medium-low to medium
- Malt: British pale ale, crystal
- Hops: Kent Goldings
- Yeast: Ale

THE STYLE AND FOOD

Earthy and malty with some fruity esters and hop characteristics, these beers can be paired with a range of foods. Seafood fried or grilled, chicken pot pie, shepherd's pie, curries, aged cheddars, and just good old burgers or pizza. Basically, you can't go wrong if you are in a pub and order an English pale as your pairing partner.

Try This First: Fish and Chips

Fish, chips, and ESB are an oldie but a goodie, and there's a reason why. The core elements, fried fish and chips, are a match made in heaven with ESB. Biscuit and caramel pale malts echo the rich fried foods, but the carbonation helps keep the palate from getting bogged down. But then, think of the whole meal: there's likely tangy, pickle-flecked tartar sauce as well, and maybe even a dash of malt vinegar. The ESB continues to shine with each element. (See page 117 for more.)

AMERICAN PALE ALE
ABOUT THE STYLE

Widely considered the original American craft beer, the style started back in 1980 with Sierra Nevada Pale Ale and the citrus-forward Cascade hop. It was actually an American interpretation of a classic English style. These days, chances are you'll still find an American pale ale on tap at most of your local breweries. There's a good reason for that: it's easy to drink, and thus friendly to craft-beer newbies, yet still complex enough to please even the most seasoned craft-beer drinker. It's characterized by fruity, citrus-like American-variety hop character, producing medium to medium-high hop bitterness, flavor, and aroma. Medium body and low to medium maltiness may include low caramel malt character. The key to this beer is balance between malt and hops, letting both shine in the flavor.

AMERICAN PALE ALE

Quantitative Style Statistics

- OG: 1.044–1.050
- FG: 1.008–1.014
- Apparent Attenuation: 72–82 percent
- ABV: 4.4–5.4 percent
- IBU: 30–50
- Color/SRM: 5–15 (gold to light brown)

US Commercial Examples: Sierra Nevada Pale Ale, Lumberyard Knotty Pine Pale Ale, Deschutes Mirror Pond, Stone Pale Ale, 3 Floyds Zombie Dust

Country of Origin: United States

Beer Sensory Notes

- Intensity: Medium
- Malt: Pale malt, caramel, and/or Munich
- Hops: American hops, typically with citrus and pine aromatics and flavors
- Yeast: Ale

THE STYLE AND FOOD

Since the bitterness is kept in check by the malt (okay, mostly kept in check), much like the English style pales, the APA is a superversatile beer when it comes to food. It pairs with almost all the American pub classics: pizza, tacos, burgers, and so on. Spicy Thai and Mexican work with an APA as well: the beer cuts the heat, livens the flavor, and brings out herbs and citrus thanks to the American hops.

Try This First: Fish Tacos with Sour Cream and Pico de Gallo

Lime and cilantro–spiked sour cream, mahimahi fillets, corn tortillas, shredded cabbage, and pico de gallo: fish tacos have a lot of tasty and diverse ingredients. Yet fish tacos, as a whole, come across as medium in intensity. There is some richness from the flavorful sour cream and of course some amount of spice, depending on how the fish is prepared and what the pico is like. The bitterness of an APA cuts through that fat, and the sweetness cools any heat at the same time.

Flavor bridges include pale malt flavors that sync with the browned corn tortilla as well as the grilled fish fillets. Any kiss of char flavor on both tortilla and fillet will also work with the pale ale's malt. The citrus and pine notes from the hops will echo the freshly chopped cilantro as well as both the sour cream and any fresh lime juice. The fat of the fish will be wiped clean by the carbonation and medium bitterness of the beer.

AMERICAN BROWN ALE
ABOUT THE STYLE

Roasted malt, caramel, and chocolate can all be found in brown ales, but these characteristics should be of medium intensity compared to darker beer styles. On the hop side, browns tend to have low to medium hop flavor and aroma, and medium to high hop bitterness. The history of this style dates back to US homebrewers, including Charlie Papazian (see page 43), who were inspired by English-style brown ales and porters. It sits in between those British styles, yet is more bitter than both—how American!

Quantitative Style Statistics
- OG: 1.040–1.060
- FG: 1.010–1.018
- Apparent Attenuation: 70–75 percent
- ABV: 4.2–6.3 percent
- IBU: 25–45
- Color/SRM: 15–26 (light brown to dark brown)

US Commercial Examples: Big Sky Moose Drool, Third Street Lost Trout Brown Ale, Telluride Face Down Brown Ale, Anchor Brekle's Brown

Country of Origin: United States

Beer Sensory Notes
- Intensity: Medium-low to medium
- Malt: Pale, crystal, chocolate, victory
- Hops: American, British, German noble
- Yeast: Ale

THE STYLE AND FOOD

Although you might believe you do not care for brown ales, we believe that once you pair the style with food, you just might change your mind. Roasted, nutty, toffee, and chocolate flavors combine with grassy citrus hops for a range of options. Try cheeses with nutty, buttery flavors, for example Comté, aged Gouda, and Manchego. Grilled and smoked meats with charred elements will harmonize with the roasted malts. Earthy, sweet, and nutty vegetables such as beets, acorn squash, mushrooms, and carrots, as well as beans, particularly black beans, are excellent pairing partners. End the meal with sweet and nutty desserts such as a maple walnut cake or chocolate- or nut-flecked cookie.

Try This First: French Onion Soup Topped with Gruyère

This soup has so much more going on than meets the eye: browned Maillard flavors (see page 204) from the beef stock and bread, and umami from the nutty and mushroomy Gruyère cheese floating atop. Of course, the char of that cheese from the broiler only brings more roasted flavors. Plus, think of the textures . . . and all that salt!

This ale's specialty roasted malts love the browned flavors of the stock and charred Gruyère. Plus, the beer's very low-level acidity meets the salt in the dish head on. The alcohol of the brown ale helps counter the intensity of the soup without being overemphasized. And, because of their bitterness, American browns can even contrast the fat of the cheese and cut the saltiness of the soup.

BELGIAN-STYLE DUBBEL
ABOUT THE STYLE

Belgian-style dubbels range from brown to very dark in color. They have a malty sweetness and can have chocolate, caramel, toffee, raisin, and plum flavors. Hop bitterness is medium-low to medium. Yeast-generated fruity esters (especially banana) can be apparent. Often

BELGIAN-STYLE DUBBEL

bottle-conditioned, a slight yeast haze and flavor may be noticeable as well. As you might expect, a dubbel is the younger sibling to the Belgian-style quadrupel.

Quantitative Style Statistics
- OG: 1.060–1.075
- FG: 1.012–1.017
- Apparent Attenuation: 79–80 percent
- ABV: 6.3–7.6 percent
- IBU: 20–30
- Color/SRM: 16–36 (brown to very dark)

US Commercial Examples: Anderson Valley Brother David's Double, New Belgium Abbey, The Lost Abbey Lost & Found Abbey Ale, Allagash Dubbel, Boulevard Nommo Dubbel, Weyerbacher Althea

Country of Origin: Belgium

Beer Sensory Notes
- Intensity: Medium
- Malt: Pilsener, CaraMunich, Special B
- Hops: Tettnang
- Yeast: Ale

THE STYLE AND FOOD

This beer has a lot to work with: dark, sweet malts and yeasty characteristics of spicy clove and banana with a subtle dark-fruit element and moderate carbonation and alcohol. It's the perfect match for caramelized nuts such as pecans, salted caramel chocolates, sweet, nutty cheeses including Manchego or Gruyère, rich tomato-based sauces or stews, or even gamey meat.

Try This First: Slow-Cooked Barbecue Beef

Beyond beef brisket, you've got so much goodness in this dish. Although barbecue sauce varies wildly by region, you'll often have cayenne, chili powder, and cumin plus brown sugar, garlic, onions, Worcestershire sauce, and often some kind of vinegar for a behind-the-scenes acid balance. The *slow* part of this meal is the cooking time in a smoker or even a crock pot: at least ten or twelve hours.

The flavor echoes in this pairing are numerous, and the alcohol and residual sugar are substantial enough to balance the richness from the meat. With any reasonable amount of heat, your brisket is not going to clash with the beer, but make it too spicy and all bets are off. The higher the alcohol in a dish, the more your tongue's pores open up, and then the palate is more perceptible to heat. The effect is that the spice is overemphasized.

As a flavor hook between beer and food, the dubbel's malt notes of dark raisin, plum, and dried cherry blend into the sauce, lending further flavor complexity to the dish. The Belgian ale yeast esters, including clove and white pepper, provide a fresh herbed boost as each sip washes down the savory beef.

ROBUST PORTER
ABOUT THE STYLE

The robust porter often features more bitter and roasted malt flavor than a brown porter, but not quite as much as a stout. Robust porters have an aroma reminiscent of cocoa, but no roast barley flavor. Their caramel, malty sweetness is in harmony with the sharp bitterness of black malt. Hop bitterness is there as well. With US craft brewers doing so much experimentation in beer styles and ingredients, the lines between certain stouts and porters are often blurred. Yet it's safe to expect a different character from robust porters than from Russian imperial stouts.

Quantitative Style Statistics
- OG: 1.045–1.060
- FG: 1.008–1.016
- Apparent Attenuation: 73–82 percent
- ABV: 5.1–6.6 percent
- IBU: 25–40
- Color/SRM: 30+ (very dark to black)

US Commercial Examples: Deschutes Black Butte Porter, Iron Hill Pig Iron Porter, Rock Bottom Moonlight Porter, Southern Tier Porter, Smuttynose Robust Porter

Country of Origin: United Kingdom

Beer Sensory Notes
- Intensity: Medium
- Malt: Munich, crystal, chocolate, black patent
- Hops: Kent Goldings, Fuggle
- Yeast: Ale

THE STYLE AND FOOD

Much like an unsweetened Baker's chocolate, with its rich bitter cocoa qualities balanced with caramel malty sweetness, the robust porter begs for a dessert pairing. So start with dessert and grab a chocolate chip cookie, some chocolate mousse, or a few salted butterscotch chocolates. For the main course, mole sauce is just begging for this beer, and so are grilled meats and veggies; root vegetables and mushrooms work especially well. If you're trying to find the right cheese, look for one with earthy sweetness, for example a Brie or Camembert.

Try This First: Meatballs in Traditional Red Sauce

Fried ground beef and Italian seasonings are the base flavors in this dish. And many recipes for meatballs have Parmesan and Worcestershire sauce as well, both of which are umami bombs. The robust porter stands up to these bold flavors as a solid intensity match. See if you find the same pleasing results from the roasted specialty malts in the porter contrasting against the acidic and umami-rich tomato sauce.

Of course, the low-roasted and dark-chocolate malt flavors in the beer play off the fried meat and any sear or char it has. The medium-aggressive hop bitterness works well to diminish the fat of the meat and meets the umami head on again. The porter almost acts like an additional, secondary sauce, blanketing the meatball and playing it up against the tomato sauce.

AMERICAN STOUT
ABOUT THE STYLE

This is a coffee- and chocolate-forward ale, but with a noticeable hop aroma and flavor, often from a citrus-forward variety. American stouts are bold, with a distinctive dry-roasted bitterness in the finish. Fruity esters should be low, but head retention is high. Oatmeal is a common ingredient in American stouts, lending additional body and head retention. Dark-roasted barley is the ingredient that truly differentiates these beers from porters.

Quantitative Style Statistics
- OG: 1.050–1.075
- FG: 1.010–1.022
- Apparent Attenuation: 71–80 percent
- ABV: 5.7–8.9 percent
- IBU: 35–60
- Color/SRM: 40+ (black)

US Commercial Examples: Rogue Ales Shakespeare Oatmeal Stout, Bison Organic Chocolate Stout, Mad River Steelhead Extra Stout, Big Wood Morning Wood, Left Coast Black Magic Stout

Country of Origin: United States

Beer Sensory Notes
- Intensity: Medium to medium-high
- Malt: Pale, black roasted barley, chocolate, crystal
- Hops: Horizon, Centennial
- Yeast: Ale

THE STYLE AND FOOD

Matching the intensity of the big, bold beer is the pairing goal here, but also look for coffee, chocolate, roast, oatmeal, and nutty sweet harmonies in foods. Start with an assertive cheese course featuring sharp aged cheddars or earthy, nutty Swiss cheese. Go for smoked and grilled fish or meats, or even full-on barbecue. For the vegetarians, how about a vegetable pot pie with mushrooms, spinach, and root vegetables such as potatoes and carrots? Dessert calls for chocolate and espresso, or perhaps an oatmeal coffee cake.

Try This First: Grilled Portobello "Steak"

This beer's bitterness, alcohol, roast, and body play oh so well with a grilled portobello's texture, high umami character, and also the mushroom's char. Since umami intensifies with acidity, many chefs prepare portobello "steaks" with balsamic vinegar, which helps boost the savory richness of the mushroom. (You also cannot go wrong by coating these earthy gems in soy sauce as you grill.)

A classic example of American stout will have notes of espresso, dark chocolate, and roast along with flavor from American hops. All of these flavors work so well with the mushroom's complex but earthy character. Lastly, the mouthfeel and body of these beers tend to be heavier on the tongue, therefore American stout also stands up to the meaty texture of the mushroom—in this case there are even texture harmonies to note.

AMERICAN STOUT

AMERICAN INDIA PALE ALE

AMERICAN INDIA PALE ALE (IPA)

ABOUT THE STYLE

Characterized by floral, fruity, citrus-like, piney, or resinous American hops, this style is all about hop flavor, aroma, and bitterness. This has been the most-entered category at the Great American Beer Festival for more than a decade, and it's the top-selling craft beer style in supermarkets and liquor stores across the United States. So it's probably a good one to figure out on the pairing front, right? And IPA is *the* style not to take for granted. Sure, it's a bitter-forward style, some would say aggressive. Yet with variants including imperial IPA, English IPA, black IPA, brown IPA, red IPA, white IPA, Belgian IPA, rye IPA, and session IPA, there is so much diversity. Even among classic IPAs, you can go from big tropical fruit to malty and herbal. Whoa!

Quantitative Style Statistics
- OG: 1.060–1.075
- FG: 1.012–1.018
- Apparent Attenuation: 76–80 percent
- ABV: 6.3–7.6 percent
- IBU: 50–70
- Color/SRM: 6–14 (gold to light brown)

US Commercial Examples: Firestone Walker Union Jack, New Belgium Ranger IPA, Ballast Point Sculpin IPA, Bear Republic Racer 5 IPA, Bell's Two Hearted Ale

Country of Origin: United States

Beer Sensory Notes
- Intensity: Medium-high
- Malt: American two-row
- Hops: Centennial, Simcoe, Amarillo
- Yeast: Ale

THE STYLE AND FOOD

Even if you love IPAs, be careful when pairing them with food. You can have a clash due to the bitter nature of these beers. In addition, IPAs can degrade fast (in a matter of weeks) and should absolutely be stored cold and enjoyed fresh. Salty and fried foods are a great place to start. Likewise, grilled meats are a sure bet. Top a dish with mango salsa and look for a sweet and spicy complement and contrast with the sweet caramel malt and bitter tropical hops to balance perfectly. Creamy risotto with asparagus and artichoke hearts harmonizes beautifully with grassy and citrus hops, and the bitter and alcohol will cut through the creaminess of the sauce. Or finish off your meal with an IPA and a lemon bar for citrus refreshment.

Try This First: Fettuccine Alfredo or Carrot Cake

Butter, cream, and Parmesan cheese—yes, this is a coronary waiting to happen. But as a treat, it doesn't get much better for cheese and pasta lovers. Add cracked pepper and fresh diced parsley sprinkled on top. Mmm, mmm, mmm, umami fat goodness. It's all a girl (or guy) could ever want . . . once in a while, that is.

American IPA is the perfect companion here. It has enough bitterness to balance the fat of this dish, and the residual sweetness of the malt lessens the sweetness of the cream sauce (sweet calms sweet). Additionally, the fresh hop flavors act like herbs on top of the dish, increasing complexity. American hops are not only known for citrus notes but also for what we call forest herbs: sage, juniper, and spruce.

Moving on, yes, we said carrot cake and IPA! This classic pairing is one that certainly makes the rounds in the beer world, so why not give it a whirl at home? We suspect it works because the two generally have an equal match of intensities. Additionally, the hop bitterness is your friend, cutting the richness of the cream-cheese frosting, and the tasty cake notes echo malt notes in the IPA. Plus the carrot cake itself loves to play against the citrus and herbal hop notes of most IPAs. Try it and see for yourself!

IMPERIAL/DOUBLE INDIA PALE ALE (DIPA)
ABOUT THE STYLE

Wait, didn't we just talk about IPAs? Yes, we did. But the imperial IPA is double special. Just as the Russian imperial stout is a unique beer compared to the American stout, so too does the DIPA deserve its own consideration. As you'd expect, this beer is bigger and bolder than the regular IPA. It has high hop bitterness, flavor, and aroma. The hop character should be dominant, though many examples of the style deliver a balanced malt character. The alcohol content is higher as well, and the body is often fuller than the IPA, too.

Quantitative Style Statistics
- OG: 1.075–1.100
- FG: 1.012–1.020
- Apparent Attenuation: 80–84 percent
- ABV: 7.6–10.6 percent
- IBU: 65–100
- Color/SRM: 5–16 (gold to chestnut or reddish brown)

US Commercial Examples: Russian River Pliny the Elder, Fat Head's Hop JuJu, Surly Furious, Dogfish Head 120 Minute IPA, Port Hop-15

Country of Origin: United States

Beer Sensory Notes
- Intensity: High
- Malt: American two-row, crystal, malted wheat
- Hops: Varies
- Yeast: Ale

THE STYLE AND FOOD

This beer comes with a large serving of hops and alcohol, but lucky for us there is a balancing kiss of sweetness from the malt. We love to pair this style with big, bold blue cheeses that can handle and tame all that bitter with intensity and a bit of salt. Add a side of honeycomb and dried apricots to harmonize with the sweetness of the malt. Salt and fat from bacon or cured ham will cut through the hop bitterness and alcohol as well. Take the ham a step further and serve it with some pineapple to complement the tropical hops and the sweetness of the malt. Or, better yet, have you ever tried pineapple upside down cake? Well now is the time—we think you will see it is a great intensity match for most DIPAs!

Try This First: All-Beef Chili

We love this pairing, as it throws tradition to the wind. After all, red wine and American lager should not be the only go-to's for chili! Mind you, there's a very broad variety of chilies: red chili, chili verde, white chili, vegetarian chili, and more. In the case of imperial IPA, start with a traditional chili recipe, and then branch out from there.

Traditional red chili is defined by the International Chili Society as a chili containing any kind of meat or combination of meats cooked with red chili peppers, various spices, and other ingredients with the exception of beans and pasta, which are strictly forbidden. Garnish is forbidden as well. Even the most basic of chilies are packed with flavor; that's what happens when you combine cayenne, chili powder, cumin, diced tomatoes, garlic, onions, salt, and ground beef. And no matter the recipe, you should expect some heat to come into play.

Imperial IPAs have a range of alcohols and intensities. If you find one version of DIPA is too much as an intensity match, then take a step down, pairing that same bowl of chili with an IPA or American pale ale, and see what changes. No matter your selection, you can rest assured it has less alcohol compared to the standard recommended wines, such as Malbec, Zinfandel, and Cabernet.

One of the first things you'll notice is the hop flavor and aroma blanketing the chili. American hops almost seem to add herb notes to the chili, sneakily acting as your forbidden garnish! Dig deeper and you'll find flavor harmony from the pale malt and browned meat, but still enough residual sugar to soothe the heat. Remember that sweet calms heat!

Note: If your chili is *hurt-so-good* spicy, if your nose runs and your mouth waters when you eat it, then look out. The hurt-so-good sensation can turn into *hurt so bad* when paired with beers that are high in bitterness and too much alcohol. Bitter forward beers often have enough residual sugar to counterbalance capsaicin heat, but when a clash of elements (capsaicin heat and bitter) is sparked, there is no turning back. Try a sliver of freshly cut jalapeño pepper and an imperial IPA, and you'll see.

BELGIAN-STYLE TRIPEL
ABOUT THE STYLE

Tripels are often on the higher end of the ABV spectrum, yet are approachable to many different palates. Complex, sometimes mild yet spicy flavor characterizes this style, along with yeast-driven complexity. The beers are commonly bottle-conditioned and finish dry. Tripels are similar to Belgian-style golden strong ales but are generally darker and have a more noticeable level of malt sweetness.

Quantitative Style Statistics
- OG: 1.070–1.092
- FG: 1.008–1.018
- Apparent Attenuation: 80–89 percent
- ABV: 7.1–10.1 percent
- IBU: 20–45
- Color/SRM: 4–9 (pale to medium amber)

US Commercial Examples: Flying Fish Exit 4, New Belgium Trippel, Green Flash Trippel, Victory Golden Monkey, Anderson Valley Brother David's Triple Abbey-Style Ale

BELGIAN-STYLE TRIPEL

Country of Origin: Belgium
Beer Sensory Notes
- Intensity: Medium
- Malt: Belgian pilsener
- Hops: Tetnang, Czech Saaz
- Yeast: Ale

THE STYLE AND FOOD

This beer has so much going on: toasted biscuit-like malts and sweetness from Belgian candi sugar; fruity, earthy, and herbal spicy notes from the yeast; subtle but apparent bitterness from hops; big sparkling carbonation and alcohol warming; and a clean, crisp finish with a hint of herbal earthiness. Basil, whether on pizza, as pesto, mixed into a dish of chicken or shellfish or salad, will be emphasized as amazing herbal sweetness.

Normally, bitter veggies such as asparagus, Brussels sprouts, or kale will be balanced by the fruity and earthy notes. Any kind of meat will partner well, whether fish, shellfish, poultry, beef, or pork. Thai, Indian, and Chinese dishes have complementing spicy qualities with a tripel. Desserts with citrus elements of lemon, orange, or lime and tropical fruits such as pineapple, banana, or passion fruit are great matches as well.

Try This First: Thanksgiving Dinner

That's right, pair this beer with a whole meal. A well-made tripel can handle all the aspects of the big dinner, from the most delicate selections to the big, bold side dishes. The high carbonation has a way of making the whole meal seem lighter and brighter. Combine that with tripel's higher alcohol content, and you have a beer that will cut, complement, and contrast without overwhelming or being overwhelmed, no matter what food has been placed on the holiday table.

Malt flavors of sweet graham crackers and toasted bread pair with the turkey's mild white meat, and the spicy yeast elements tie in the flavors of dressing, glorious gravy, and mashed potatoes. In addition to the spicy phenols contributed from tripel's yeast strain, there are also earthy, herbal elements and fruity esters such as pear and apple, which help lighten and spice up cranberry relish, marinades or dressing, spicy sweet potatoes or butternut squash, glazed carrots, and many of your other favorite side dishes. And whatever desserts are served (because you know there are always more than one), they are a great potential intensity match. Thanks to the high carbonation, the beer will also scrub the palate between bites.

BELGIAN-STYLE SAISON
ABOUT THE STYLE

Commonly called farmhouse ales and originating as summertime beers in Belgium, saisons are not just warm-weather treats. US craft brewers brew them year-round and have taken to adding a variety of additional ingredients. Often bottle-conditioned, with some yeast character and high carbonation, Belgian-style saison may have *Brettanomyces* or lactic character and fruity, horsey, goaty, and/or leather-like aromas and flavors. Specialty ingredients, including spices, may contribute a unique signature character that varies greatly by brewery.

Quantitative Style Statistics
- OG: 1.055–1.080
- FG: 1.004–1.016
- Apparent Attenuation: 80–93 percent
- ABV: 4.4–8.4 percent
- IBU: 20–40
- Color/SRM: 4–14 (pale to light brown)

US Commercial Examples: Funkwerks Saison, The Lost Abbey Red Barn Ale, Ommegang Hennepin, Allagash Saison, Brooklyn Sorachi Ace

Country of Origin: Belgium

Beer Sensory Notes
- Intensity: Medium-high
- Malt: Pilsener, Munich, malted wheat
- Hops: Noble, Styrian or East Kent Goldings
- Yeast: Ale

THE STYLE AND FOOD

Saisons go with so many foods, you really should try them with much more than we recommend here. Known for their high carbonation levels, spiciness, and fruitiness—often with a touch of tartness and some earthy and musty qualities—they are wrapped up with a hint of malt and a drying finish that give the entire beer balance. Take this refreshing beer and combine it with light or heavy dishes, then sit back and watch this style work its pairing magic! Spicy dishes harmonize with the lively carbonation and fruity, spicy, and earthy qualities of the beer. Funky, pungent cheeses are balanced with the funky pepper characteristics. Fatty and sweet breakfast foods shine when combined with the high carbonation and toasted breadiness as well.

Try This First: Goat Cheese with Hot Pepper Jelly or Vegetable Pad Thai

Buy a goat cheese that's simple, clean, and acidic, but with that touch of goat milk funk. Or go ahead and get one with more "goat" if you'd like! The hot pepper jelly should bring sweetness and a bite of spice. The two will complement each other in every way. Creamy texture, tart acid, and a hint of salt from the cheese will balance to perfection with the sweetness and spiciness from the jelly. What could make it any better?

Beer, of course! Specifically saison. The carbonation, bitterness, tartness, and moderate alcohol level of the saison complements the creamy, clean acidity of the goat cheese and balances the sweet and spice in the jelly. You might even be fooled into thinking you are eating a Thai dish.

Hey, did we say Thai food? We are going with vegetable pad Thai and tofu that's on the spicy side for our next pairing. The combination of pepper, ginger, and/or cilantro; umami and salt from soy sauce; creamy sweetness from sugar and coconut milk; earthiness from vegetables; and some sour from lime makes this a complex dish. When saison is thrown into the sensory picture, there is a complement of malt and yeast, fruity sweetness to go with the sugar and coconut, and all that is balanced by the umami and salt from the dish. Vegetable earthiness and musty, earthy yeast elements work together as well. And the tart and spice from the beer balances with lime acidity and pepper spice for a marriage of harmony.

BELGIAN-STYLE SAISON

AMERICAN BARLEY WINE
ABOUT THE STYLE

These ales range from amber to deep red or copper-garnet in color. A caramel and toffee aroma and flavor are often part of the malt character, along with high residual malty sweetness. This is often a boozy but deliciously complex beer, and the fruity-ester character is often high as well. As with many American versions of a style, this barley wine is typically more hop-forward and bitter than its British counterpart. Low levels of age-induced oxidation can harmonize with other flavors and enhance the overall experience because the beer is cellared for longer periods of time. In fact, some breweries sell them as vintage releases.

Quantitative Style Statistics
- OG: 1.090–1.120
- FG: 1.024–1.028
- Apparent Attenuation: 73–76 percent
- ABV: 8.5–12.2 percent
- IBU: 60–100
- Color/SRM: 11–18 (copper to dark brown)

US Commercial Examples: Anchor Old Foghorn Ale, Tröegs Flying Mouflan, AleSmith Old Numbskull, Uinta Cockeyed Cooper, Hair of the Dog Doggie Claws, Sierra Nevada Bigfoot

Country of Origin: United States

Beer Sensory Notes
- Intensity: High
- Malt: Pale, crystal, pale chocolate, Special B
- Hops: Magnum, Chinook, Centennial, Amarillo
- Yeast: Ale

THE STYLE AND FOOD

A strong, complex beer featuring dark fruits and alcohol means you are going to have to look for foods that can match this intense beer style. It sounds challenging, but really this big beast is a beauty. Think plum, fig, and date, and perhaps fruitcake. Yes, you can actually eat fruitcake, and the good ones are rich with molasses and brown sugar, along with a mix of fruits that will complement the same elements in the barley wine. Bold blue cheeses will bring a matching intensity, and in fact a cheese plate complete with walnuts and charcuterie would be a fine idea. Or how about blue cheese atop a steak or burger? With the alcohol as high as it is in this beer, you just know that it's going to cut through big, rich foods and create balance.

Try This First: Aged Cheddar

A high-quality cheddar is silky and smooth when young, and as it ages so does the sharpness of the flavor. It's crumbly, nutty, and so familiar to so many people that it ends up coming across as a very comforting cheese. Most of the popular cheddars are medium-low to medium on the cheese intensity scale. However, when pairing a big beer like this, we are going to recommend an extra sharp aged cheddar (older than one year) that is dense, intense, and rich.

The bitterness of an American barley wine is your friend when pairing with aged cheddar. It will contrast with the sweetness of the cheese and the milk fat rich character as well. High alcohol is going to lift the milk fat up off the palate, and the result will be even more flavorful bites. American hop–centric flavors of citrus and pine and biscuit malt notes counterbalance cheddar's sharp butter and nuttiness for a classic pairing.

AMERICAN BRETT BEER
ABOUT THE STYLE

Brett beer and sour beer are not synonymous. Brett beer may contain acidic components from wild yeast or bacteria, but the presence of acidity in all *Brettanomyces* beers should not be assumed or even dominant. These unique beers vary in color and can take on the hues of added fruits or other ingredients. The evolution of natural acidity can develop balanced complexity. Horsey, goaty, leathery, phenolic, and some fruity acidic character derived from *Brettanomyces* organisms may be evident, but it is generally in balance with other components of the beer.

Quantitative Style Statistics
American Brett beers come in a variety of styles, the range of style statistics accompany what style the beer was brewed in.
- OG: Varies
- FG: Varies
- Apparent Attenuation: Varies
- ABV: Varies
- IBU: Varies
- Color/SRM: Varies

US Commercial Examples: Russian River Sanctification, The Lost Abbey Framboise de Amorosa and Cuvee de Tomme, Logsdon Peche 'n Brett, The Bruery Tart of Darkness, Boulevard Love Child series

Country of Origin: United States

Beer Sensory Notes
- Intensity: Varies
- Malt: Varies
- Hops: Varies
- Yeast: *Brettanomyces*, ale/lager possible

THE STYLE AND FOOD

Light or dark, with fruit or without, but always with the balance of funkiness, these beers are truly intriguing and interesting. What to pair with them will really depend on the malts and additional ingredients used to brew and mature the beer you choose.

Still, use the wild side to pair up funk with funk, and look first to bloomy, pungent, stinky, washed rind cheeses. We're talking about Gorgonzola, Roquefort, Époisses, Taleggio, Camembert, even an aged goat Gouda. Be sure to add fruit to match any fruit addition in the beer, and don't forget sourdough bread for a bridge through the breadiness of the beer (which may also be tart). If your beer has an earthy funk, look to mushrooms, root vegetables, and any earthy foods to

complement the barnyard elements. If your Brett beer has some peppery qualities, then match those with spiced meat filled with umami, for example pork carnitas. Desserts are generally a sure thing when they have acidic lemon or tart raspberries, peaches, or cherries.

Try This First: Chinese Hot and Sour Soup
This is a flavor balancing act for food if ever there was one. Salt, umami, oil, spice, sweet, and sour: how can all of this be in a soup? The texture of wood ear mushrooms is as unique as the fungus's appearance. They give the soup that earthy bitterness that rounds out the entire experience.

Now for the beer. Again, we have to say this is an incredibly broad style. Brett beer can be light or dark, fruited or not fruited, bitter or not. Still, generally the focus is on the funk; you know, the barnyard, earthy, fruit, and tart character. The tartness or just plain sourness of the beer offsets the sour from the soup, and you are left with the subtle impression of tart, but a lot of earthiness and umami. A salt-like aftertaste is followed by sweet. There are a lot of sensory notes to take in here . . . you might have to have another bowl of soup with another beer.

BELGIAN-STYLE FLANDERS
ABOUT THE STYLE

If ever there was a beer style to convert wine drinkers, it's the Belgian-style Flanders. Overall, these beers are characterized by slight to strong lactic sourness. This style is a marvel in flavor complexity, combining malt, yeast, microorganisms, acidity, and low astringency from barrel aging. Cherry-like flavors are often found, and sometimes a cocoa-like character as well. Oak or other wood-like flavors may be present, even if the beer was not aged in barrels. Even *Brettanomyces*-produced flavors may be there at a low level—that funk we just talked about above.

Quantitative Style Statistics
- OG: 1.044–1.056
- FG: 1.008–1.016
- Apparent Attenuation: 71–82 percent
- ABV: 4.8–6.6 percent
- IBU: 8–25
- Color/SRM: 12–25 (copper to very dark)

US Commercial Examples: New Glarus Oud Bruin, The Bruery Oude Tart, New Belgium La Folie

Country of Origin: Belgium

Beer Sensory Notes
- Intensity: Medium-high
- Malt: Vienna, Munich, Special B, aromatic
- Hops: Kent Goldings
- Yeast: Ale, *Brettanomyces*

BELGIAN-STYLE FLANDERS

THE STYLE AND FOOD

This beer style is a marvel of versatility and complexity, with multiple chances for flavor echoes. It's a great opportunity to leverage higher-than-usual acidity in a beer. We use it for absolutely any part of a beer dinner: as a welcome beer at dinners for a big wow factor while palates are fresh, slipped into the first course as a counter to rich soups or dressed salads with funky cheese, allowed to shine as an entrée beer pairing next to roasted duck and gamey meats, and with dessert (try it with chocolates that have fruit notes and nuts).

Try This First: Lentil Soup

Good lentil soup recipes have glorious flavors to go with brown malts. It's also a more complex soup than you might think. There's the stock (scratch-made chicken or veggie), root vegetables such as carrots and onions, and spices that include coriander and cumin. Both the lentils (red, brown, or green) and red tomato bring umami and tannins to the party as well.

Some lentil soup recipes call for a splash of vinegar. In the same vein, a squeeze of lemon to the soup helps lessen salt and tannins. Or better yet, pair the soup with a beer that also has browned malt flavors, acidity, and sometimes tannins—our Flanders. This is a pairing based on contrast of taste elements; the tart acidity of the beer style matches up against the umami and salt of the soup. Yet we also have flavor harmonies of Munich malt with the soup stock, lentils, and vegetables. In this home-run pairing, pay specific attention to how the beer's acidic aspects truly lessen the high salt content and at the same time finds flavor harmonies and echoes that make you want to live off lentils!

GERMAN-STYLE DOPPELBOCK
ABOUT THE STYLE

Originally made by monks in Munich, this style is very food-friendly and rich in melanoidins (see page 205) reminiscent of toasted bread. This copper to dark brown beer is a showcase for malty sweetness—but that's not to say it's cloying. The malt character should be fresh and lightly toasted, showcasing Munich malt more so than caramel or toffee. Doppelbocks are full-bodied, and their alcoholic strength is on the higher end. Since *doppel* means "double," it's clear this style is a bigger and stronger version of the lower-gravity German-style bock beers.

Quantitative Style Statistics
- OG: 1.074–1.080
- FG: 1.014–1.020
- Apparent Attenuation: 75–81 percent
- ABV: 6.6–7.9 percent
- IBU: 17–27
- Color/SRM: 12–30 (copper to very dark)

US Commercial Examples: Samuel Adams Double Bock, Great Dane Uber Bock, Bell's Consecrator Doppelbock, Tommyknocker Butt Head Bock, Starr Hill Snow Blind

Country of Origin: Germany

Beer Sensory Notes
- Intensity: Medium-high
- Malt: Pilsener, Munich, Vienna, CaraMunich
- Hops: German noble
- Yeast: Lager

THE STYLE AND FOOD
Most doppelbocks deliver advanced melanoidins (see page 205), smooth alcohol character (from the lagering), and various other browned malt flavors. Sip slowly and you might find hints of grapes and prunes as well. Of course, that means this is a beer for rich, earthy, and roasted foods such as mushrooms, sausages, pork, duck, and ham. But don't forget about the sweet side, which helps the beer work with a wide variety of foods: chocolate, cheeses, including smoked Gouda or smoked Swiss, root vegetables, including butternut squash, or even hearty legumes such as lentils.

Try This First: Devils on Horseback (Goat Cheese–Stuffed Dates Wrapped in Bacon)
Cheese stuffed and bacon wrapped should be enough to get anyone moving toward the grocery store. As you'd expect, the intensity of these morsels is pretty high, and thus we need a big enough beer style with hopefully some flavor resonance to match. As far as flavors are concerned, we're talking both date and fig flavors, a subtle creaminess from the goat cheese, and sweet, salty bacon.

Doppelbock's browned malt and pruney flavors make a great match with both the browned bacon and the date. Intensity-wise, doppelbock packs enough of a punch both in flavor and in alcohol. The higher residual sweetness in the beer even helps counter the perceived sweetness of the dates, so you get more date flavor and find your way to the gooey goat cheese.

BARREL-AGED BEERS
ABOUT THE STYLE
A wood- or barrel-aged beer is any lager, ale, or hybrid beer, either a traditional style or a unique experimental beer, that has been aged for a period of time in a wooden barrel or in contact with wood (chips, spirals, or cubes). The brewer's intention is to impart the beer with the unique character of the wood and/or the flavor of what has previously been in the barrel, such as bourbon. A variety of types of wood are used including oak, apple, alder, hickory, and more.

Quantitative Style Statistics
- Barrel-aged beers come in a variety of styles, so the range of style statistics accompany what style the beer was brewed in.
- OG: Varies
- FG: Varies
- Apparent Attenuation: Varies
- ABV: Varies
- IBU: Varies
- Color/SRM: Varies

US Commercial Examples: Port Brewing Older Viscosity Ale, Ballast Point Victory at Sea Rum Barrel-Aged, Anderson Valley Bourbon Barrel Stout, Avery's Black Tot Imperial Oatmeal Stout, Deschutes The Abyss, Brooklyn Black Ops

Country of Origin: Undetermined

Beer Sensory Notes

- Intensity: Varies
- Malt: Varies
- Hops: Varies
- Yeast: Varies

Barrel-aged beers often take on the character of the wood as well as the character of the spirit that was previously aged in the barrel.

THE STYLE AND FOOD

This grouping of beers is so varied that each brewery's example is unique. You could say that makes pairing foods challenging, but we prefer to see the infinite variations as new opportunities. There are also helpful generalities. It's safe to say a barrel-aged beer tends to have a higher level of alcohol than its non-barrel-aged counterpart. That means in addition to tannins from the wood, you can expect increased intensity in the mix. Those tannins from the oak act in a similar way to bitterness from hops, so foods with some substance and fat often do well with these beers. Grilled red meats, wild game, and aged nutty cheeses such as a cave-aged Gruyère are all a good match for strong tannins and alcohol barrel intensities. Pair with foods that are too delicate, and you'll barrel them over (pun intended) since these beers are super complex. But pair with foods that are too intense, and you'll negate the beer's personality. Keep nutty, chocolate, vanilla, and coconut in mind as your pairing partners for both beer and food, and you can't go wrong with a bourbon or whiskey barrel–aged beer. German chocolate cake, anyone?

Try This First: Dark Chocolate–Covered Fruit and Nuts or Black Bean Mole Chili

Remember, there are no rules, so if you want to start dinner with chocolate, then start it with chocolate! With such a huge variation when it comes to barrel-aged beers, why not throw in something that should stand up to whatever the barrel and the beer might be? The chocolate is sure to complement any vanilla, coconut, and chocolate elements from the barrel. Various nuts such as pecans, walnuts, almonds, and hazelnuts should make for another complement. Fruit is interesting because it can work really well by complementing the fruity characteristics of the beer, or it can be a bit of a contrast if the alcohol is on the very high side. Either way, it is an interesting and a learning experience, and hey, you started your meal with chocolate!

As for the mole, we think they're best when you can add a bit of the beer to the mix when you cook it. Smoked characteristics from the chilies in combination with a hint of bitterness from dark cocoa really can hold up to a big barrel-aged beer. Use different peppers in addition to poblanos (when dried, they're referred to as anchos), such as pasillas and guajillos. In this dish we are looking more for medium smoky heat and a ton of flavor. Mix black beans, beer, broth, cocoa, and chilies with garlic, salt, a dash of cinnamon, olive oil, and tomatoes, and you have one fine mole.

For the purpose of this pairing, we are going to use a dark beer that could have been aged in bourbon, rye, rum, brandy, or another spirit barrel. The roasted elements of the malt balance with the roasted, smoky characteristics of the chilies. Those same malts also complement the umami flavors of the black beans. Bitterness from the cocoa contrasts with the sweetness of caramel malts and vanilla from the oak. This pairing is a warm one, not just from the chilies but from the alcohol as well.

CHEESE, CHOCOLATE, AND OTHER SURE THINGS

CHEESE

You might not know it, but cheese and beer are quite similar. Sure, beer's basic ingredients are water, malted barley, hops, and yeast whereas cheese's basic ingredients are water, lactose (milk sugar), fat, protein, and minerals. But barley is in the grass family and cows eat grass, bringing the two closer together . . . and that's before you consider that both beer and cheese go through fermentation and then have to age in order to properly condition or ripen. Both are living foods that need to be stored properly. And both come in hundreds of varieties and contain a multitude of aromas, tastes, and textures.

At many points in history, the two have also overlapped on the production side. They were both farmhouse-produced products. They were both produced at monasteries. And in more recent times, in the 1970s and 1980s, cheese went through a revolution much like the one that's ongoing for craft beer. Artisans chose to break away from the mainstream and start making small batches of farmstead cheeses as a rebellion against the yellow slices of "cheese" in the supermarket.

MILK'S ROLE IN CHEESE

Just like barley is for beer, milk is very important when it comes to flavor for cheese. In this book we are going to concentrate on milk from three specific animals: cow, goat, and sheep. They can be used independently of each other or in blends of two or more milks. (Blending different milk types can give cheese complex characteristics.)

Of course, cheese is influenced not just by the animal producing the milk but how and where the animal is raised—even when it is milked. Yes, there will be a difference between milk from a cow eating clover in a field in the spring and that same cow's milk collected in the winter after it has been eating silage. Goats that are raised in pastures in Vermont produce different milk than goats raised in rocky terrain in the Pacific Northwest. In short, different species, environments, climates, and different grazing habits will ultimately produce different milks, and thus different cheeses.

Why are cheeses different colors? On the natural side, beta-carotenes in the grass that cows eat are stored in fat globules in the cows' milk. Depending on the grass source, the milk can range in color from pure white to more of a yellow color. However, goats, sheep, and water buffalo don't store beta-carotenes in their fat, so the color doesn't get passed to their milk and their cheese is always white. Not all cheese color comes from grass, of course. In processed cheeses, all sorts of dyes can be added to achieve a consistent yellow color. This started decades ago when industrial cheese makers started using dye from annatto tree seeds to create a consistent cheese color from inconsistent milk supplies. This factory-processed cheese color eventually became the most common color for cheese in the United States. Luckily, that's changing.

Cow Milk: When it comes to dairy, most people think of products made from cow milk first. It is by far the most common milk for everything from yogurt to cheese.

When it comes to cheese, cow milk has a variety of built-in flavors. It can be mild and buttery, earthy and barnyard, acidic, fruity, salty, caramel, and grassy. Hundreds of types of cow milk cheeses are produced. It's safe to assume that almost all of the most common cheeses are made from cow milk, unless the label says otherwise. Some of the most common cow milk cheeses are cheddar, Brie, Camembert, Gruyère, Stilton, Gorgonzola, Gouda, Muenster, Havarti, and Parmesan. They have a huge range of textures and flavors, from mild cheeses such as mozzarella and Monterey Jack all the way to strong, aged cheeses such as Gorgonzola and Danish blue.

There are as many different types of cheese as there are beer styles.

Cow milk is naturally unhomogenized (cream rises to the top), and the fat globules are large, so most milk has to be mixed to fuse the cream with the milk. You will see that other animal milks differ in this regard.

Goat Milk: Although goats typically eat grass, they've also been known to eat herbs, trees, shrubs, and bark—you name it, goats will eat it. While this varied diet will affect milk flavor, and hence cheese flavor, there's no denying that goat milk and cheeses have a distinctive set of tastes and aromas.

Although goat milk tends to be low in fat, it does contain a very high percentage of fatty acids such as caproic, caprylic, and capric acid. (*Capra* is Latin for "goat.") These fatty acids are what give the milk and cheese that "goaty" aroma. Additionally, goat milk does not contain the protein agglutinin, allowing fat globules to stay mixed in suspension in the milk, or naturally homogenized. The smaller fat globules and natural homogenization help set the lower fat content of the milk. About ten pounds of goat milk is required per one pound of cheese, like cow milk.

Goat milk cheese typically has a creamy and smooth texture; tangy, tart, citrus, and earthy notes; and a clay-like consistency. Some of the most common goat milk cheeses are chèvre style (*chèvre* is the French word for goat) such as Garrotxa and Humboldt Fog, but you can also find goat cheese varieties of feta, Gouda, blue, and cheddar as well.

Sheep Milk: Sheep were actually raised for milk before cows, but they produce less milk than cows overall. In an age of efficiency, this matters to the people raising animals for milk or milk products. Still, sheep milk will yield more cheese percentage-wise than cow or goat milk. On average, it takes six pounds of sheep milk to make one pound of cheese, compared to up to ten pounds of cow milk per pound of cheese. This is because of the high concentration of fat solids, or curds, in sheep milk. That means cheeses made with sheep milk have a higher fat concentration than goat or cow milk cheese, yet it is typically easier to digest sheep milk cheeses because the fat globules are small and concentrated.

Sheep, like cows, are grazers that tend to eat plants located near the ground, including grass, clover, etc. Sheep milk cheese has characteristics such as earthy, sweet, nutty, rich, and soft, as well as funky and gamey. Typical sheep milk cheeses include feta, ricotta, Manchego, Roquefort, Pecorino Toscano, and Pecorino Sardo (*pecora* is Italian for "sheep").

AGE AND CHEESE CLASSIFICATION

The importance of age is another thing that cheese and beer have in common. That fresh beer you tasted just before packaging is going to taste much different in one week, thirty days, or ninety days. Some beers, such as pilseners, are best fresh, while other beers, such as barley wines, increase in complexity as they age. For beers containing *Brettanomyces* or other bacteria cultures, this is doubly true.

Cheeses are the same way: some are meant to be aged, while others are not. Just like beer, the environmental conditions in which you store your cheese will determine if you are cellaring or aging your cheese for maximum flavor. A soft cheese, for example chèvre, is matured for a relatively short time, from two weeks to two months. Soft ripened cheeses, think Camembert or Brie, have bacteria added to the starter, so they age from the outside in. The mold creates the rind on the outside, and the bacteria then work their way inside. Environmental conditions will determine proper aging time. As the cheese ages, the rind changes color from white to yellow to brown and eventually mottled, and the interior changes from crumbly and chalky to soft and eventually to runny liquid. The middle stage is where the cheese is considered ripe and best to eat. On the opposite end, hard cheeses that rely on non-starter bacteria, natural microbes that change the composition of the cheese, ripen from the inside to the outside. The longer the cheese ages, anywhere from a couple of months to several years, the stronger and more flavorful the cheese.

Categorizing cheese in a simple and straightforward way will help you narrow down what to expect. However, the problem you'll quickly encounter is that there is great variability in cheese categories. Each country has its own system for identification, and cheese comes in hundreds of varieties with variations within each variety. The US Dairy Export Council claims that there are four hundred varieties of cheese available from US cheese makers alone, for example. (When you combine this with brewers who use different ingredients, recipes, and equipment, and are in all kinds of environments and climates but brewing beer in the same styles, it gets very hard to make generalized recommendations for pairings!) This is why when you pair cheese and beer, we recommend you always deconstruct what you are tasting, pick out the pieces and parts, and assess how they will play together. This will give you the upper hand when it comes to successfully putting together an amazing pairing. Ultimately, while you can start with guidelines and recommendations, it all comes down to tasting a particular beer and particular cheese together.

But we have to start somewhere, right? Cheese styles can come from milk type, texture, country of origin, what form it comes in, whether it's vegetarian or not, color, and more. Since cheeses will vary in moisture content and thus texture and mold growth, there will be variations not only from batch to batch but also from day to day in the same cheese. (Once oxidation sets in, be aware that the cheese will change.)

PAIRING CHEESE AND BEER

The chart on page 152 is meant to get you moving in the right direction. But if you take a look and feel overwhelmed, we have some dead simple advice: **start with what looks interesting to you**. When you're at the store, if you want the cheddar with the cayenne rub, then by all means get it! Then work backwards: cut that cayenne with something sweet and malty, say an amber ale. Or go the other way and try something strong and hoppy, maybe an imperial red or an imperial/double IPA. You have to experiment to learn.

Whether you're looking over the grid or shopping, the biggest thing to keep in mind is to **match intensity**. Sure, by this point in the book you are probably saying, "Yes, I get it," and we're sure you do. But we're going to hammer it home anyway: you are ultimately looking for balance. You can complement or contrast, but one component cannot stand head and shoulders above the other if the pairing is going to work.

Once you're sure the intensities will work, you'll need to **consider order** if you're tasting multiple cheeses and beers. Although we are firm believers in doing what you want, you can wreck your palate early in a tasting. This means you need time to reset, and time to reset means

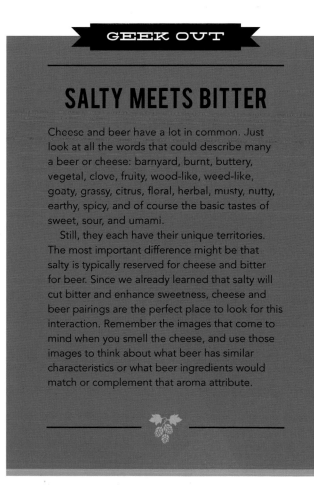

GEEK OUT

SALTY MEETS BITTER

Cheese and beer have a lot in common. Just look at all the words that could describe many a beer or cheese: barnyard, burnt, buttery, vegetal, clove, fruity, wood-like, weed-like, goaty, grassy, citrus, floral, herbal, musty, nutty, earthy, spicy, and of course the basic tastes of sweet, sour, and umami.

Still, they each have their unique territories. The most important difference might be that salty is typically reserved for cheese and bitter for beer. Since we already learned that salty will cut bitter and enhance sweetness, cheese and beer pairings are the perfect place to look for this interaction. Remember the images that come to mind when you smell the cheese, and use those images to think about what beer has similar characteristics or what beer ingredients would match or complement that aroma attribute.

STYLE	DESCRIPTION	CHEESE EXAMPLES	BEER PAIRING POSSIBILITIES
Fresh cheese	Unripened, unaged; no rind; short shelf life; high moisture; mild, lactic, or acidic; sweet, lemony, or citrus; possibly grassy and herbal	Mascarpone, queso blanco, feta, ricotta, chèvre	Fruit beer, wheat, Belgian-style wit, pilsener, blonde ale, Kölsch
Soft ripened/ bloomy rind	Fresh and aged to encourage mold growth on exterior to create rind; ripens from outside in; bloomy, creamy, hay, mushroom, pepper, earthy, and butter	Brie, Camembert, aged chèvre, Cowgirl Creamery Inverness, Cypress Grove Humboldt Fog, Mt. Townsend Seastack, Bucherondin, Sharpham	Bière de Garde, brown ale, Belgian-style white, abbey dubbel, Belgian-style strong golden, saison, sour ale, Belgian-style tripel
Semi-soft cheeses	Moisture content decreases with age; little or no rind; smooth, creamy, becomes more firm with age; mild, nutty, herbal, pungent	Monterey Jack, brick, Muenster, fontina, Havarti, Swiss, Port Salut	Hoppy pilsener, brown ale, Bière de Garde, doppelbock; abbey dubbel, amber lager, saison, pale ale
Natural rind (dry rind)	Rind forms spontaneously from whatever is in the environment; mild, sweet, floral, nutty	English Stilton, Gloucester, Lancashire, Beecher's Old Man Highlander, Tomme de Savoie, clothbound cheddars, Vermont Shepherd	Bitter, brown ale, blonde, saison, abbey dubbel, amber ale, pale ale, Belgian-style tripel, Belgian-style strong golden, Märzen
Washed rind	Washed with brine and/or alcohol; specific molds (esp. *B. linens*) encouraged to break down the interior of cheese; orange/pink rind; pungent, barnyard, meaty, garlicy; smoky	Chimay, Taleggio, Époisses, Livarot, Cowgirl Creamery Red Hawk, Stinking Bishop	Abbey dubbel, quadrupel, and tripel, Belgian-style strong golden, barley wine, Belgian-style pale ale
Semi-hard	Still has some moisture and is usually firm and/or crumbly; could be soft when young, hard as aged; Swiss-style included; sweet, spicy, nutty, buttery, etc.	Gouda, cheddar, Colby, Edam, Swiss, Gruyère, Manchego, Comté, Appenzeller	Pale, brown ale, bock, abbey dubbel, Belgian-style quadrupel, amber lager, doppelbock, ESB, Belgian-style strong golden, Märzen
Hard	Low moisture content or dry in texture; long shelf life of one year or more; can crumble or be grated; granular, grainy, crunchy, caramelized, nutty	Aged cheddar, aged Gouda, Asiago, Bellavitano, Parmesan, Pecorino, Romano, cotija	IPA, double/imperial IPA, barley wine, Bière de Garde, Belgian-style dark strong, dunkle, imperial stout
Smoked and flavored	Any cheese that has been smoked to give it a unique smoky flavor; cheese may have seeds, herbs, nuts, fruit added for flavor	Chèvre, cheddars, Swiss, Gouda, blue, mozzarella, Wensleydale	Dependent on cheese style
Blue veined— creamy and mellow or bold and strong	Innoculated with *Penicillium* and pierced to allow oxygen, which promotes mold growth inside and outside; found in all categories except fresh; can be creamy, dense, buttery, spicy, tangy, metallic, herbal, salty, gritty	Cambozola, Gorgonzola, Stilton, Roquefort, Danish blue, Maytag blue, Vaquero	Barley wine, Belgian-style tripel, Belgian-style strong, imperial/double IPA, Rauchbier (smoked), imperial stout

Information found in the chart above is a style/type generalization based mostly on texture and mold growth or rind but is a combination of information from a plethora of different resources (Gwen's own research, the American Cheese Society, www.cheese.com, www.world-of-cheese.com, www.cheese-types.com, www.cheeselibrary.com, *Cheese & Beer* by Janet Fletcher, *Tasting Beer* by Randy Mosher, and anything (book, lecture, podcast) from Garrett Oliver, who is our beer and food pairing hero).

Move over, wine—beer and cheese are natural companions!

you'll miss out on some of the cheese and beer fun. Order also plays into the overall intensity of the pairings, so moving from simple to complex, mild to strong, and so on is the way to go. Luckily, this works perfectly for cheese, since the young, fresh, moist cheeses have a shorter window of tasting time and should be tasted first for that reason as well.

When it comes to the cheeses with rinds, simply move from natural to bloomy and then to washed. Any blues should be last, with a few exceptions. (Blues vary in pungency, and that pungency increases with age. So you can work a creamy and mild Cambozola, Blue Castello, or Saga into the middle of a tasting.)

You could also go in the order of milk type, starting with the milder fresh or chèvre goat cheese; then go to a sheep milk cheese, which is nutty, earthy, and slightly funky; and finally try a cow milk cheese that is aged and hard with grassy barnyard notes—or a smoky blue. Whatever you decide, tasting each cheese prior to pairing is always your best bet for choosing the best order.

— Fred Bueltmann —

Fred Bueltmann is a maverick presence in both beer and food and is the owner of New Holland Brewing Company. His book, *Beervangelist's Guide to the Galaxy*, has many pairing gems.

What's your pairing mantra?

I believe mindfulness is the most important tool in learning to pair intuitively. Tasting and pairing is personal, tactile, and romantic, so much so that a comparison to sex sheds an interesting light on the topic. If you think about it, they have a lot in common. We indulge in the delight and pleasure of our senses, and both can please us emotionally. Most importantly, you know the difference between when something is deeply personal and when it's mechanical. It's difficult to list or describe, but you know it when you feel it, and when it's good . . . you want to do it again!

Well said, Fred. What about some general best practices or rules?

Well, in my book you'll find my patented galactic travel rules on pairing. They include:

Listen to your palate (your brain is a liar).
Honor ingredients; use good techniques.
It's not about you.
You're not alone.
Flavor first.

How would you define pairing?

Pairing, whether intentional or not, is when the beer and the food excite something in each other. They can harmonize and accentuate signature flavors, or they can contrast with each other in dynamic and pleasing counterpoint. Sometimes the beer changes your perception of the food; other times, it's the other way around. Directing the change is something of a skill, but it all starts with recognizing that you are looking for an exchange of energy or flavor between the two.

When it comes to teaching, you're well known for a particular rant on how hard it can be to communicate taste. Will you share that with us?

At the heart of it is something I believe in, which is describe flavors to communicate, not to impress.

Describing food is similar to the way a good novelist might describe a wooded path. She might describe the color of the leaves or the way the light shines through the trees . . . perhaps the smell of yesterday's rain. As a reader and a human, I am completely capable of deciding whether I like the sound of that path or not, though—the writer doesn't need to tell me how to feel about it. She just needs to get me to imagine the path as if I were there. The same goes for food and for beer.

Photo Credit: Steph Harding

A SAMPLE SET OF CHEESE AND BEER PAIRINGS

For this set of pairings, we'll start off with a chèvre that's mild, possesses a tart acidic bite, and has a creamy mouthfeel paired with a beer that's light and bright with some carbonation and possibly some fruitiness or tartness, such as a German-style hefeweizen or a Belgian-style wit. The tartness and creaminess of the cheese will play off the clove and banana of the hefeweizen or the coriander and orange in the wit. With the same cheese, you could play it safe with something like a German pilsner, German-style Kölsch, or blonde ale. Or, you can go for something that brings out the full "goat" in the cheese such as a Belgian-style saison. You'll find the cheese emphasizes the spicy fruitiness of saison, too.

Follow the fresh goat with a cheese that's a tad more bloomy, perhaps a Camembert. You can also break things up by having accompaniments for your cheese—in fact, you should do both! Accompaniments are superfun to pick out while you are choosing your cheeses. Just go to the jam/marmalade area of the store and let yourself be inspired by fruit ingredients, then go to the dried fruit and nuts area and see what speaks to you. Or, pick up honey, olives, pickles, and other flavors that spark your interest. Don't forget about breads and crackers. Sourdough breads really bring out hidden acidities in cheese as well as beers, whereas sweet breads help emphasize sweetness in both the cheese and beer.

End the three cheese pairings by going in one of two directions. The first would be something like a Manchego with a Belgian-style dubbel. The nuttiness and sweetness of the cheese perfectly complements the sweetness of the malts.

Alternately, you can wrap things up with a Cambozola and an American imperial IPA. The contrast of the creamy, sweet funkiness of the cheese with the alcohol and intense hoppy bitterness of the IPA brings a complex interaction that is mind blowing. The intensity of the flavor impact is not everyone's cup of tea, though. Some would prefer the Cambozola with an imperial stout, which will emphasize the roast, nuttiness, and earthiness in a more complementary way. Honey would be a great accompaniment with the cheese and either beer combination.

CHOCOLATE

The history of chocolate as we know it is a complex journey, but it's safe to say chocolate has been a treasured food for a long, long time. The Mayan and Aztec cultures used cacao pods for currency and trading. Residue on pottery from excavations in places such as Honduras has shown that cacao was fermented into an alcoholic drink. Through the nineteenth century, chocolate was refined and eventually made more consistent thanks to Dutch processing.

GEEK OUT

SERVING SIZES

Since we are talking about cheese and are about to get into chocolate as well, this seems like a great place to mention serving sizes. When you are doing a pairing/tasting that involves many beers and food items, remember that smaller portions are better for you and your guests' enjoyment. Quickly burning out from either food or beer is highly likely if you serve too much. For your beer, you do not need more than four ounces, and really two to three ounces is even better if you are sampling more than four beers. Cheese and chocolate are both recommended in one-ounce tasting portions.

Chocolates can vary greatly based on how they're made, other ingredients, and fillings.

(Dutching is when cocoa beans have been washed with an alkaline solution that neutralizes the beans' overall acidity and gives chocolate a milder, mellower flavor, as well as a darker color.) Perhaps it's no surprise that in recent history, chocolate has had an artisanal revolution of its own as people look for less-processed, sustainably sourced chocolates as opposed to mass-made milk chocolate bars. (If you really want to nerd out on chocolate history, we recommend *The True History of Chocolate* by Sophie and Michael Coe.)

MAKING CHOCOLATE

Chocolate begins as bean pods on the *Theobroma cacao* tree. Each tree has anywhere from twenty to sixty pods, and each pod has thirty to forty seeds. Once these pods are harvested, they are split open and placed in bins or baskets. Yeast and bacteria begin the fermentation process, which can take two to eight days. Ethanol, lactic acid, and acetic acid will be produced. The longer the fermentation time, the less astringent and bitter and the more fruity and floral the cacao will be. Beans are generally dried for five to seven days after fermentation ends and then shipped off to a chocolate manufacturer.

Beans are then cleaned, roasted, and graded before the shell is removed to extract the nib. Now we are getting to the meat of the cocoa bean: the nibs! Nibs can be used in some chocolate confections as is, but they are mostly ground into a paste, which is called cocoa or chocolate liquor (though no alcohol is present). In about equal parts, the chocolate liquor is made up of cocoa butter, which is fat, and cocoa solids. At this point in the process, you basically have what we consider unsweetened chocolate.

To get to the next step in making chocolate, the cocoa liquor is heated so it can be poured into blocks. Chocolate liquor is then blended with cocoa butter in varying quantities to make different types of chocolate. The chocolate liquor may also be pressed to remove a portion of cocoa butter (fat), leaving the cocoa solids. Cocoa butter is used to make finished chocolate or for other products, such as cosmetics and pharmaceuticals. The cocoa solids can be crushed into cocoa powder.

TRUFFLE AND BEER PAIRING

Gwen: While at Flying Dog Brewery I had the great fortune of working with an amazing chocolatier by the name of Randy Olmstead. He has made artisanal chocolates that have been served in the White House, at Washington embassies, and at several SAVOR events in Washington, DC. He uses ingredients that include spirits and beer, as well as balsamic vinegar, lavender, Old Bay Seasoning, teas of various flavors, passion fruit, wasabi, chilies, ginger, bacon, blood orange, and more.

Anyway, once a month at the brewery we would do an evening of strange pairings to introduce locals to the beer as well as to vendors in the area and, best of all, how beer pairs with virtually anything. The focus would be on a theme such as cheese, chocolate, cupcakes, candy, ice cream, soups, chicken wings, etc. We were open to whatever vendors wanted to do. Some of the pairing evening themes were weirder than others, and at the end of the evening I would always ask for a show of hands for who thought this pairing night surely wasn't going to work. It could range from a quarter to well over half.

Chocolate was something we did several times. Randy taught me that when you talk about the percentage in chocolates, you are referring to the total chocolate from the bean. That means the cocoa solids (powder) and the cocoa butter. When a chocolate is labeled as 70 percent cocoa, that might mean 35 percent cocoa solids and 35 percent cocoa butter, but it also might mean 25 percent cocoa solids and 50 percent cocoa butter. The flavor of a higher percentage of pure chocolate will be more bitter and intense overall, but Randy says that the division of cocoa solids to butter, as well as the nib quality and roasting process, will all play a factor in aroma and flavor.

However, his creative truffles had all sorts of flavors beyond chocolate. Here are some examples of beer and chocolate pairings we did together:

- Salted dark chocolate caramel truffle/peanut butter truffle with American amber lager: Sweet, toasted malt, sweet caramel and peanut butter, and the balance of salt. This is like the best peanut butter cup you've ever had.
- Maple truffle/hazelnut dark chocolate truffle/espresso truffle with American imperial porter: Nutty, roasted, slightly drying, with a smooth, creamy finish.
- Old Bay milk chocolate truffle/key lime truffle with German-style hefeweizen: Acidic, toasted, citrus, spicy, clean and crisp finish.
- Cayenne truffle with Belgian-style IPA: Fruity and creamy with sweet malt and chocolate.
- Irish coffee truffle with English brown ale: Pleasant roasted bitterness throughout, with a creamy finish.
- Lavender truffle with Belgian-style tripel: Herbal and fruity with toast and roasted notes; finishes with a lingering, pleasant herbal bite.
- Pistachio white chocolate truffle with smoked lager: Nutty, roasted, toasted, and smoky, with all the elements harmoniously balanced.
- Passion fruit dark chocolate truffle with American IPA: The tropical fruit is magically in this pairing from the chocolate and the hops. So refreshing.
- Wasabi ginger truffle with Belgian-style wit: This one is surprisingly nutty and not overwhelming spicy, with a slight sweet finish.

The last process is called conching, and this is where the chocolate paste is kneaded to develop the chocolatier's desired texture and flavors. Time and temperature will play a big role in how the final chocolate turns out.

Knowing where chocolate comes from and how it is made will help you deconstruct how different chocolates' aromas and flavors are going to play out when paired with beer. Above, I mentioned that baking chocolate is unsweetened chocolate, pure chocolate liquor that

Beer's kilned and roasted malts have many flavor synergies with chocolate.

has no sugar added, but it may have added emulsifiers such as lecithin and possibly vanilla for some flavor. Cocoa powder is what remains after the cocoa butter has been pressed out of the cocoa liquor. Residual fat levels in cocoa powder can vary, so the flavor can also vary. Unsweetened or bitter chocolate is the liquid cocoa liquor poured and molded into blocks.

Each country has different regulations that define what should constitute types of chocolate. The US FDA divides the identity standards for chocolate and chocolate ingredients into the following categories: cacao nibs, chocolate liquor, sweet chocolate, milk chocolate, buttermilk chocolate, skim milk chocolate, mixed dairy product chocolate, and bittersweet chocolate. Bittersweet and semisweet chocolate should have a minimum of 35 percent chocolate solids with the addition of sugar, more cocoa butter, and vanilla. Milk chocolate is at least 10 percent cocoa liquor, cocoa butter, 12 percent milk or milk solids, sugar, and flavorings such as vanilla. Sweet chocolate should have a minimum of 15 percent cocoa liquor, cocoa butter, more sweetener than semisweet chocolate, and flavoring additives. White chocolate does not contain cocoa liquor. It is made up of a minimum of 20 percent cocoa butter, less than 55 percent sugar, 14 percent milk or milk solids, vanilla, and lecithin. The US FDA has not set a regulation or definition for chocolate that is labeled dark chocolate. The European Union has defined dark chocolate as containing a minimum of 35 percent of cocoa liquor, cocoa butter, sugar, and sometimes vanilla. What about truffles? These are ganache, and the base is semisweet chocolate and cream, butter, sugar, and liqueur, if you like (I do mean alcohol now) coated with cocoa powder, sugar, or nuts. They can also involve dark, milk, or white chocolate.

CHOCOLATE TYPE	WHAT'S IN THE CHOCOLATE	CHOCOLATE DESCRIPTORS	BEER PAIRING POSSIBILITIES
Unsweetened/ bitter	Raw, unadulterated chocolate: 100 percent refined cocoa liquor with 50–55 percent cocoa butter, no added sugar	Dark, intense, bitter, roasted chocolate. Used mostly in baking, but why not try it for pairing?	Fruited lambic or any sour; Belgian-style dubbel or quadrupel
Dark (sweet dark)	Chocolate liquor (range is 30–90 percent), sugar, additional cocoa butter, vanilla, emulsifiers, and no milk solids	Very dark in color, rich, bitter chocolate, slight sweetness, high in creamy cocoa butter	Stout, porter, Belgian-style dubbel, imperial IPA, barrel-aged strong beer, imperial stout, barley wine, sour and fruited sour
Bittersweet	Considered dark chocolate: chocolate liquor, sugar, additional cocoa butter, vanilla, emulsifiers, and no milk solids. Must contain a minimum of 35 percent cocoa solids; higher quality equals higher cocoa solid percentage	Rich dark chocolate with additional sugar sweetness and smooth, creamy cocoa butter	Stout, porter, imperial IPA, Belgian-style saison, dubbel, quadruple, or tripel, German-style hefeweizen, lambic
Semisweet	Considered dark chocolate: chocolate liquor, sugar, additional cocoa butter, vanilla, emulsifiers, and no milk solids. Must contain a minimum of 15–35 percent cocoa solids; higher quality equals higher cocoa solid percentage	Rich dark chocolate with a bit more additional sugar sweetness than bittersweet and smooth, creamy cocoa butter	ESB, stout, porter, English-style sweet stout (oatmeal, chocolate, milk), American IPA and pale ale, Belgian-style dubbel or quadrupel
Milk chocolate	Cocoa liquor (10–25 percent minimum), additional cocoa butter, sugar, lecithin, more than 12 percent milk solids	Sweeter, lighter color, milk addition, mild, less-intense chocolate	German-style doppelbock, American or English pale ale, American brown ale, German-style Märzen/Oktoberfest, American amber ale
White chocolate	Cocoa butter, sugar, milk solids, vanilla, emulsifiers. Contains no cocoa liquor.	High quality will be ivory white to cream colored, milky sweet, smooth, creamy, no chocolate flavor	Belgian-style wit, sweet stout, brown ale, fruited lambic, fruited wheat

PAIRING CHOCOLATE AND BEER

When we see pairing articles discussing beer and chocolate that say you really should stick with dark beer for the best pairings, we're flabbergasted. Chocolates have all sorts of subtle flavors—caramel, licorice, coffee, toffee, and vanilla—but can also incorporate fruit flavors such as raisins, berries, apples, and tropical fruits such as pineapple, banana, and passion fruit. Adding ingredients such as nuts, herbs, and spices such as mint, lavender, heather, ginger, Old Bay, chilies, and teas only expands the possibilities of what beers will pair with them.

Sure, you should absolutely consider dark beers such as stouts and porters, but fruity hefeweizens and Belgian styles can be amazing, too. Consider "out there" pairings, including IPAs with passion fruit chocolates and wits with wasabi ginger–infused chocolate. You'll find exciting things, for example how the tropical fruit aromas from the hops in the American IPA and the tropical fruit in the chocolate are a beautiful complement. Belgian strong ales and saisons are must-tries as well. Oh, and fruited sour beers can be wonderfully complementary with the lactic sour and butter in chocolate. Even lighter beers such as golden ales or Kölsch and pale ales that have subtle malt sweetness will play very well with flavored chocolates. And since every beer lets you harness the power of carbonation to cut through the fat of the chocolate coating your palate, you'll have some amazing flavor chemistry going on in your mouth.

So clearly there are plenty of options. How do we go about narrowing them down for specific chocolates? As with other foods, it's best to start by deconstructing. Use the potential basic taste interactions found on page 159 to begin your beer and chocolate pairing advantage.

Let's say you want to start with what's the most comfortable and do the dark beer and chocolate pairing. And why not, since porters and stouts already have the chocolate and coffee notes that you know are going to complement the chocolate? But dark chocolates will also pair nicely with Belgian-style fruit lambic, perhaps a kriek, framboise, or peche. The sour and tart fruit will balance with the sweet of the chocolate.

Belgian-style dubbel or quadrupel has the nutty, raisin-like molasses that will complement the sweetness in the chocolate. Watch the cocoa percentage that we spoke of earlier. Higher percentages will help match intensities of the bitter in the malt roast to the bitter in the chocolate. As the chocolate type decreases in bitter intensity, so should your beer's roasted bitter intensity. Hoppy beers' bitter intensities can be hard to match with chocolates, but are definitely worth the effort. Tastings are for sure advised here. Look for citrus characteristics in the chocolate to match the citrus of the hops in the beer. White chocolate is much less bitter, since it is void of cocoa liquor, and will contrast nicely with bitter hoppiness. Milk chocolates are good to try with American amber ale, brown ales, and American pale ale. Saisons, wheats, and wits have acid and citrus notes, so find a flavored chocolate to complement or contrast: wasabi, ginger, black pepper, clove, nutmeg, banana, key lime, lemon, etc.

SWEET PAIRINGS

As we continue to look at pairings, you have by now realized that we are ultimately looking for the potential interaction of the key ingredients that are concentration- or intensity-driven. However, you've also realized that perception often equals reality. For example, on at least a weekly basis I hear someone in the tasting room make the comment, "Oh, I don't like dark beer." So I ask if they like chocolate and coffee. They say yes. Then I hand them an American brown ale brewed with chocolate and coffee, and what do you know? That person is now interested in dark beer and more open to possibilities.

This same principle applies to pairings. Use particular foods or particular beers to get people over the hump. Whether it's the nostalgia of Girl Scout cookies or someone's favorite Halloween candy, use their perceptions and prejudices to the advantage of the pairing.

GIRL SCOUT COOKIES

Holy wow, there are some amazing ingredients in these little cookies. There's butter, coconut, caramel, peanut butter, lemon . . . the list goes on! One of the best things about Girl Scout cookies is that everyone grew up with a favorite. Find out what your guests like, and there is no better way to end an evening than with a beer and a cookie they remember fondly from

Pairing beer with Girl Scout cookies puts a grown-up spin on a childhood favorite.

childhood. And sure, you can wait until your local troop holds its annual fundraiser, but if you read the pairings and just can't wait, you can order them online now as well!

- Pair Samoas (caramel, chocolate, and coconut) with porter, Belgian-style quadrupel, or American brown ale. If you can find a coconut porter, even better! You'll discover melt-in-your-mouth sweet caramel, brown fruits such as fig and date, dark chocolate, and buttery biscuit—and don't forget the harmonizing flavor of coconut throughout.
- Pair Thin Mints with a coffee- or chocolate-infused stout or porter. It's like a peppermint patty that goes to eleven.
- For Rah-Rah Raisins run with the milk theme and grab a milk stout. Milky creaminess with chocolate, roasted undertones and oatmeal cookie and raisins will remind you of an expensive latte.
- Trefoils are those rich shortbread cookies, and they pair oh so well with either a Bretted saison, a Belgian-style pale ale, or a Belgian-style tripel. Oh, sweet, bready pastry with tropical fruit and a bit of earthiness, you are so satisfying.
- Lemonades made their name by being the most popular Girl Scout cookie with a citrus component. For the beer, amp up the citrus with a clean, citrusy session IPA. This pairing is refreshing, with a fizzy citrus quality that tastes like summer in your mouth.
- Tagalongs are delightfully rich with peanut butter and chocolate. They go great with a Belgian-style dubbel or quad, though you can't go wrong with an American brown ale brewed with coffee or chocolate (or both!). That sweet, nutty caramel and a kiss of chocolate balance the cookie and the beer perfectly.
- Do-Si-Dos are a peanut-butter-packed sandwich cookie. They go with a wide range of beers, from imperial reds and winter ales (especially those that are caramely) to American amber ale and Belgian-style dubbel. Sweet caramel malts blend with the nutty peanut butter for this not over-the-top pairing.

FLAVORED CANDY CORN

And you thought Girl Scout cookies were as nostalgic as it could get. Ha! That fall treat from childhood, candy corn, now comes in all kinds of flavors. What seems like a little ball of sweet wax can change completely once paired with beer.

- A Belgian-style dubbel takes a caramel apple–flavored candy corn and plays up the fruit along with the sweet, nutty notes of caramel.
- Chocolate-flavored candy corn and an American imperial stout combine to make a Tootsie Roll–like flavor.
- Candy corn flavored with pumpkin spice paired with a German-style Märzen/ Oktoberfest give the impression of pumpkin pie.
- Apple cider–flavored candy corn paired with a saison results in a fruity, fizzy, and tart mouthful of flavor.

CAKE

Whether it's a birthday, a holiday, or just a Thursday night, there's no wrong time for a cake and beer pairing. You can use mini cupcakes or cut the cake into bite-size pieces for easy sampling. Keep in mind that cake is more complex than you might think. The cake, any filling, and the frosting or icing choice will all play a huge role in these pairings. Use the following to get started, but feel free to customize and tailor to match your own cake preferences.

- Lemon cake and buttercream icing with a German-style hefeweizen: The creamy mouthfeel from the icing and the yeast combines with the slightly acidic fruity and citrus notes perfectly. You'll find the sweet toasted malt and lemon characteristics pop out and the finish is light and refreshing.
- Red velvet cake and buttercream icing with a British-style barley wine: There's a balance of sweetness from the cake and the beer, with hints of brown fruits, including plums, dates, and cherries. Then the alcohol cuts through the buttercream elements of the cake. It's magic in your mouth!
- Carrot cake with cream cheese icing and an American IPA or American pale ale: There's a complete balance and harmony from the sweetness of the cake with the hoppy bitterness of the beer.
- Peanut butter cake with vanilla icing and an oatmeal stout: Nutty, vanilla aromas mingle with the stout's full, creamy mouthfeel and subtle roast.
- Cheesecake with raspberry glaze and a framboise: The acid from the beer cuts through the fat from the cheesecake. Lactose tartness and raspberry sweetness from both beer and cheesecake make for a wonderful complement.
- Chocolate bourbon cake with buttercream icing and an American imperial stout: Big, bold chocolate and roast with the sweet complement of buttercream. You might think this sounds like too much, but try it and you'll find with this pairing, too much is just enough.

ICE CREAM

I scream, you scream, let's pair some ice cream, frozen yogurts, and sorbets! Ice cream comes in so many flavors with so many different ingredients, the possibilities are endless. Although wine and ice cream are often an awkward match, beers can create some stunning pairings. Not only that, but the carbonation in beer is going to really help cut through the richness of the cream in ice cream.

- Lemon sorbet with a Belgian-style wit: Citrus with a bit of sweet malt in the beer combines with the lemony tartness of the ice cream for a most refreshing pairing.
- Hazelnut ice cream with a coffee beer or English-style milk stout: Creamy, nutty, and roasted coffee notes get together to create the perception of a hazelnut latte.
- Salted caramel ice cream with a Belgian-style dubbel: Salty, creamy, raisiny, caramely, salty, and vanilla sweet . . . it's a flavor explosion of basic tastes!
- Mint chocolate-chip ice cream and American imperial stout: The crunchy addition of chocolate chip bits is a fun texture treat. When the chocolate, roasted characteristics of the stout are combined with them, and with the mint aroma, you'll feel like you just ate the best peppermint patty ever.
- Pineapple Greek frozen yogurt (not low fat!) with a dry-hopped pilsener: Sweet pineapple and sweet toasted malt complement each other, while the slightly hoppy bitterness and the carbonation lift the creaminess off your palate.

You'll find there's a surprising amount of flavor and aroma complexity in chips and dips when you pair them with beer.

SAVORY PAIRINGS

It's so fun to explore the sweet side, but let's not forget about the savory! Chips and dips, nuts, pizza, wings—there are so many delicious possibilities for every one of these foods. And let's not forget about cheese. Whether you're making a pepper jack grilled cheese or a bowl of gorgonzola mac-and-cheese, there's a beer for that!

CHIPS AND DIPS

The salty crunch of chips is a natural match for beers of all stripes. In fact, flavored chips with different beers can make for some fun pairings. Bring in the dips for some next-level flavor matching. It's easy to forget as you munch away at a party, but salsas, queso, and guacamole are packed with both strong and subtle flavors that make for interesting pairings. Plus, who won't thank you for bringing chips, dips, and beer to the next gathering?

- Roasted tomato and chipotle corn salsa with pilsener or golden ale: The toasted malts and carbonation combine with the roasted, smoky, and earthy characteristics of the salsa in such a way that you'll find this seemingly simple pairing calling for another bite, then another sip, then another bite . . .
- Queso dip with British-style barley wine: This may seem crazy, but the higher alcohol and carbonation cut right through the richness of the cheese. Sweet malts complement the dairy sweetness of the queso but cut the spiciness of any pepper, and the finish combines sweet, salty, and savory.
- Corn, black bean, and roasted red pepper salsa with American brown ale: Roasted chocolate malts complement the earthiness of the black beans. The mouthfeel is silky; the finish is sweet and roasted.
- Guacamole with a hoppy American pale ale: Citrus from the hops meets the lime in guacamole, toasted malt meets corn chips, and the carbonation cuts and lifts fat so nothing is overwhelming—it's all in harmony.
- Pineapple salsa with German-style hefeweizen or Belgian-style saison: The acidic tart and sweet notes from the salsa play with the creamy, yeasty mouthfeel and high carbonation from the hefe. It all combines in a most interesting crisp, clean finish with a touch of complex spice.

PIZZA

Pizza is one of those foods that everyone can agree to order, but then try agreeing on toppings. Since there are so many varieties of pizza, approach pairing by pizza type and refine from there.

- Cheese pizza with an American amber ale: Let's start with the classic pizza and classic beer for pizza pairings. Sweet toasted malts are sure to complement the baked crust and the cheeses, hops will cut through tomato acidity, and carbonation will lift and balance fat. This extremely simple pizza can be easily overwhelmed, so play this pairing safe if you choose a different beer.

- Spicy pizza with American pale ale: If the sauce on the pizza is kicked up with spice or if you load up your pizza with toppings such as jalapeños, spicy sausage, or crushed red pepper, you should find a good match in a pale ale. The subtle sweet and malty backbone of the pale will cut through the capsaicin heat and leave you with a balance of sweet umami tomato, rich cheese, and toasted bread.
- Barbecue pizza with a Belgian-style dubbel: Barbecue pizzas feature barbecue sauce and often different cheeses such as Gouda. You'll find the sweet of the dubbel's malt balances with the sweet of the switched-out sauce. The fruity and nutty qualities of the beer are sure to complement barbecue-friendly cheeses, as well as any smoke notes.
- Pepperoni, sausage, and other meaty pizza with an English-style IPA: A more intense pizza calls for a more intense beer. IPAs, especially those with earthy and spicy hops, will complement the same characteristics in the meats while the alcohol and carbonation will cut through the fat and grease.
- Pesto pizzas (often with artichoke hearts, sun-dried tomatoes, etc., as toppings) with a Belgian-style golden strong ale: Lemon-like citrus, herbal pesto, and fruity sweetness all get along, and you'll find the salt is emphasized yet balanced. If you have sun-dried tomatoes on top as well, you'll have additional complexity with tomato acid, umami, and sweetness.

NUTS

Nuts are good for you, and they have a plethora of textures and flavors that include buttery, creamy, bitter, sweet, caramel-like, crunchy, roasted, salted, and so on. Sounds like a pairing about to happen!

- Salted, roasted peanuts and Bohemian-style pilsener: The salt on the nuts cuts through the bitterness of the hops, allowing the sweetness of the malt and the sweetness of the nuts to balance each other perfectly.
- Sweet pecans with a Belgian-style dubbel or quad: Two beers with one nut are a great contrast in how interactions change your perception. Paired with the dubbel, there is a salty and savory overall perception, but with the quad it's so sweet and bready, you'll feel like you're eating pecan pie.
- Jalapeño cheddar almonds and pecans with an American IPA: The nut and sweet malt make for a great creamy complement that helps cut through the spice of the pepper. Hops make sure the spicy pepper still has a tiny punch, though. With really spicy nuts, it can be kind of a challenge to see if this pairing will get too hot for you to handle.
- Bloody Mary–flavored peanuts and a German-style hefeweizen: Toasted malts and salty peanuts with the fruity spice of the yeast and the sweet of the tomato all make for a balanced and complex pairing. These flavored peanuts are not a specific brand, because everyone seems to be making them. Now that you are on the lookout for crazy pairing partners, we're just guessing you will notice these everywhere.
- Ridiculously spicy over-the-top nut mix with an American amber ale: Think of those "hotter than hell" or "spicy enough to burn your face off" nut mixes you see in the

PAIR WITH JERKY!

While images of truck stop–procured processed beef may have sprung to mind, the truth is there is a lot of great jerky out there. Just like beer, artisans are creating fine flavored jerkies from a variety of meats with a staggering number of spices. Meat types range from game meats such as venison, duck, elk, buffalo, ostrich, alligator, wild boar, and yak to fish including salmon, tuna, and trout. Of course, there is still plenty of beef and turkey jerky as well. If you are a vegan or vegetarian, there are even jerkies for you out there!

Just like the wings suggestions on page 166, your pairing-focus ingredients are the spices and rubs. The original jerky spice is salt and pepper, but why go with original when you have variety out there waiting? You've got teriyaki, garlic, sweet-and-sour, smoked, barbecue, Thai, Jamaican jerk, basil citrus, maple cinnamon, and chili lime, among others. Teriyaki has sweetness, black pepper, and sesame spice, so let's try a beer with some body and sweet malt, say a German-style Märzen/Oktoberfest. Sweet-and-sour, on the other hand, would match nicely with a lambic or a Belgian-style tripel. Barbecue makes me think of a beer with sweet malt, the lifting power of carbonation, and some spicy notes. How about an American amber ale, American pale ale, or Belgian-style dubbel? Let's finish with chili-lime jerky and an imperial IPA for a kick of pepper, a kiss of sweet, and a citrus fruit hug.

store and think "do I need to try those?" Now you have a reason. Let the sweet malt and sweet nutty flavor cut through that spicy assault and leave you with a creamy, almost roasted impression.

WINGS

We aren't talking about the run-of-the-mill pub hot wings, although if you are pairing buffalo wings, go with an American pale ale to cut through the heat and emphasize the sweet or a Bohemian-style pilsener that can still cut the heat but gives a crisp, clean finish. The hops in both these beers will help to cut the grease as well. Nevertheless, we are talking about wings that focus on different spices and sauces to give you the variety and sensory experience you are craving. The sauces are really what you are focusing on, because that is where your pairing ingredient is most important.

- Raspberry wings with a Belgian-style tripel: Berry fruitiness from the sauce and the fruity notes from the yeast in the beer complement and balance each other with a bouquet of sweetness, not to mention that the high carbonation helps lift and harmonize the flavors. If you can't find wings with this kind of sauce, then use plain wings with a raspberry glaze or jam on the side.
- Barbecue honey mustard wings and a German-style Helles: Yum to the sweet, acidic, and spicy sauce as it blends with the beer's sweet toast of malt and then finishes with kiss of hop bitterness. A bit of sour bite from the mustard is the perfect ending on this pairing.

- Thai peanut wings with a California common: This one is definitely a crowd-pleaser. Nutty peanut sauce that has a hint of caramel combines and balances with the sweet toasted malt and leaves you with a creamy pepper mouthfeel. You will be addicted and wanting more.
- Santa Fe chipotle wings with an imperial porter: This pairing is so complex because it is continuously changing. It starts with chocolate malt and smoked pepper spice, similar to a mole sauce, then you'll find it gets more roasted and sweet, with a sun-dried tomato finish.
- Jamaican jerk with a British-style barley wine: The sweetness of the malt and the sweetness of the sauce complement each other and emphasize the garlic and ginger. Alcohol cuts through the spicy pepper, and the finish is sweet like candy.

MAC-AND-CHEESE OR GRILLED CHEESE

With these classic comfort foods, the riffs of different cheeses, pastas, and breads (and toppings) are endless. Try one of the suggestions below, or make a few and invite some friends for a tasting party of bite-size treats!

- Cheddar and Gruyère cheese on multigrain bread with American brown ale: Rich, buttery, nutty, and salty cheeses find a complementary pairing friend with the American brown ale. The richness will emphasize the coffee, chocolate, roasted, and nutty, malty characteristics. For a change of pace, switch out the multigrain bread and make whole-wheat mac-and-cheese instead; now change up or add a second pairing beer, a Belgian-style dubbel. A bit more sweetness from the grains of the bread or pasta, as well as the beer, and the nuttiness of the cheeses will shine with dubbel's earthiness.
- Lobster mac-and-cheese with a Belgian-style wit or German-style hefeweizen: Preparations can vary, but this is typically one rich dish. Cleanse your palate and break up the butter and cheese with the citrus and spicy characteristics of wit or hefe. Let the high carbonation cut through the richness and lift away the heaviness of the fat.
- Triple-crème Brie on sourdough bread with an American sour or Belgian-style saison: Look for toasted, earthy, and tart notes combining for a lively mouthful in this pairing. You'll find the beers will add additional complexity—spicy and floral or maybe fruity—for the perfect funky pairing. You can always add a tart Granny Smith apple to kick your tart side up. Get funky now!
- Gorgonzola mac-and-cheese with an American imperial/double IPA: This beer's alcohol and hops are going to cut through the richness of this big, bold cheese, as well as the fatty butter and creamy mouthfeel. You'll also see that DIPA matches the funk intensity of the cheese with its dank, citrus hop flavors for an explosion of complexity.
- Pepper Jack mac-and-cheese or grilled cheese with an American pale ale: The pale ale can't be beat for spicy foods. It balances them in a slightly sweet, satisfying way. And just as with the DIPA and Gorgonzola, you'll find hop aroma mingles perfectly with the subtle grassiness of the cheese.

BREAKFAST OR BRUNCH (OR BRUNK)

Is there any really good reason not to start your first meal of the day off with beer? We didn't think so. Sweet breakfast pastries or coffee cake with a coffee stout, coffee porter, coffee brown ale—I think you can see where we are going here. The roasted malt and coffee notes perfectly match up with the buttery, sweet pastry dough. French toast, pancakes, and waffles can be eclectic depending on the syrup and fruit, but you'll have butter and caramel notes, which make us think of a Scotch ale/wee heavy, a Vienna-style lager, or an American brown ale. If you add fruit, then go with fruited wheat, which will have toasted, bready characteristic as well.

Did you throw in chorizo, pork sausage, or bacon? Well, then pair that with an imperial red for sweet malt, spicy hops, and some alcohol to cut through the fat. More of the traditional steak-and-eggs kind of breakfast person? Then grab a porter or stout for the matching char and roast and the balance of sweet coffee and chocolate. If you're craving huevos rancheros, pair those steamy corn tortillas with a pilsener or Helles to complement the sweet and grain notes.

Gwen: Donuts of all types are a breakfast item you simply must try with a variety of beers. Let's start with the maple-iced donut, which seems to be the one that's always fought over. We pair it with either a Belgian-style dubbel or a Belgian-style quad, so the alcohol cuts through the fat but balances earthy and sweet to cure anyone's sweet tooth. Raspberry-filled donuts, on the other hand, we pair with a framboise. The beer's tart fruit and high carbonation pull all the ingredients together for fruity, fizzy, sweet fun. Chocolate cake donuts with oak-aged stout are another favorite—think bitter roast and sweet chocolate meet vanilla from the oak. Last but not least, for the fritter folks, apple fritters and Belgian-style blonds combine for a fruity, earthy breakfast bite. Now go get your dozen and start pairing!

Two thumbs up for beer with breakfast!

BEER DINNERS

Around the world there are millions of meals paired with beer each year. Yet a beer with dinner is different from a beer dinner. A beer dinner can be many things. It can be as informal as a picnic or as formal as a multicourse meal at a fancy restaurant, and anything in between. What makes a beer dinner a beer dinner, though, is the thought, care, and pride behind it: the focus on the way beer and food work together.

When hosting a beer dinner—or lunch, breakfast, or brunch, for that matter—the goal is to take beers and food to the next level. But you can't let perfection intimidate you. No matter if you feel your pairing skills are ready for prime time or not, the only true way to learn is to practice, practice, practice, practice, practice.

When you get right down to it, a beer pairing event is just like any other event: it's all about the experience for your guests. If you approach hosting a beer dinner with that in mind, you're guaranteed success. This means when planning a dinner, you should not only consider the beer and food menu, but also the location, atmosphere, and so on. Guests will be eating and drinking, sure, but they'll soak up other details that affect whether they leave happy or not. They'll leave with different impressions of the event based on whether it had a loud, party-like atmosphere or a quiet, intimate feel. They'll certainly remember the company, whether it was old friends or a bunch of new people. In short, there are many, many layers to any experience, and at a pairing event you should consider more than just the food and drink, because after all, the goal should be to make a memory.

Whether you're trying to host an intimate tasting with a few friends or a large, formal event with plenty of beer experts, this chapter will put you on the path to success.

THEMES

Ever hear of a newspaper article without an angle, a play without a story, or a fund-raising event without a cause? So, too, should all pairing events have some form of theme. There are so many possible themes, it can be tough to narrow it down and pick one. As with all aspects of a beer dinner, consider the type of event you want to have and the size—and level of beer experience—of your audience when selecting a theme. For example, beer nerds may love a Maillard-mania beer dinner, where browned flavor reactions are the star of the show, or an evening of sour beers. However, your friends who are new to craft beer would probably have more fun with a theme such as beers from your state or a dinner where each guest selects a beer and you provide the pairings.

BEER DINNER THEME OPTIONS	EXAMPLES
Beer style	You could try all IPAs, barrel-aged beers, malt-centric beers, American sours, rare/vintage beers from multiple years, or do an ale vs. lager showdown!
Beer by geography	Try only US breweries, only breweries from your state, East Coast vs. West Coast, or Belgium vs. America.
Craft beer vs. wine	Serve a craft beer and wine option with each course.
ABV	Draw a line: try beers that are only under 6 percent ABV or the reverse.
People	Here the two organizers each pick one beer to be served with each course, and guests vote on which they like better. Other options: chef vs. chef dinner, Cicerone vs. sommelier, brewer vs. brewer, brewer vs. homebrewer, husband vs. wife (yikes!), mother vs. son, father vs. daughter, Republican vs. Democrat, you get the idea.
Types of food	Pair to types of food such as off the hoof, from the sea, vegetarian, or gluten free.
Types of techniques	Feature particular cooking techniques, such as Malliard-mania or caramelized food and beer delights.
Fundraiser	Craft brewers in the United States commonly use their beers as a tool to raise money for other causes. A great added theme to any beer pairing occasion would be to use it as a chance to support a good cause. Note: If you're doing this officially, for tax purposes be sure to follow proper donation procedures tied to nonprofit causes.
Seasonal	There's something for every season: a fall harvest field party, winter ales and winter vegetables, spring seasonals and spring dishes, and summer saisons and summer dishes. In fact, that brings us to seasonal menus!

SEASONAL THINKING

Seasonal beers are some of the most popular beers in the United States. Perhaps it's because these beers are not always available year-round and their ingredients, flavor profile, or inspiration is tied to the season of release. If you pick a theme tied to the season, you open up the option of presenting a meal that showcases flavors of the moment both in beer and in food. The big caveat is that any of these beer styles might be made and be available at other times of the year. Unlike wine, beer is made all year long because hops can be dried and preserved along with malted barley. So when it comes to seasonal beers, there might be tradition, but there are no hard-and-fast rules on when production has to happen.

Note: Be wary of a beer marketed as a seasonal when it's on the shelves or menu after the season it's tied to. Most brewers are organized enough to release their seasonals early (in the weeks or month prior to the start of that season), but unfortunately some retailers do not track out-of-date beers or ones that are past their prime. Think of beers like bread or milk (but with a longer expiration date). Store them cold and drink them fresh unless you know they're meant to be cellared. The first place to check is the bottle or can of beer. Hopefully, the brewery has packaged it with key dates, either the date the beer was made, the "best by" date, or both. Many brewery websites share their shelf life for specific beers as well. Third-party sites also provide information on beer brands that are widely available.

BEER	FOOD
SPRING German-style Märzen, bock, and doppelbock, American amber ale, Irish-style red, Irish-style dry stout, bière de Mars, wheat-centric beers, and gruits **SUMMER** Summer ale, American cream ale, California common, German-style Helles, pilseners, German-style Kölsch, hefeweizen, and Maibock, Belgian-style saison (means season), fruit beer **FALL** Harvest ale, German-style Oktoberfest, pumpkin beer, fresh/wet hop beer, brown ales, German-style Eisbock **WINTER** Winter warmers, Scotch-style ale, English-style old ales, barley wines, robust porter, American stout, imperial stout, winter lager, Christmas/holiday ales, Belgian-style lambic	**TIED TO EACH SEASON** Vegetables, foraged food, herbs **MEAT IS GENERALLY NOT SEASONAL** **SEASONAL CHEESES** Think about it. World-class cheese comes from fresh milk. Fresh goat and sheep cheese, for example, is tied to the lactation cycle of the animal and what they are eating during the year. Generally speaking, consuming these cheeses from spring to fall is likely your best bet. For aged cheese, you have more options tied to cheese type and suggested shelf life from the cheesemonger. **EXCEPTIONS** Go to any farmers market, fresh produce section, or specialty food store and ingredients vary greatly based on Mother Nature, terroir, and geography.

A SAMPLE PAIRING MENU

What follows is an American craft beer–themed dinner that is sure to wow the taste buds. We've also provided tasting notes and strategy.

Welcome Tipple: Great Divide Samurai Rice Ale
Four ounces in small pilsner glass at 38°F (refrigerator cold)

It's a good idea to begin any evening with some social time and a refreshing palate. It lets guests whet their whistle and relax. A four-ounce pour of Samuri rice ale will deliver a much more flavor-forward start to the evening than a mass domestic lager, yet is similar in body,

— Chef Adam Dulye —

Chef Adam Dulye is a powerhouse in the world of beer. He is a Culinary Institute of America graduate who has helmed kitchens with a craft beer focus from the mountains of Colorado to San Francisco. He is now executive chef for the Brewers Association and CraftBeer.com.

Craft beer is considered an ingredient by many chefs today. Why?

Not only craft beer but wine and cocktails are evolving into more complete parts of the dining experience. By looking at craft beer as food, you bring the flavors of the craft beer into the dish and take into account the whole experience on a diner's palate. The question of what to drink has often been asked before what to eat, and that is slowly changing to a question of what can we pair for you. Craft beer can wake up the palate, contrast with a cooking method, cleanse the palate, harmonize with a dish, and more. Given all the ways craft beer can affect a dish and a palate, the question of what craft beer to pour now starts way before the question of "Can I get you something to drink?"

Why is craft beer so versatile when it comes to pairing with food?

When looking for a pairing, a chef will look to what will complete the dish on the palate. Not only to complement but to bring an added element that is not present in the dish. Craft beer has endless possibilities in this arena. From notes of lemon to peppercorns, chocolate, and beyond, there is a craft beer out there that can complete almost any pairing. The carbonation helps keep the palate awake and is a natural palate cleanser that can allow for the movement of more than just lighter to heavier tastes and textures. Craft beer gives the chef the freedom to move the menu in a way no other beverage has before. One major reason as well is the timing of

craft beer and the relationships brewers are able to create with chefs. Craft beer has the advantage of going from idea to glass in just a few months, whereas no other beverage can do that, and brewers and chefs are now more than ever grasping the concept that something unique can be created in what, compared to wine and spirits, is just a short amount of time.

What are your three favorite all-time pairings and why?

It's hard to pick three top pairings, as each experience brings something new. The time and place of the pairing most definitely can add to a pairing becoming the new experience to beat. Here are three that are time tested, palate tested, and ready to be put into play.

Roasted quail or duck with brown ale or dubbel: One of my favorite beers to pair with is a brown ale. Sadly, not many are being made right now, but if you can find one, the light roasted malt notes and balance of hops go perfectly with the roasted game bird.

Carrot cake and IPA: As IPAs become hoppier and hoppier, the reaction on the palate of carrots brings a natural sweetness to calm the bitter. In the form of carrot cake, you also get the added benefit of some extra fat in the bite that allows the IPA to reveal more than just hops. As an added benefit, it's always great to finish with a beer that no one was expecting with dessert.

Saison and asparagus: Maybe it's because nothing else goes with asparagus or maybe it's that saison and asparagus were made to go together. Either way, the combination of the two is nothing short of simply amazing.

Photo Credit: © BREWERS ASSOCIATION

intensity, and alcohol. This is a refreshing yet flavorful craft beer with a dry finish that piques the appetite. In general, medium-low alcohol or session beers are an inviting yet mellow way to start the evening (see page 180 for more on this).

Course 1: French Onion Soup Paired with Ska Buster Nut Brown Ale and Samuel Adams Double Bock

Three ounces each in small rocks glasses served at 42°F (take out of the refrigerator fifteen minutes before service)

Your guests will be welcomed to the table by a warming bowl of French onion soup. The soup has browned flavors from the reduced beef stock, umami from the stock, and the cheese, and it also has bread flavors from the slice of bread that is cradled between stock and cheese.

The stock base will bridge nicely to the toasted bread crust–flavored Munich malts of the double bock and the pale malt flavors of the nut brown ale. The umami-rich soup flavors cry for a richer, more robust beer. The double bock's 9.5 percent ABV deliver similar intensity as the soup. On the other hand, the Ska brown ale is an English-style brown ale that has much lower alcohol, 5.1 percent ABV. This beer is lighter and drier than the Samuel Adams, with nutty bread crust notes from its Victory and Munich malt base that complement and echo the flavors of the stock and bread. The brown ale proves that a lower ABV beer does not always get pummeled by increased food intensity. Try it and you will see!

Course 2: Smoked Arctic Char en Papillote (in Parchment), Walla Walla Onions, Apples, and Fromage Blanc Paired with Funkwerks Saison

Four ounces served in Belgian-style tulip glass at 50°F (take out of the refrigerator twenty-five minutes before service)

Funkwerks Saison is 6.8 percent, medium in alcohol intensity. The saison's pepper phenols, and flavors of lemon, orange, and ginger are like the spicing the char would beg from a creative chef. Char is in a similar flavor family as Atlantic salmon and will do well with a medium-intensity beer with a sturdy by not aggressive bitterness. The bitterness will calm down the richness (fat) of the fish, letting more of the smoke flavors carry over, and will also help cut the fat from the fromage blanc. The smoke of the fish will also marry with the yeast notes of the saison. The lingering sweetness of the onions will find any residual sugar from the sasion to match. The saison's drying finish should refresh and leave one's palate more dialed in to sensing the apple, too.

Course 3: Coffee-Stuffed Donuts, Espresso, Crunchy Coffee Ice Cream, and Hot Fudge paired with Stone Coffee Milk Stout

Four-ounces served in white wine glass at 45°F (take out of the refrigerator 15 minutes before service)

For dessert, the beer is high on coffee, meaning the coffee flavor is strong and exhilarating. Other ingredients include British mild ale malt and lactose milk sugar. It's only a 4.2 percent ABV beer, but still has girth due to the medium body and lingering sugar. It has 40 IBUs, so there is some significant bitterness, too.

There are so many flavor harmonies in this pairing, especially between the beer's coffee and roasted malt and the dessert's espresso. And of course, there's the hot fudge, which marries beautifully with the milk sugar and pale malts of the stout. The beer's bitterness matches the espresso bitterness to help tame it, thus featuring the other flavors even more.

By the way, you may think, what is the theme on the above pairing menu? The dishes and beers present a meal to remind the world that US craft brewers make world-class beer that can stand up to any dish from a variety of nations.

OTHER CONSIDERATIONS
WATER

Although not commonly listed on the menu, water is key to successful beer dinners. Letting your guests have as much water as they want in between sips of beer lets everyone consume more responsibly. Staying hydrated is important, as it not only helps flush your body of toxins, it also slows down your rate of consumption.

Note: We recommend serving water without ice. When water is colder, almost everyone tends to consume less of it.

Julia: I'll never forget one huge day of beer appreciation when I attended All About Beer Magazine's *World Beer Festival in Durham, North Carolina. This festival is fantastic. The venue is the Durham Bulls Athletic Park, where everything is set up on the actual baseball field. The event has three hundred beers and two back-to-back tasting sessions in one day. When I attended, I presented at both sessions, walked the festival grounds and sampled, plus in between festival sessions and after, I toured breweries. For the curious, the breweries I toured that day were Fullsteam (a self-dubbed plow-to-pint brewery and very food/agriculture focused) and Bull City Burger and Brewery (a very green and locally minded brewery. Try their pretzel-crusted pickles— not to be missed!).*

Wow, it was a crazy, huge, fun tasting-filled day. How did I get through it? Simple. I kept refilling a water bottle that I had with me, and I only would take one or two sips of each sample (it's OK to pour out extra beer from your glass and not finish it). When I was at the breweries, I certainly sampled but would order flights, which are usually small four-ounce glasses of several different beers.

Anyhoo . . . I sampled a lot that day, but because my appreciation was spread out over a long period of time and the festival had good access to water (which was frequently refilled), I was able to maintain my composure and simpy have a great time without getting blotto.

Water with ice looks refreshing, but you'll find that guests consume more water when it's served without ice.

A welcome beer can set the tone, even if it's just a small sample.

GLASSWARE PLACEMENT

For seated dinners, tell your servers or guests to place the most recent beer served right above the plate and knife. That way, if you are discussing a specific beer for the most recent course, everyone has a point of reference. Many beer styles can look alike, too, so a strategy on which beer is placed where is a smart one. Beers from a previous course can be shifted right as the meal progresses.

THE WELCOME BEER

For any beer dinner or pairing meal we are a part of hosting, we like to ensure there is always a welcome beer. Think about it. People often come to a meal such as dinner both thirsty and hungry, at the end of a day. Sometimes they even come straight from work. You don't want them mentally distracted as to when the appreciation and savoring will begin. Upon arrival, welcome them fully with something that will whet their whistle and pique their appetites. A common ounce amount for our welcome beer is four to six ounces, depending on alcohol level of the beer. Praise the welcome beer, people, for it sets the tone and properly helps get everyone in the mood for more.

INCORPORATE BEER INGREDIENTS INTO THE MEAL

Beer's ingredients can be used to cook (see Chapter 9: Cooking with Beer) with in the meal and, crazy enough, even for decoration. Malt and hops are present at many a beer dinner.

Ale-peritif, anyone? This was an idea used at a Great American Beer Festival media luncheon, where we plated and served two-row pale malt, chocolate malt, Cascade hops, and Saaz hop cones as a sensory course. We had guests tasting the malt and splitting open hop cones. It was a gem of an addition, very interactive and also educational. If you do this, it's smart to know key information about each ingredient: Lovibond color of the malt, potential diastatic power of the malt (the ability for malt to convert to fermentable sugars during the brewing process), alpha acids of the hops, source/producer of each ingredient, and flavor descriptors of each. Guide guests through each ingredient, and have them share what they are sensing. Tasting as a group helps bring everyone together and provides one more layer of shared experience.

MENU ALTERNATIVES

This is a valuable base to cover. At minimum, most dinners we've hosted and attended have accounted for the vegetarians (with Gwen being one of them!). This will ensure things are more thought through. If working with a chef, he or she should help with this effort and present you with a vision for the courses gone veggie. From there, getting an idea from your guests regarding who is a vegetarian will help ensure you have the right amount of food.

We've run into situations where we ask invited guests in advance to indicate if they are vegetarian, but then during meal service, more than that total number ask for the veggie meal. Dilemma! If you are hosting a dinner at a venue, have some sort of ticketing system to confirm the number of vegetarians, or assign predetermined seats for vegetarians to help prevent issues. That way, those who asked in advance for the veggie meal get one and you don't come up short because new people decide on the fly that they wanted one too.

Beyond that, there are dangerous allergies that chefs are used to accommodating but we at home might not think of, for example shellfish, nuts, dairy, wheat, and more. Give your

SESSION BEER

For the welcome beer, consider a session beer. Any style of beer can be made as a session beer—lower in strength—but that will not guarantee it's a winner. The goal should be to reach a balance between the style's character and the lower alcohol content. Drinkability is a factor in the overall balance of these beers. Session beer should not exceed 5 percent ABV. This beer style is not defined by specific flavors or aromas, which can place it in almost any style category. Instead, what makes a session beer is primarily refreshment and drinkability.

Quantitative Style Statistics
- OG: 1.034–1.040
- FG: 1.004–1.010
- Apparent Attenuation: 75–88 percent
- ABV: 4.0–5.0 percent
- IBU: 10–30
- Color/SRM: 2+ (straw)

Examples

Full Sail Session Premium Lager: This was one of, if not the first, session beers in the post-Prohibition era marketed as such. It helped spur the session beer movement. We love everything about this beer, including the chunky bottle and the easy, throwback quenching yet flavorful qualities. Feeling lucky? Bet against the rock-paper-scissors under the cap.

21st Amendment Hell or High Watermelon Wheat: Available only April through September, with watermelon added after the initial fermentation. This beer is light yet packed with pleasing fruit flavor and aroma.

Odell Loose Leaf: An American pale ale at 4.5 percent ABV. Toast and earthy malt with a slight touch of sweet balanced with grassy, citrus, fruity hops, and a crisp finish. Great carbonation and a pleasant subtle bitter aftertaste make this beer refreshing anytime.

Saint Arnold Fancy Lawnmower: An ale style beer fermented at cooler lager temperatures, the Lawnmower centers on spicy Hallertau hops. Bagging *two* past Great American Beer Festival gold medals in the Kölsch category (2010 and 2007) is no small feat. One taste of this beer, and you will tangibly have an understanding of what sessionable is.

Julia: Utah Provo Girl is a 2011 gold medal winner for the session beer category at the Great American Beer Festival. The base style is a German-style pilsener. This beer works well as a session beer, as we watched in motion when we served it at a media dinner we hosted at Colicchio & Sons in New York City.

guests (and chef) a chance to work around food restrictions by finding this information out in advance, and remember to also consider how those restrictions might alter the pairing. Today there are many adults with a gluten intolerance or celiac disease. The good news is there is an ever-increasing number of gluten-reduced and gluten-free beers in a variety of styles.

Our suggestion is to list both of these questions somewhere, such as on the RSVP form, or ask when confirming the reservation or seat at the dinner. Prompt attendees to contact you by a specified date if they have specific allergies or food restrictions.

Keep in mind beer pairing synergies when dishes are changed up. Many a chef can be your guide on what alternative menu items will still provide flavor harmonies with the beer chosen for the listed main course.

EXECUTION

We've talked about the philosophy behind pairing meals, the importance of access to the chef, striving to conduct a test tasting (see page 77), picking a theme, and more. Now let's talk execution.

1. During the meal, formally present each food course and beer. This is not considered interruptive and is in fact what the people came to hear! If you skip this, your guests miss getting the behind-the-scenes information. If the chef is on hand, have him or her, or a representative from the establishment, speak about the food when it is served. If this is a home meal, you should fill this role. Also, somebody should be ready to present the beers, including the story behind the brand, the flavor profiles of the beer, any special ingredients and unique brewing processes, IBU, and ABV. Be ready to describe what craft beer and food interactions you perceive so others can relate to what you are experiencing, and discuss your approach behind each pairing.

Tip: Don't be afraid to pick up a glass, hold it by its stem, and use a clean fork or knife to gently tap the glass. This classic technique that we've all seen at weddings when the bride and groom kiss is a sure bet to get people's attention in a classy way.

2. Shoot for good timing; start and end on time. Busy peeps very much appreciate this, especially if they paid to attend! The only thing worse than a dinner that is not good is a dinner that runs way too long that you regret attending in the first place. If you say the dinner will end at a specific time, work it out so that the meal service and speakers stick to this.

3. Leave them satisfied but not oversatiated. This point ties to menu development, but it's important for beer, too (see Tip 7). In a nutshell, gluttony is not glorious. So serve reasonable portion sizes of food when you're serving multiple courses. You want your guests to leave inspired and refreshed, not tired and overwhelmed. In beer dinners, nuance and finesse will make or break the overall impression—not sheer quantity.

4. Table setting: Leave the glassware on the table unless prompted by a guest to remove it. Often a different beer from a previous course is worth trying with additional dishes. Experiment, experiment, experiment should be the mantra, and guests should have the

THE LARGEST BEER DINNER EVER

Julia: I've had the pleasure of attending the largest seated beer dinner ever hosted by the Brewers Association, for the World Beer Cup in 2012, which was hosted in the beer mecca of San Diego. Chef Adam Dulye (see page 175) , whom I've been privileged to work with for several years, designed the menu. The dinner was attended by nearly 2,100 people, with many of them in black-tie attire and some in flip-flops (gotta love brewers' eclectic ways). Here is the menu to whet your appetites and inspire your inner pairing gods and goddesses.

BREWERS ASSOCIATION MENU
Saturday, May 5, 2012
World Beer Cup Dinner

FOR EACH TABLE
Charcuterie and Cheese
Hampshire Pork Pâté de Champagne
Rillette of Liberty Farm Duck
Winchester Aged Gouda, Temecula, CA
Mt. Tam Triple Crème, Point Reyes
Assorted Artisan Breads
Pickled Market Vegetables & Cured Olives
Hand-Ground Yellow Mustard
California Strawberry Jam
Candied Hazelnuts
**Malheur Bière Brut, Brewery Malheur,
Buggenhout, Belgium
2006 Silver, Other Belgian Ales**

FIRST COURSE
Braised California White Sea Bass,
Spring Root Vegetables,
Oyster Mushroom Puree, Fava Gremolata
Vegetarian: Oyster Mushroom Risotto,
Spring Root Vegetables, Fava Gremolata
**Pale 31, Firestone Walker, Paso Robles, California
2010 Gold, American Style Pale Ale**

SECOND COURSE
Rotolo of Spinach, Parsnip & Roasted Hen,
Parmesan Brodo
Vegetarian: Rotolo of Spinach, Parsnip
& Pine Nut, Parmesan Brodo
**Sculpin, Ballast Point, San Diego, California
2010 Gold, International Pale Ale**

THIRD COURSE
Grilled Eye-of-Beef Rib, Potato Gratin,
Fig Reduction, Truffled Deckle Pot-au-Feu
Vegetarian: Butter Bean Cassoulet,
Spiced Carrot, Preserved Fig
**Troegenator, Tröegs Brewery, Hershey, Pennsylvania
2010 Gold, 2008 Bronze,
Traditional German-Style Bock**

FOURTH COURSE
Single-Source Chocolate Cake,
Dark Chocolate Pudding,
Salted Cocoa Nib Caramel, Fudgsicle Sorbet
Caramel Popcorn for the Table
**Left Hand Brewing Company Milk Stout, Left Hand
Brewing Co., Longmont, Colorado
2008 Gold, Sweet Stout**

opportunity to do so on their own instead of regretting that a beer from the previous course was pulled from the table too early. The con is you end up with a more crowded and full table setting, but a second benefit is that less table clearing cuts down on a lot of distracting noise and lessens conversation interruptions.

5. Should guests pour the beer themselves or have it poured for them? It depends on the setting. When in a restaurant or bar, you will usually have servers pouring for you. At home, this is a great chance for people to pour for themselves. Have guests pass the bottle around. However, when guests serve themselves, make it clear how much they should pour. You can test this out in advance with a glass of water and the type of glass you plan to use. Then show your guests the glass filled to the correct level and ask that they don't go beyond. This step prevents guests from getting shorted and discourages overpouring.

6. Leave the bottles on the table. Our joke is that we all like to fondle the bottles, but actually it's no joke! So much of what we enjoy about beer goes beyond the flavor and ties to the story of the producer and the packaging as well. When you're not serving draught beer, presenting each bottle or can is a chance for your guests to glean insight to that story via the label and package. Trust us when we say that if you put one empty bottle or can of each beer served in reach of the guests, you will see them automatically pick it up, read the labels, and take pictures of the package for both memory's sake and to share on social media. This enhances the educational aspect of the meal and also helps with memory retention of the brands served.

7. Portion size for beer is very important to consider, whether you're hosting the meal at your home or at a venue. Think about it: if you have a dinner that is three to five courses, you'll multiply the ounces per course by the number of beers for the total. Beyond planning purposes regarding how much beer you'll need, it's essential for responsible appreciation to be aware of the number of ounces served per guest. (Some beer dinners present two beers per course, so that, too, is something to consider.)

> 3 courses × 1 beer per course (3 ounces per beer) = 9 ounces
> 3 courses × 2 beers per course (3 ounces per beer) = 18 ounces
> 4 courses × 1 beer per course (3 ounces per beer) = 12 ounces
> 4 courses × 2 beers per course (3 ounces per beer) = 24 ounces
> 5 courses × 1 beer per course (3 ounces per beer) = 15 ounces
> 5 courses × 2 beers per course (3 ounces per beer) = 30 ounces

Add to the above a welcome beer of four to six ounces, and you can see how quickly the total ounces per person add up. This also ties into what type of glass to use. Traditional beer style glassware examples are your best bet when serving a full beer (twelve to sixteen ounces), but not necessarily when you are presenting small three- to four-ounce pours. The small amount of beer poured into a larger standard size glass will lose carbonation more quickly, and not look as appealing.

A well-executed beer dinner leaves everyone talking about the pairings.

8. Serving temperature: Depending on the glass shape, thickness, and size, different beer styles will warm up at different times. Proper serving temperature varies based on beer style, too. Standard refrigerator temperature is 38 degrees Fahrenheit and the temperature at which most American lager is meant to be served. However, beers bigger in alcohol and body will do well to be served warmer, say 42 degrees Fahrenheit and up. Some, such as robust barrel-aged beers, are best at cellar temperatures (55 to 65 degrees Fahrenheit). To serve beers at 38 degrees, take them straight from the refrigerator and serve. To get closer to 42, take them out of the refrigerator ten to fifteen minutes before service. To serve at cellar temperatures, try taking the beers out of the refrigerator one hour before service.

9. Use glass tags to let guests label what beer is in what glass. This helps lessen confusion if you're leaving previously served beers on the table.

10. A common technique is serving two different beers with one course. This technique helps bring more beers into the mix and creates a fun experience for guests, as there is always one of the two beers that a person likes more than the other. Or flip the script and try serving two foods with the same beer. That could set the stage for great enjoyment and discovery as well.

BEER DINNER CHECKLIST

Julia: I've been a part of organizing beer dinners all over the United States, including at Eleven Madison Park, Gramercy Tavern, and Colicchio & Sons in New York; The Tasting Kitchen in Los Angeles; Blackbird in Chicago; Lyons Fork in Lyons, Colorado; and many more. Here is a checklist of items my team uses when planning a formal pairing event.

TO DO	GENERAL	OTHER THOUGHTS
☐ Date	Vet the date in advance to ensure you have as few competing conflicts as possible. You want a date that doesn't have other similar events stealing your thunder or potential attendees' attention. Check beer event–centric websites such as www.ratebeer.com, www.beeradvocate.com, and www.craftbeer.com to search beer events by date.	What is the occasion tied to this dinner? Many venues time beer dinners to slower nights of the week (Monday or Tuesday). Many beer dinners happen during one of the seventy-five or more beer weeks that happen in the United States (see www.craftbeer.com for a list). Maybe a brewery representative is available to attend your dinner and thus that drives the date.
☐ Venue and beer options	How will the dinner be marketed? Your goal should be a sellout of the event or that most guests who were invited attend. Is there an anniversary of the establishment or brewery, special milestone, or occasion to celebrate (Colorado just reached 300 breweries!). Pegging the timing of your event to a milestone or newsworthy item will help with marketing.	Find out in advance: · Can you bring the beers in, or are you restricted to only what they offer on their menu? · What distributor does the venue work with, and can you expand your beer options even if it means special orders? · Can the venue handle draught beer during your dinner or only bottle service?
☐ Marketing	Serve a craft beer and wine option with each course.	If your event is ticketed, places to market the beer dinner include: · Mentions via the websites/newsletters/social media channels of the breweries (contact the brewery to see if they will market it), the venue, the speakers, local liquor stores that might sell the beers you are presenting, local media (newspaper, radio, TV), and guests who plan to attend. · Make it easy by drafting a press release about the event, publish it, and send the link out for sharing to the above parties. · Tag attendees and speakers in your social media efforts, thus prompting them to promote your posts plugging the event. · Repeat mentions via social media are within reason, for example, "Only xx tickets left!" (and information on where to purchase them). Help shake the trees and create a sense of urgency. · Send out links to media articles tied to the event or beers you plan to serve. This is also good for top-of-mind awareness (TOMA).

☐ Capacity	How many people can attend? · Too few seats and it may not be worth all the effort. · Too many seats and you risk not selling out.	There is no magic number. It all depends on the costs you have to cover and the cost per head for the venue (or not—if hosting at home, what is your space restriction and how many people can you comfortably seat?)
☐ Seating arrangement	How will the room look? You'll need to consider table shape, number of seats, and table configuration. Common types of tables: · Seated rounds · Banquet tables · Feasting tables · Classroom seating · Cocktail style/standing (not recommended)	If there are lots of planned speakers standing at a podium or on stage, ensure nobody's back will be facing the presentation area.
☐ Theme	Each beer dinner should have a theme.	See page 172 for ideas.
☐ Menu	You will want to print your final menu and present it at each seat for guest reference. Timing is key regarding when you print the menu. Last-minute ingredient or beer switches are common, especially based on shipping issues (beer) and seasonally specific fruits and vegetables (food).	Ensure you have a deadline to determine the final menu. Route the menu to the chef and speakers. Insist that beers are physically at the venue at least one week in advance of the event date. This gives you the proper time for bottle-conditioned beer to settle, beers to chill properly, and most importantly, it gives you time to secure backup beers if something does not arrive on time or arrives broken.
☐ Timing of service	Make it clear to your servers what time you want each course served (or keep track of this yourself if you are serving). There is nothing worse than a beer dinner that goes too long. Having an in-person pre-event meeting right before the event starts, with the servers, is very wise.	Servers should know if they need to pull still-full beer glasses as the meal progresses or wait until prompted by the guest. Many guests like to go back to previous beers to try them with later courses or may not be done sampling the beer when asked by the server.
☐ Table setting	What will the final table setting look like?	Discuss in advance: · Centerpiece · Color of tablecloths and napkins · Style of napkin fold · Table decorations, including beer ingredients as options · Menu placement · Glassware pre-set or not · Party gifts

☐ Traffic flow	Where will your guests be when they arrive? Is that the same room as the meal itself? Make sure you don't have a bottleneck where guests get checked in and where they stand and mingle. Keep the check-in line out of the way of other traffic.	Coat check service is something to sound out in advance, especially since there can be a cost. If you are having the meal at home, where will guests put their coats and who will tell them this? Also, is coat check service an add-on cost covered by you, the dinner host, or is it paid for individually, by those who use it?
☐ Speakers	Make sure your speakers and the venue are all on the same page and understand your expectations. A prep phone call with all speakers on the call together is a very helpful step and ensures there is a general dynamic between all speakers. Also, predetermine if you need A/V equipment or not for music, microphones, and presentations (PowerPoint, videos, etc.).	Who is speaking? How did you prep them? Have you vetted what they plan to say? Do they know the timing of the meal? Will brewer representatives be invited to speak? Will the chef speak? What do you plan to say and when? How long will they get to talk? (Communicating this item is key.) Where will they stand? Will speakers be offered free tickets to bring guests?
☐ Ticket sales	Who will conduct the ticket sales: the venue, a ticketing service, or someplace else?	Will the venue allow on-site ticket sales if you are not sold out in advance? How will this work and where will the ticket sales happen? Will you accept both credit cards and cash? Will tickets account for dietary restrictions?
☐ Glassware	Decide on glassware after you confirm the beers. Ask the venue what your options are.	Sometimes beer dinners use so many glasses that the venue has to rent them. If necessary, be sure to plan for this in your budget. See glassware list below for common options.
☐ Run of show document (BEO)	If this is a ticketed event, document the entire "run of show" in a master document. Some venues will do this for you in a document called a BEO, which stands for banquet event order. This includes all anticipated costs, the agenda, beer and food menu, table setting, room layout, service timing, and more. Common costs to expect include food cost, corkage fee (if there is one), deposit, valet charges, coat check, gratuity (this can be pre-set at even higher than 20 percent), venue space charge, and glassware rental. You don't have to agree to everything a venue lists in its initial BEO. Before signing on the dotted line, discuss any items that seem unnecessary to you. Plus, sometimes fees listed can be negotiable.	In addition to the BEO document, document all information on each beer as well as what each speaker plans to say. That way, if a speaker doesn't show up you have backup notes to present the information yourself.

☐ Corkage fee	This is a fee some venues require to offset the fact that you are bringing in special beers not provided by them.	Common corkage fees vary. I've hosted dinners at multiple-star and diamond restaurants where the cost can get quite high. One example is $30 per 750 ml bottle (equally split out for smaller bottles). Gasp. My hope is that none of you are ever subjected to this cost, but be aware you might be if the venue is deemed worth it.

Even simple table settings should be well thought out in advance.

CHAPTER

— **9** —

COOKING
WITH
BEER

As you might expect, we both love cooking with beer. But we're not alone. In a CraftBeer.com poll, 36 percent of those surveyed said they cook with beer at least once a week, and 26 percent said once a month. That means more than 60 percent of us beer lovers may be cooking with craft beer regularly!

Part of the fun is that you don't have to be formally schooled when it comes to cooking, and the same applies to cooking with beer. Beer is a flavor-based ingredient that can be used on its own (imperial stout ice cream float, anyone?) or as an addition to just about any recipe. The flavor possibilities are limited only by your imagination.

Julia: Before I start cooking dinner, I like to pull a beer from the fridge without checking the label and pour a few ounces into a glass. Tasting blind with a fresh palate lets me dial in to the flavor components of a beer instead of paying heed to preconceived notions I may have about a beer style or brand. It's a fantastic way to work on beer style identification, of course, but it's also a chance to say, "Hmm, I wonder if this beer could work its way into my dinner?" Liquid inspiration! Only through experimentation like this, trying new beers and trying them with and in food, will you develop the instincts needed to be a better taster and a better chef.

The whole point of adding any ingredient to a dish is to help balance the overall result. And in this respect, we believe beer has many advantages over liquor or wine. It is generally lower in alcohol (and thus easier to cook with and avoid big boozy notes), it delivers deep and complex flavors that have tremendous resonance with so many foods (grilled, roasted, smoked, herbed, and spiced), it can add bitterness thanks to hops, and it has residual sweetness that can be *very* beneficial. Additionally, beer has carbonation, and based on the style of beer, it has varying acidity. Both these things can be used to your advantage in many situations.

So what are our surefire places to work beer into your cooking repertoire? There are the usual suspects, including beer chili, beer-battered fish, beer cheese soup, beer-simmered bratwurst, beer-steamed clams and mussels, and more. However, since most of us did not grown up with craft beer in our households, we can go further with our initial attempts.

Take a classic such as beer chili. Why not try making it with a pumpkin beer instead of a American lager for a subtle hint of spice? Or, if you want to use dark beer in a soup, try integrating beer into a coconut curried soup rather than creating just the straightforward beer cheese soup (for which most recipes call for, gasp, "a bottle of beer," as if to say all beers are the same). Stouts are made for peanut-butter brownie bars, bacon can be candied with a wide variety of beers, and a brown-ale vinaigrette brings life to plain buttered squash.

But those are the dishes to our tastes. In short, we recommend bringing the beers you love to the dishes you already enjoy cooking and eating. See what simple substitutions can do, and of course, continue on in this chapter for some helpful information as you experiment and learn what beer not only brings to the dinner table but also to the dishes themselves.

BEER'S FLAVOR ELEMENTS

Beer is both a beverage made up of its own ingredients and an ingredient in and of itself. However, the latter, beer as an ingredient, is the main thing to consider when using beer to cook.

Embrace the characteristics of your particular beer. If you want to add a tart, light fruit element, then use a Belgian-style saison. Looking to make a dish with coriander? Go for a beer with coriander built in, for example a Belgian-style wit. If you're making polenta and want to emphasize its bready and corn notes, try a German-style Helles or Kölsch. And a bourbon chocolate cake with barrel-aged beer will become even more intense.

Note that using heat to change the character of beer is so important that it will get its own section, starting on page 203. But first, on the pages that follow, we'll dissect some of the dominant flavor elements of beer when used in cooking: alcohol, carbonation, bitterness, residual sugar, acidity levels, and salt.

ALCOHOL

When cooking with fermented beverages, some alcohol remains in the final dish. The US Department of Agriculture's Nutrient Data Laboratory has extensive data on this very topic. The cooking methods they tested include mixing alcohol into a cold dish, adding alcohol to a boiling liquid, flaming (lighting the alcohol on fire), and baking for various lengths of time. The definitive conclusion is that anywhere from a small amount (4 percent) to a large amount (more than 50 percent) of the original alcohol can remain in the dish, depending on the cooking method, temperature, cooking and standing time, amount of alcohol added, and other factors. The takeaway: no matter if you use beer, wine, or spirits, it's important to share with your guests that you've cooked with alcohol.

THE FISH FRY

Julia: The best party I ever hosted was a Friday fish fry in my old mountain hometown of Nederland, Colorado. It was one of those parties that hit the mark for me and fired on all cylinders: friends, food, fun, and drink.

My now husband and I had just started dating, and we decided to bypass the ever-popular potluck in favor of a fish fry for our friends. We brewed homebrew for it, too, of course. We made an English-style extra special bitter (ESB). We kegged half the batch and bottled the other half.

We bought the best cod fillets we could find and used the ESB in the fish batter recipe. With about fifty guests, as the evening went on the fried fish got more and more flavorful, since the oil became increasingly seasoned with each filet that swam amid the greasy heat. When the keg kicked that night, we moved on to the bottle-conditioned ESB. I remember going to snag some of those bottles from their hiding place under the stairs and offering them up to guests while the height of happiness (and aroma of frying oil) filled the air.

The flavor harmonies of the ESB's English pale malt (caramel, biscuit, honey, and earthy Maris Otter malt notes), the breading in the fish batter, and the fried oil were simply simpatico! The beer and food fell into each other like two high school kids on their third date. And I haven't even mentioned how that earthy English hop flavor found its way to the dill in the tartar sauce. Trust me when I say this: once you go homemade tartar, you don't go back.

High heat burns off alcohol.

Julia: From where I sit as a mother, so little alcohol usually remains that I do not hesitate to serve dishes that include beer to my young children. As long as it has been cooked, I'm good with it. However, I will not serve them food that contains beer and has not been heated.

Sean Paxton, the homebrew chef, shared some additional information on the science of cooking with alcohol: Water boils at 212 degrees Fahrenheit, whereas ethanol (alcohol) has an evaporation point of 173 degrees Fahrenheit. So the longer a dish containing alcohol is held above 173 degrees, the less alcohol will be retained in the finished recipe.

This lower boiling point can be used to your advantage. When cooking with beer or other forms of alcohol instead of just water, you can affect the texture and outcome of all sorts of dishes. Take classic beer-battered fish, for example. Since ethanol in the batter will evaporate before the water in the food will, the beer batter will heat up more quickly. The battered crust will thus brown quickly while the fish inside cooks evenly at a slower speed, preventing your fish from drying out and being overcooked.

Demonstration: Bananas Foster is a crazy great dessert that includes butter, brown sugar, spices, alcohol (banana liquor and also dark rum), and bananas. We love it spooned over vanilla ice cream. Anyway, if you take any recipe for bananas Foster and mix up the sauce, take a taste of the sauce before cooking it. You'll find you taste a lot of the banana liquor and rum; the flavor is more intense, and it stands apart from the rest of the dish before it's cooked. However, once the liquor and dark rum are simmered—or even intentionally flambéed—you'll find the flavors now blend much better and the alcohol component is subtle rather than in your face. That change in flavor came about because you cooked some of the alcohol out of the dish.

CARBONATION

Beer's carbonation can be an incredible attribute in batter, too. Tempura batter, crunchy breadcrumb-based onion ring batter, southern fried chicken batter: the list goes on. Gases, specifically oxygen in this case, dissolve into solution at low temperatures, so as a cold beer warms up, carbon dioxide is released. Hence, when you dip the cool beer batter into the hot oil, carbonation is released quickly.

Beer has a secret advantage over other carbonated beverages because it contains carbohydrates as well as proteins. These act as natural foaming agents, meaning they bind to the carbon dioxide gas, holding it for a little longer than, say, champagne, allowing the batter to

Batter can be airier, fluffier, and tastier thanks to beer's carbonation and flavor.

BEER, BREAD, AND YEAST

Bread and beer are both fermented by our friend yeast. In fact, bread uses *Saccharomyces cerivisiae*, just like beer! Think back to page 16, where we talked about yeast and its contributions to beer. If yeast cells are added to the wort at the right temperature, they start to eat starch sugars and then secrete ethanol (one specific type of alcohol) and carbonation (CO_2). In addition to flour, a touch of sugar, and a pinch of salt, any basic bread recipe also includes yeast (typically dry yeast that must be rehydrated).

When the rehydrated yeast is combined with flour and sugar, it begins to eat the sugars. Just as in beer, bread yeast produces carbon dioxide and ethanol as by-products, and these gassy bubbles get trapped in the dough, causing it to rise. Eventually, most of the yeast cells will die before the dough goes into the oven, but for those yeast cells that are still alive and well, the oven's heat just intensifies their sugar-eating powers and they continue to produce carbon dioxide, hence bread continues to rise for a short period of time in the oven. Ethanol's boiling point, when it starts to turn to gas and evaporate, is 173 degrees Fahrenheit, so as bread continues to bake at a higher temperature, the ethanol and carbon dioxide originally produced by the yeast will be expelled from the loaf. (As a side note, many quick-bread recipes get their rising action from baking powder instead of yeast, so yeast is not the only option when it comes to leavening bread.)

fluff up and be more airy. And of course, using beer means that you have another flavor you can add if you choose. Try using the same beer in your batter that you're going to drink with your food, or go with elements such as smoke from a Rauchbier, sweet from a German-style Märzen/Oktoberfest, or acidic from a sour beer. As always, a test tasting will reap rewards, since not all recipes are guaranteed to work with all beers.

Demonstration: Time for you to throw your own fish fry. Beer-battered fish and chips are a timeless pair that has many variations and approaches, but the common theme is beer. Use your favorite recipe for beer batter and split it in half. In one version, skip the beer and just use water in the batter. In the other half, use an English-style bitter or American amber ale. What you'll notice is that the batter with beer will not only taste more appealing, it should also be fluffier and airier thanks to the carbonation.

BITTERNESS

It is commonly known that if you cook something down, meaning you evaporate the liquid, you concentrate solids and intensify flavors. However, heat also volatizes some aromatic compounds, so many delicate aromas can leave the dish as it is being heated. Bitter is not aromatically based. It is one of your basic taste elements, along with its other friends, sweet, sour, salt and umami. So when beer is cooked and ethanol evaporates, hop aromatics will be lost, but the bitter flavor remains and is often enhanced.

The most common methods to avoid adding harsh bitterness to your dishes are to either avoid cooking with beer styles that are higher in bitterness or else skip exposing those bitter beer styles to heat. Just as you match intensities in pairings, you will need to think about the intensity of your food when cooking with hoppy beers. Less intense foods call for lower IBUs. We also recommend that any beer above 50 IBUs stay out of the pan, even for the biggest, boldest dish; instead, use a high-IBU beer for a last-minute whisk or drizzle, or, failing that, simply pair it with the dish instead. Additionally, it's good to be aware that when a high-temperature burning or charring reaction occurs during cooking (see page 204), an even harsher bitterness can occur.

Don't let this scare you when it comes to hops and bitterness. Using bitterness as a contrast to sweet works great, so why not use subtle hop bitterness together with honey sweetness for beets, chard, or even green beans? Bitter citrus harmonizes with sweet citrus in dressings and salads, curry dishes, root vegetables, chicken, and fish. Dishes that use bitter ingredients, such as chamomile, horehound, ginger, dandelions, thistle, yarrow, and even cinnamon, are dishes in which beer with higher IBUs could be substituted or used as a cooking partner for a balance of resinous character. We haven't even hit on chocolate, which already has a sweet, fat, salt, and bitter of its own, so why not make a chocolate beer ganache for a topping? Pickled veggies and mustards are great when infused with hops. Be adventurous and test the bitter side!

A Marriage of Beer and Pickles: Dogfish Head Craft Brewery and Brooklyn Brine Company (which makes pickles) teamed up to make Hop-Pickle, which is made with 60 Minute IPA, caramelized onions, and Cascade hops. The recipe is said to have come together fully when Cascade hop oils were introduced. These pickles are a classic example of hops being added both as a flavor from the hop oils and as a bittering ingredient from the IPA.

Pickled vegetables come in so many varieties; why stick with just one?

RESIDUAL SUGAR

As we discussed on page 102, just about all beer has a final gravity higher than water, thanks to its residual sugar. The average FG for beer styles listed on www.CraftBeer.com is 1.014, with some styles being as low as 1.000 (Belgian-style lambic) and others being as high as 1.032 (American-style wheat wine ale).

— Lucy Saunders —

We credit Lucy Saunders, author and educator, with many firsts in beer and food. Saunders has twenty-five years of experience cooking with beer, studying baking and pastry followed by apprenticeships at beer-centric restaurants in London and Brussels. She is a food writer who is passionate about beer and the author of five cookbooks, most recently *Dinner in the Beer Garden* and *The Best of American Beer and Food*, as well as a frequent guest lecturer and teacher.

What are your favorite types of foods that include beer as an ingredient?

I use beer as an ingredient in braises, baking, and barbecue most often, plus sauces and marinades made with beer make it so easy to add color and flavor to basic recipes like chicken breasts and grilled vegetables.

It's always good to start by tasting your ingredients. For example, taste your fresh sliced vegetables or herbs with a sip of beer. Knowing which flavors in your raw ingredients are the most intense lets you balance salt and seasonings and adapt your cooking technique. A fresh carrot that's just been picked will taste different from a carrot that's been shipped and then refrigerated for weeks. The difference in flavor will guide your preparation in a recipe, which will also influence the possible pairings.

What are the things everyone should keep in mind when cooking with beer?

It just drives me nuts when recipes say that to settle out the carbonation, it's best for a beer to be opened and set at room temperature overnight, or worst of all, the recipe says to use stale beer. What you're really introducing is a host of unpleasant oxidized flavors. Just get out a really big mixing bowl, decant the beer and whisk it, and let the foam settle to get a beer that is less carbonated but still retains fresh flavors.

To me, hoppiness is a greater factor in culinary usage than beer's acidity. Hops can be tricky in high-heat techniques. I prefer to use the hoppiest beers in fresh, raw recipes such as vinaigrettes or IPA white-chocolate whipped cream.

We've read that you make refrigerator pickles with beer. What does beer bring to the table as an ingredient in pickles?

My refrigerator pickles are made with blanched fresh vegetables immersed in a beer and malt vinegar seasoning blend, and allowed to steep. It's part marinade, part pickle, so they must be kept refrigerated for food safety. You can make them even in an afternoon by slicing the vegetables thinly so the flavors are absorbed quickly. Beer makes it fun, and adds another layer of flavor.

Most beers generally have a higher final gravity and residual sugar content than wine. Sugar in cooking is an asset, since sugar can balance sweet, tannins, bitter, roast, capsaicin heat, salt, and acid. So you can use certain beers as a flavored sugar source to help along dishes that might have called for sugar anyway. Also, as you heat beer, ethanol and water evaporate, making those residual sugars even more intense.

Beer additions to sauces, dressings, gravy, marinades, batters, brines, and glazes, for example, can deliver both flavor and residual sugar. Here are some styles to keep in mind when you need that added sweet boost: American-style wheat wine ale, German-style doppelbock, Scotch ale/wee heavy, American and British-style barley wine, English-style old ale, American imperial porter, Baltic-style porter, English-style sweet stout, imperial stout, and German-style weizenbock.

When you experiment using beer to boost sweetness, remember that you may want to lessen the sugar in the recipe. You can always sweeten the dish some more after it's done, as long as the dish is not dependent on sugar as a chemical catalyst while cooking. If beer is used as a replacement for liquid that is not sweet, including water, vegetable, beef, or chicken stock, keep this increased sugar in mind while also taking into account the contrasting bitterness from the beer.

You'll really notice the residual sugar in beer when you reduce it to make a beer syrup.

Demonstration: Grab a doppelbock or another sweet and strong beer style, such as an English-style old ale or a Scotch ale/wee heavy. Slowly simmer the beer down until it's a thick syrup; it should coat the back of a spoon. Once cool, taste the syrup and create a mental profile of all the sweet goodness you get from just one beer. Store the syrup in a mason jar in your refrigerator and use it whenever you want a jolt of sweet, beery flavor. Whisk into vinaigrettes, pour it into marinades, or spike sauces to your heart's content.

ACIDITY

The benefits of using beer's acidity in cooking is tied to improving taste. Remember how when pairing, acidity in beer can lessen the impact of salt, fat, and acid in food? The same principles apply when cooking.

For an example with a light amount of science, let's look at fondue. You'll find most fondue recipes call for the addition of wine because of the tartaric acid. The acid binds to casein protein from milk in cheese and helps to keep the molecules separated and in liquid suspension. Without the acid addition, these proteins will clump together and coagulate into a mass of gloppy cheese. Not very dippable when we are talking about fondue, now is it? While it's not overtly as acidic as wine, beer still provides enough acid to work the same way. And the bonus is you have a wide range of flavors to match with cheeses: roasted, smoked, sweet, nutty,

Brining with beer not only adds flavor to meat, but it also helps keep meat moist as well.

bready, toasty, or how about some hoppy herbal notes? You could even go a step further and use sour beer as the liquid base in your fondue.

A more extreme example can be found in ceviche. When the acid additions to this recipe are low enough in the pH range, they denature proteins in the small pieces of seafood you find in ceviche. Typically, you'd use lemon or lime, but try a very acidic beer like an American sour ale or Belgian-style lambic next time. Note that this no-heat "cooking" process does not kill food bacteria (which heat does). At levels below 4.0 pH, you have a better chance of preventing bacterial growth, though. Also, since lower temperatures stave off microbes, marinate in the fridge.

Acidic agents such as beer can also preserve the appearance of your foods. When a recipe tells you to soak your artichokes in lemon water to prevent oxidation, change that acidic agent to beer and get some added flavor as well.

To sum it up, beers with varying acidity levels can be used as an ingredient when acid is needed in a dish.

pH

Did you know pH stands for "power of hydrogen"? pH is used to express the degree of acidity and alkalinity in a water solution, usually on a logarithmic scale ranging from 1–14, with 7 being neutral, 1 being the most acidic, and 14 being the most alkaline. pH ranges vary, but common ranges for beer are 3–4.5 pH. Now here's a cool concept to put pH measurements into perspective. Just like the Richter scale for earthquakes, pH is logarithmic. What this means is that every point on the scale is ten times more or less acidic or alkaline than the point next to it. A pH of 3 is 1,000 times more acidic than a pH of 6. Crazy, huh?

Another item that's very important to note is that pH levels can and do vary from beer style to beer style, brand to brand, and batch to batch. So many things alter pH in beer, including the type of yeast, generation of yeast, addition of yeast nutrient, the gravity at which a beer finishes, the water used, bottle conditioning, and so much more. It's not uncommon for some craft brewers to regularly anticipate a wavering of pH plus or minus 0.3. So one beer brand could have a pH of 4.1 in one batch and 4.4 in another. This wavering does not tie to quality. It ties to the variability of beer's ingredients and its terroir.

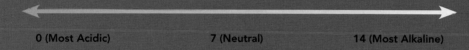

0 (Most Acidic)	7 (Neutral)	14 (Most Alkaline)

Now let's review acidity ranges for common liquids in the kitchen.

COMMON pH LEVELS OF SOME LIQUIDS

PH	TYPE OF LIQUID	BRAND TESTED
7.42	Water	San Diego tap water
5.33	Black coffee	Ryan Bros.
4.60 3.2	Beer	Port Brewing Mongo IPA The Lost Abbey Cuvee de Tomme
3.82	Orange juice	Minute Maid
3.52	Red wine	Venteux Syrah
3.32	Soda	Sprite
3.16	White wine	Kim Crawford Sauvignon Blanc
2.61	Vinegar	White distilled vinegar
2.56	Lemon juice	Bottled lemon juice
2.45	Soda	Coke

— John Holl —

Beer writer and *All About Beer* magazine editor John Holl has authored a triumph of a book titled *The American Craft Beer Cookbook*. In it, he provides 155 recipes from US brewpubs and breweries, each with thoughtful suggested pairings.

Based on your experience traveling and writing your cookbook, what breweries stand out for beer and food pairing?

Thankfully, we're now in an age when that list could fill several books. It's a far cry from even a decade ago, but now there is a real effort on behalf of brewers, chefs, and consumers to find those perfect pairings. On the larger side of craft, places like the Brooklyn Brewery and Samuel Adams go to great lengths to work with chefs and make better-than-generic suggestions on food pairings for their specific beers. Their suggestions are usually inspired.

There are also smaller breweries doing wonderful things. I'm a fan of what Lakefront Brewery does on Friday with their midwestern fish fry menu. From malty lagers to hop-forward ales, there is a lot of variety and tons of flavors pulled from relatively simple foods. The Haymarket Pub and Brewery in Chicago does a great job coaxing nuances from their Belgian-inspired beers to match their hearty food menu. Pizza is as versatile as beer, and at Earth Bread + Brewery in Philadelphia, both are made lovingly and expertly, and finding the right pairing—guided by your server—is a fun journey.

The fact is this: if a brewery isn't thinking about food when they are making beer, and if what's coming from the kitchen isn't made to match the liquid, those places are going to lose a lot of ground very quickly.

What role do you see for chefs at today's breweries/brewpubs?

In a brewery position, the chefs are really ambassadors for beer and food. They need to have the knowledge and confidence to articulate the flavors of not only the food but the beer as well. Showcasing the complements or contrasts in a pairing is paramount. This is no small feat, because there are so many dynamic flavors that can be found in a beer, especially when a brewer uses nontraditional ingredients. Finding food inspiration in a background flavor of a beer can elevate the whole meal experience. A chef is the first wave in that movement.

What are some of the most unusual beer pairings you've ever had, and at what breweries?

I've had Epic Brewing Company beers paired with flavored popcorn, Allagash Brewing Company sours made into sorbet, all manner of tropical fruits and wild game expertly prepared and paired with ales of all stripes. Unusual is more and more common in this diverse beer world, and when done well, it can quickly become a familiar favorite.

Photo Credit: Timothy Ivy

SALT

It's commonly thought that salt, when used in moderation, is a gateway to goodness because it acts as a flavor enhancer. Salt can be applied to all kinds of foods, including chicken, steak, tofu, or veggies, with a variety of techniques for different periods of time in order to permeate the cells. Salt then denatures, or breaks down, the protein and relaxes the fibers into submission, also known as tenderizing. Moisture can be lost, gained, or retained, depending on the duration of contact, medium used, temperature, and size of the item. Acid acts in a similar fashion to salt in that it also helps break down proteins and acts as an antimicrobial agent.

Although only one or two beer styles are actually salty (hello, Gose!), beer can be used in conjunction with salt to enhance flavors even further with a couple of techniques.

Marinating: A marinade is a combination of wet and/or dry ingredients (rubs) used to infuse flavor into food while also increasing its tenderness. Whatever food you are marinating will determine the amount of time the food should sit. Most vegetables take much less time with a marinade than a thick piece of meat would (if you don't want them oversalted or overseasoned). If you are using a dry rub, initially water will be drawn out of the food by osmosis, but once the water mixes with a small amount of salt in the rub, the same process of osmosis will draw the water back in, along with the salt and seasoning. With a liquid marinade, you are coating the surface of the food with flavors that will be cooked in, but you are also denaturing the protein, which helps change how liquid is retained in the cells.

Since beer is acidic and acid breaks down the protein fibers in food, adding beer helps food become more susceptible to flavor-inducing ingredients (with beer being one of them).

For example, chicken marinated in a German-style hefeweizen isn't just tender and juicy, that juiciness is now chock-full of fruity and bready characteristics. Or take a barbecue marinade made with a bourbon barrel-aged stout. It's sure to infuse some intense bourbon, vanilla, dark chocolate, and sweet roasted characteristics into steaks or portobello mushrooms while keeping them moist and flavorful.

Brining: Brining, although similar to marinating, is specifically designed to permeate all the food cells with salt (commonly there's up to 10 percent salt in brine). Unlike marinades, which are primarily focused on the surface area of food, brining penetrates and saturates the food. The science behind this process is osmosis: because the surrounding brine has a higher concentration of salt than the internal cells of the food, the salt is drawn to the area of lower concentration, which is inside the cells. As the item remains in the brining solution, water flows freely back and forth, and the salt begins to denature the proteins cells. These denatured protein cells are large molecules and cannot flow back and forth, and they begin to bond to the water molecules. That means that eventually more water will be retained inside the food cells. The result is a higher degree of tenderness and moisture than with a marinade (the moisture retention is especially valuable when brining large meats that often dry out, such as a whole turkey). And guess what? Beer is a great addition to brines as well!

For an example, look no further than the Tipsy Turkey, invented by Homebrew Chef Sean Paxton. Rather than brining as usual, Sean tweaked the recipe to incorporate a holiday ale or Christmas beer. The brine recipe accentuates the flavor profile brought by the beer style. The finished turkey will be full flavored, well-seasoned, incredibly moist, and have a lingering essence of the brew used in this beer brine. For a video of Julia making this recipe, see www.craftbeer.com/recipes/tipsy-turkey-video.

HEAT

To heat or not to heat? When cooking with beer, it makes a huge difference. As you've seen in the preceding section, when it comes to beer, heat will intensify some flavor elements while others will dissipate. Taste elements will become stronger as the liquid is reduced, and aroma compounds will be cooked out instead. So a beer's bitter and sweet tastes will become stronger while any yeasty esters or hop aromas will decrease. But heat is so important that we have to address it on its own as well. Let's look at the types of heat you'll encounter and some reactions that apply to beer.

Heat causes many reactions in cooking.

Heating is the movement of energy from a hotter object to a cooler object and can be transferred in three different ways: conduction, convection, and radiation. As energy is transferred to molecules, they begin to vibrate, which then causes the other molecules to get excited and begin to vibrate. **Conduction** is a common form of heat when cooking: heat is transferred by direct contact with the heat source, so cooking occurs from the outside to the inside. It's what happens when you're pan frying or grilling. The level of heat on the surface and the time of exposure to the surface will determine how much energy is transferred to the inside of the food. **Convection** is when heat is transferred by liquid or gas/air. For example, blanching, poaching, boiling, deep frying, baking, and steaming are all forms of convection heat. By cooking with convection heat, items cook more slowly and evenly throughout, but still from the outside to inside. Radiation is when heat is transferred through heat waves, light waves, or radio waves and does not require contact. **Radiation** causes molecules (water, sugars, fats/oils) to vibrate, causing friction. The friction becomes heat, which transfers through the inside of the food item, cooking it evenly. Radio waves are what your microwave uses to cause water molecules to vibrate and create friction, which in turn creates heat. It also happens when you hold an item near a heat source but not touching it, like marshmallows on a stick over a campfire. Molecules will continue to vibrate and change places after being removed from the heat in an attempt to equalize the cold and hot areas. Time, temperature, thickness, and moisture content are all going to play a part in when your food is ready.

In addition to the three ways heat is transferred, there are also two different heat types: dry heat and moist heat. Dry heat uses air or fat; think of everything from broiling and grilling to roasting and frying a tender cut of meat. Moist heat, on the other hand, applies water or steam for longer cooking times and is often used for less tender cuts of meat. Methods for moist heat include braising, simmering, boiling and poaching in water.

MAILLARD REACTION

The Maillard reaction, discovered over 100 years ago by Louis Camille Maillard, is a non-enzymatic browning reaction. As you might have guessed, no enzyme is required for non-enzymatic reactions; however, the presence of heat, sugar from carbonyl groups on carbohydrates, and amino groups on proteins are required to create flavor and color changes in food and beverages. Put a little more simply, the sugars and amino acids are separate individual molecules, of which there are many. Then we turn up the heat. Once the temperature starts to increase, sugars react and hook up with the amino acids. Since there are different sugar molecules and different amino acid molecules, you end up with a plethora of resulting flavors—and that is just the beginning of the chemical molecule rearrangements.

In general, heat above 285 degrees Fahrenheit is required for the reaction to begin, but Maillard reactions can still occur at lower temperatures. A good example of a reduced Maillard reaction is self-tanning products, which often brown the skin through the chemical reaction between amino acids in your skin and ultraviolet light.

However, in this book what we are interested in is what the Maillard reactions produce in food: for example, the browning of bread and flavors that occur such as cracker, biscuit, popcorn, or tortilla. There's also the flavor of meat, which changes from roasting, grilling, or frying. And don't forget about the color and flavors of coffee, chocolate, and of course, beer!

CARAMELIZED MALTS

Julia: As a homebrewer, I'd be remiss not to mention other examples of beer's main ingredient and how it can also be used in cooking. Caramelized malt (sometimes called crystal malt) can serve as a great ingredient in food. How is it made? In the presence of water and kernels of green barley, wheat, or rye that have not been germinated, malt undergoes a mash in the hull at about 150 degrees Fahrenheit (the same temperature at which beer is mashed). This converts the grain's starch to sugar. The malt is then dried over a higher heat, which crystallizes the sugar. There are zero enzymes, as with most specialty malts, so it is not a fermentable to beer. In beer, malt is primarily known for its color, but it can also provide body and mouthfeel (via dextrins, which are sugars that cannot be fermented by brewing yeast), some sweetness, and improved foam stability. The sweetness varies by type of caramel malt. Flavor ranges include a light malty sweetness to an actual caramel flavor, toffee, dark fruit, raisin, or burnt sugar. Sounds like a food ingredient to me!

Caramel malt, along with many other forms of malt, can serve as a formidable ingredient in many baked goods (malted cookies, anyone?) or even a base for bread. To find caramel malt and a plethora of other fun ingredients that happen to also make beer, walk into any homebrew shop or order online.

Since the original discovery of the Maillard reaction, quite a bit of food chemistry research has focused on the chemical compounds that create all the interesting aromas, flavors, and texture and consistency changes in food. At the time of writing, there are thought to be three stages to the Maillard reaction and thousands of compounds that are formed! Researchers have discovered that different temperatures, pH levels, ingredient combinations, and moisture levels all affect the outcome of the aroma and flavors of your food. With so many amino acid and sugar combination and reaction possibilities, the complexity of flavors only grows.

If you want to get geeky, the amino acid reactions of valine produce rye-bread aromas, while proline and cysteine are the primary ones for cereal-like aromas and flavors. Lysine and cysteine reactions lead to cracker and meat aromas and beer aroma begins with the reactions of amino acid glycine. Not to mention, chemical rearrangements into compounds like 2,3-butanedione produce aromas and flavors for both popcorn and grilled red meats. (If you would like to dive deeper into the science of all the stages, check out the article *The Maillard Reaction Turns 100* published in 2012 in Chemical & Engineering News.

Still, what it all comes down to is that we enjoy the benefits of the Maillard reaction when we drink beer and eat foods like bread, grilled or roasted meats, coffee, cookies, chocolate, and so on. Let's hear it for chemistry!

CARAMELIZATION

Caramelization is also a non-enzymatic browning reaction that requires heat transfer to remove water and break down sugar into thousands of different molecules. The end result is toasty, nutty, buttery, and sometimes floral or fruity caramel syrup that can be amber to brown. It can even be black, but as you push caramel that far it will get quite bitter as well—that's more of a burnt sugar syrup than a classic caramel.

The temperature at which caramelization begins is sugar-type dependent. Fructose caramelizes at 230 degrees Fahrenheit; sucrose, glucose, and galactose at 320 degrees Fahrenheit; and maltose at 356 degrees Fahrenheit. That last one is important. It means if you are caramelizing or doing a reduction sauce with beer, you are going to have to get it up to at least 356 degrees to start caramelizing all the sugars that are available. Of course, variables such as moisture content, pH, cooking conditions, etc. are going to have an influence on the amount of time that it takes for caramelization to occur as well.

So how do you know if you're caramelizing something or if it's undergoing a Maillard reaction? Here's a handy chart.

TECHNIQUE	MOIST OR DRY HEAT	MALLIARD REACTION	BEER-STYLE FLAVOR SYNERGIES
Baking	Dry	Yes	
Boiling	Moist	No	
Braising	Both	Yes	
Broiling	Dry	Yes	**MOIST HEAT:** Dark lagers, pale ales, IPAs, brown ales, Scottish ales, bocks, porters, stouts, strong ales
Frying	Dry	Yes	
Grilling	Dry	Yes	
Poaching	Moist	No	
Roasting	Dry	Yes	**DRY HEAT:** Wheat beers, pilseners, some Belgian styles, some wild/sour beers
Steaming	Moist	No	
Sautéing	Dry	Yes	
Stewing	Moist	No	

KATZ The ART of FERMENTATION CHELSEA GREEN

Anne Taintor *someone* has to set a bad example CHRONICLE BOOKS

 The TRUE HISTORY of Chocolate 3rd EDITION

 TASTING BEER MOSHER Storey

TASTE What You're Missing — The Passionate Eater's Guide to Why Good Food Tastes Good — BARB STUCKEY fp

ASBC HANDBOOK SERIES Practical Guides for Beer Quality FLAVOR

OLIVER THE OXFORD COMPANION TO BEER OXFORD

FIX Principles of Brewing Science

THE BEST OF AMERICAN BEER & FOOD PAIRING AND COOKING WITH CRAFT BEER SAUNDERS

FLETCHER CHEESE & BEER

THE BREWMASTER'S TABLE GARRETT OLIVER DISCOVERING the PLEASURES of REAL BEER with REAL FOOD

He said BEER She said *wine* Old & Calagione DK

MASTERING CHEESE McCALMAN & GIBBONS POTTER

208

RESOURCES AND WORKS CITED

Bamforth, Charles W. *Flavor: Practical Guides for Beer Quality*. St. Paul, MN: American Society of Brewing Chemists, 2014.
A definitive source on all things flavor.

Bueltmann, Fred. *Beervangelist's Guide to the Galaxy: A Philosophy of Food & Drink*. Holland, MI: Black Lake Press, 2013.
This book takes your mind and palate on a wild and rewarding ride.

Calagione, Sam, and Marie Old. *He Said Beer, She Said Wine: Impassioned Food Pairings to Debate and Enjoy: From Burgers to Brie and Beyond*. New York: DK, 2009.
This is such a fun and interactive book that educates while it inspires, and chances are you'll end up trying your own beer vs. wine dinner at home.

Chartier, François. *Taste Buds and Molecules: The Art and Science of Food, Wine, and Flavor*. Boston: Houghton Mifflin Harcourt, 2012.
Check out this one if you're looking for a science-based book on both food and flavor.

Cicerone Certification Program Master Syllabus. https://cicerone.org/files/Master_Syllabus_v2.pdf.
Whether or not you're training to become a Cicerone, the course and study materials are a great body of work that truly shows the depth of beer.

Coe, Sophie D., and Michael D. Coe. *The True History of Chocolate*, 3rd ed. London: Thames & Hudson, 2013.
A marvelously detailed history of chocolate, and how it shaped and was shaped by history.

www.CraftBeer.com
A passionate and informative source of information on craft beer and pairing. If you ask us, you should click over there right now! (Then again, we might be biased.)

Culture: The Word on Cheese. www.culturecheesemag.com.
Subscribe and you'll receive six issues a year filled with basic to advanced information all about, you guessed it, cheese!

Dodd, Jacquelyn. *The Craft Beer Cookbook: From IPAs and Bocks to Pilsners and Porters, 100 Artisanal Recipes for Cooking with Beer*. Avon, MA: Adams Media, 2013.
Jacquelyn's book is full of mouthwatering recipes and photos that make you shout, "I want to try that!"

Fletcher, Janet. *Cheese & Beer*. Kansas City, MO: Andrews McMeel Publishing, 2013.
A great primer on cheese, beer, and why they go so well together.

Hanni, Tim. *Why You Like the Wines You Like*. Napa, CA: privately printed, 2013.
A cutting-edge approach to why we like what we like to drink and eat.

Harrington, Robert J. *Food and Wine Pairing: A Sensory Experience*. Hoboken, NJ: Wiley, 2007.
One of the best textbooks in existence on food and wine pairing with the same principles that can apply to beer.

Holl, John. *The American Craft Beer Cookbook: 155 Recipes from Your Favorite Brewpubs and Breweries*. North Adams, MA: Storey Publishing, 2013.
Take a tasting tour of some of the most creative and pleasing brewery kitchens in the United States.

Katz, Sandor Ellix. *The Art of Fermentation*. White River Junction, VT: Chelsea Green Publishing, 2012.
An in-depth but approachable guide and history to all things fermentable.

Mornin, Brian, and Stephen Beaumont. *The Beer Bistro Cookbook*. Bolton, ON: Key Porter Books, 2009.
A very accessible book filled with practical and tasty recipes and pairings.

Mosher, Randy. *Tasting Beer: An Insider's Guide to the World's Greatest Drink*. North Adams, MA: Storey Publishing, 2009.
A masterpiece on enjoying beer.

Oliver, Garrett. *The Brewmaster's Table: Discovering the Pleasures of Real Beer with Real Food*. New York: Ecco, 2005.
A groundbreaking book that documents the world's beer styles and classic food dishes that pair well with them.

———. *The Oxford Companion to Beer*. New York: Oxford University Press, 2011.
The bible on all things beer.

Papazian, Charlie. *The Complete Joy of Homebrewing*, 4th ed. New York: William Morrow Paperbacks, 2014.
This book turned more people on to homebrewing and the virtues of beer than any other book on planet earth.

Paxton, Sean. The Homebrewed Chef. www.homebrewchef.com.
Anything Sean Paxton writes is worth reading!

Saunders, Lucy. *The Best of American Beer and Food: Pairing and Cooking with Craft Beer*. Boulder, CO: Brewers Publications, 2007.
A groundbreaking book that captures innovative, creative, and tasty recipes and beer pairings.

———. *Dinner in the Beer Garden*. Shorewood, WI: privately printed, 2013.
A down-to-earth book that dives deep on fresh garden ingredients and beers that pair beautifully with them.

Shepherd, Gordon M. *Neurogastronomy: How the Brain Creates Flavor and Why It Matters*. New York: Columbia University Press, 2012.
An in-depth examination of the biological and chemical reactions in our brains while eating and drinking.

Stewart, Amy. *The Drunken Botanist*. Chapel Hill, NC: Algonquin Books of Chapel Hill, 2013.
For those who thirst for more knowledge of where, how, and why we drink and eat what we do, this book is a captivating read.

Stuckey, Barb. *Taste: Surprising Stories and Science about Why Food Tastes Good* . New York: Atria Books, 2013.
A book filled with aha's. It's a page-turner on food and how we perceive.

Wolke, Robert L. *What Einstein Told His Cook.* New York: W.W. Norton & Co., 2002.
A fun read, this book is packed with interesting science facts about food and cooking.

OTHER WORKS CITED BY CHAPTER

Chapter 1

del Olmo, Álvaro, Carlos A. Blanco, Laura Palacio, Pedro Prádanos, Antonio Hernández. "Pervaporation Methodology for Improving Alcohol-Free Beer Quality through Aroma Recovery." *Journal of Food Engineering* (2014): 133. doi:10.1016/j.jfoodeng.2014.02.014.

Langstaff, S. A., and Lewis, M. J. "The Mouthfeel of Beer—A Review." *Journal of the Institute Brewing* 99 (1993): 31–37. doi:10.1002/j.2050-0416.1993.tb01143.x

Caul, Jean F. *The Profile Method of Flavor Analysis* New York: Academic Press Inc., 1957.

Chapter 2

The *American Society of Brewing Chemists Beer Flavor Wheel* design combines the original flavor wheel developed by M. C. Meilgaard, C. E. Dalgliesh, and J. F. Clapperton in 1979 with updated, detailed terminology provided by experts. www.asbcnet.org/store/Pages/WHEEL1.aspx.

Howard Hughes Medical Institute (HHMI). "Humans Can Distinguish at Least One Trillion Different Odors." ScienceDaily, accessed April 1, 2015, www.sciencedaily.com/releases/2014/03/140320140738.htm.

University of California—Riverside. "How Cells in the Nose Detect Odors: Braking Mechanism in Olfactory Neurons Helps Generate Amazing Diversity of Sensors." ScienceDaily, accessed April 1, 2015, www.sciencedaily.com/releases/2012/11/121114172941.htm.

Meyerhof, Wolfgang, Claudia Batram, Christina Kuhn, Anne Brockhoff, Elke Chudoba, Bernd Bufe1, Giovanni Appendino, and Maik Behrens. "The Molecular Receptive Ranges of Human TAS2R Bitter Taste Receptors. *Chem Senses* 35, no. 2 (2010): 157–70. doi:10.1093/chemse/bjp092.

Zhao, Grace Q., Zhang, Y., Hoon, M. A., Chandrashekar, J., Erlenbach, I., Ryba, N. J., and Zuker, C. S. "The Receptors for Mammalian Sweet and Umami Taste," *Cell* 115, no. 3, (October 31, 2003): (255–66). doi:10.1016/S0092-8674(03)00844-4.

Liman, Emily R. "Thermal Gating of TRP Ion Channels: Food for Thought?"
Sci. STKE 2006, no. 326 (2006): 12. doi:10.1126/stke.3262006pe12.

Chapter 3

CraftBeer.com. "CraftBeer.com Tasting Sheet," accessed March 30, 2015, www.craftbeer.com/wp-content/uploads/2015/01/BeerTastingForm12_14.pdf.

Technical Committee of the Brewers Association. *Brewers Association, Draught Beer Quality Manual.* 2nd ed. Boulder, Colorado: Brewers Association, 2011. www.draughtquality.org/wp-content/uploads/2012/01/DQM_Full_Final.pdf.

Chapter 4

Tabasco. "Tabasco FAQ," accessed March 30, 2015, www.tabasco.com/mcilhenny-company/faqs-archives/#how-hot-is-each-flavor.

Papazian, Charlie, "Umami: It's Not About the Marriage—It's About the Child." CraftBeer.com, accessed March 30, 2015, www.craftbeer.com/beer-and-food/umami-its-not-about-the-marriagemdash-its-about-the-child.

Chapter 6

CraftBeer.com. "CraftBeer.com Beer Styles," accessed March 30, 2015, www.craftbeer.com/beer-styles-guide.

Chilicookoff.com. "The Rules and Regulations for Cooks at the World's Championship, State, Regional and District Cookoffs," accessed March 30, 2015, www.chilicookoff.com/Event/Event_Rules.asp.

Chapter 7

American Cheese Society. "Cheese Glossary," accessed April 1, 2015, www.cheesesociety.org/i-heart-cheese/cheese-glossary.

Cheese.com, accessed April 1, 2015, www.cheese.com.

"Cheese Types," Cheese-types.com, accessed April 1, 2015, www.cheese-types.com.

"Cheese Glossary and Types of Cheese," CheeseLibrary.com, accessed April 1, 2015, www.cheeselibrary.com/cheese_glossary.html.

Coe, Sophie D., and Michael D. Coe. *The True History of Chocolate*, 3rd ed. London: Thames & Hudson, 2013. 17–32, 253–61.

US Food and Drug Administration. "Code of Federal Regulations Title 21." Vol. 2, Subpart B. Requirements for Specific Standardized Cacao Products. www.accessdata.fda.gov/scripts/cdrh/cfdocs/cfcfr/CFRSearch.cfm?CFRPart=163.

Chapter 8

Adam Dulye and Brewers Association. World Beer Cup dinner menu, Saturday, May 5, 2012.

Chapter 9

"Does Alcohol Really Boil Away in Cooking?" OChef.com, accessed March 30, 2015, www.ochef.com/165.htm.

"Poll: How Often Do You Cook with Craft Beer?" CraftBeer.com, accessed March 30, 2015, www.craftbeer.com/craft-beer-muses/tips-for-cooking-with-craft-beer.

"What Does pH Stand For?" Chemistry.about.com, accessed March 30, 2015, http://chemistry.about.com/od/ph/f/What-Does-Ph-Stand-For.htm.

Everts, S. "The Maillard Reaction Turns 100." *Chemical & Engineering News* (2012): 58–60.

Hartings, M. "The Maillard Reaction." *Sciencegeist*. http://sciencegeist.net/the-maillard-reaction/.

"Why Foods Brown—The Maillard Reaction." *Science of Food and Cooking*, http://web.mnstate.edu/provost/BCBT100%20Browning.pdf.

WorldofChemicals.com. "Food Browning by Maillard Reaction." www.worldofchemicals.com/456/chemistry-articles/food-browning-by-maillard-reaction.html

"What is Caramelization?" ScienceOfCooking.com, accessed March 30, 2015, http://scienceofcooking.com/caramelization.htm.

ACKNOWLEDGMENTS

Thank you to both our chosen charities, which hopefully see a lift from the sales of this book. Gwen's chosen charity is Best Friends Animal Society, which has a powerful and worthy mission to bring about a time when there are no more homeless pets. Julia's chosen charity is The Foundation for Alcohol Research, which helps build a base of knowledge regarding how alcohol affects health, its use in society, and the benefits and detriments related to consumption. Thank you to Jackie Dodd (http://thebeeroness.com), a gifted, talented, passionate, and beautiful photographer, writer, and foodie. Thank you to The Lost Abbey and Jeff Bagby (Babgy Beer Company) for letting us shoot photos at your amazing locations. We would like to personally thank all of those pioneers who have plowed the way for the rebirth of craft beer and artisanal foods. Bravo! We also thank those who are continuing to travel with us, changing laws, rules of production, and being amazing anarchists in this slow food and beverage movement. Most of all, we give thanks to those of you who will continue to push the boundaries beyond what we could ever dream of. We are never bored and always amazed with the creativity of those around us. Keep inspiring!

Gwen: At the top of my list always is my better half, my rock, and best friend, my husband Bill. You are the Zen in my life! Thank you to Gene Lee, who taught me to be an honest taster. Thank you, Julia, for the amazing book journey that was—and will continue to be—a fun, enlightening adventure. A big thanks to Thom O'Hearn for keeping us focused and Voyageur Press for believing in our journey. An apology to my sister, Tammi: I should not have tormented you with foods you didn't like when we were kids. I was wrong, and I promise never to do that again!

Julia: Yay for the husbands, and mine is Greg Ucker! Thank you, thank you, and thank you for the time and patience, belief, and encouragement. Some women buy shoes; I buy food and drink and want to talk through every morsel—thank you for indulging me. Thank you to my parents and brother Bill. Thank you to all my coworkers at the Brewers Association (every single one of you). Thank you to Charlie Papazian, who started a movement with just a kettle and carboy. Go homebrewers! Thank you to each and every single craft brewer who brews not only to give us the gift of craft beer but also to make the world a better place. Rock on, Gwen: you are truly the sensory goddess. As you say, "Maryland girls rule!" Thank you to Voyageur Press and Thom O'Hearn for your steadfast yet patient prodding!

ABOUT THE AUTHORS

Julia Herz is the craft beer program director at the Brewers Association and publisher of CraftBeer.com. She has been featured on *The Splendid Table*, The Food Network's *Unwrapped*, CNBC's *Closing Bell*, *Good Morning America Live*, and numerous other national media outlets. She also is a certified Beer Judge Certification Program (BJCP) beer judge, Certified Cicerone, and devout homebrewer. She tweets about craft beer as @HerzMuses.

Gwen Conley is the director of brewery production and quality at Port Brewing/The Lost Abbey in San Marcos, California, one of the most highly regarded and award-winning breweries in the United States. Previously, she worked as quality assurance and sensory director at Flying Dog Brewery and as a flavor panel leader for Ball Packaging Corporation. In a previous life, she was a microbiologist, environmental chemist, and biology teacher. She is a veteran judge at the World Beer Cup and the Great American Beer Festival, and an instructor for the American Brewers Guild and the University of California, San Diego Extension Brewing Certificate program. She tweets about beer as @SensoryGodess.